T0361037

IT Performance Management

IT Performance Management

Peter Wiggers
Henk Kok
Maritha de Boer-de Wit

Routledge
Taylor & Francis Group

LONDON AND NEW YORK

First published by Butterworth-Heinemann

This edition published 2011 by Routledge
2 Park Square, Milton Park, Abingdon, Oxon OX14 4RN
711 Third Avenue, New York, NY 10017, USA

Routledge is an imprint of the Taylor & Francis Group, an informa business

British Library Cataloguing in Publication Data
A catalogue record for this book is available from the British Library

ISBN 0 7506 5926 2

Contents

Foreword

Ever since the beginning of computing there has also been an interest in performance management. However, since the early 1990s this interest increased significantly. Perhaps because of controversial statements such as Nobel laureate Robert Solow stating 'you can see the computer age everywhere but in the productivity statistics'. Perhaps also because, slowly, there is actually something to choose from. We are no longer eagerly waiting for the next technological update to release another technical bottleneck. After all, why measure if you are unable to change your course?

IBM staff have a tradition in writing performance measurement books. Noteworthy examples are T.J. Lincoln, *Managing IS for Profit* (1990), and G. Hogbin and D.V. Thomas, *Investing in Information Technology* (1994). This book is a new milestone. A lot has changed since the early days of performance measurement. The lifecycle approach to measurement has, for example, been adapted. This implies that measurement requires a continuous approach and should no longer be restricted to one-off investment appraisals. Performance management is also not restricted to a financial analysis alone, but supported by a comprehensive set of both financial and non-financial/qualitative techniques. I am unaware of another book that provides such an extensive analysis of the topic at hand.

An ample list of topics is addressed, including outsourcing and organizational issues. Many original ideas are proposed. As the authors themselves state, this is predominantly a practitioner's book. This only makes the book stronger. The hands-on experience of the authors shows in almost every sentence.

I have little doubt that this book will be a valuable asset for many professionals. These may be IT professionals, but also business managers who are searching for methods and techniques to improve the business contribution of IT. Given the amount of practical experience illustrated, this book will also appeal to many business students who need to be introduced to this area.

Improving IT performance management is currently more important than ever before. This book provides an enormous amount of well-structured information. The reader is left without an excuse not to start today.

Egon Berghout
Professor of Business & ICT
University of Groningen

Acknowledgements

First of all, we want to thank Annemarie, Ans and Remco for their support and patience during the past year. Without them we could never have written this book.

The themes of this book became central in our thinking only a few years ago. At the end of 1998 the leadership of Martin van der Meer brought us together in a team with a mission: 'The CIO has a cost problem.' This became the start of our work as consultants in the area of IT performance management.

Our different backgrounds provided a fruitful mix of skills and experiences in the following years, finally resulting in this book. We therefore have to thank especially IBM and Essent for giving us the opportunity to work in this area. Many clients and colleagues that we were able to work with have given us the opportunity to create and sharpen a lot of the ideas in this book. We specifically want to pay tribute to the International Knowledge Network for IT Cost and Value at IBM, a global community alive and kicking.

Special thanks go to colleagues who reviewed draft versions of the script. The comments of Cormac Petit, Martin van der Meer, Rogier Geleijns, Egon Berghout, Wim den Hartog and Richard Jarrett were an important contribution to the end result.

The *IBM System Journal* kindly granted permission for the reuse of the figures from the articles of Boynton, Victor and Pine (1993a, b) and Henderson and Venkatraman (1993). The working council for CIOs at the Corporate Executive Board kindly granted permission to reuse the global standardization chart in Chapter 4. The Economist Intelligence Unit kindly granted permission for the reuse of the IT value continuum and the value measurement method table in Chapter 5.

IBM is a registered trademark from the International Business Machines Corporation. UNIX is a registered trademark from The Open Group. SAP is a registered trademark from SAP AG. EVA is a registered trademark from Stern Stewart & Co. Other companies and services may be trademarks as well. All trademarks are acknowledged. We have used the terms 'he', 'his', etc. for readability. Please note that 'she', 'her', etc. would apply as well.

Finally, we are very interested in what our readers get out of this book. We hope it will encourage you in introducing IT performance principles in your own organization. Please do not hesitate to share your experiences with us.

Peter Wiggers
Henk Kok
Maritha de Boer-de Wit
email: it_performance_management@hotmail.com

1   Introduction and framework

1.1 Introduction

The subject of this book is the performance management of information technology (IT). It addresses the way organizations should balance the demand and the supply of information technology, optimizing the cost and maximizing the business value of IT.

We have written this book because we feel that this is the time to make a comprehensive overview of the thoughts and theories of multiple disciplines in the field of strategic management, financial management and information technology. Of course the idea of combining these three disciplines is not unique. In the early 1990s, the application of business economics techniques for information technology, referred to as Information Economics (named after the publication of Parker, Benson and Trainor, 1988), was popular. Ten years later, a lot has happened. It's time for an update.

In business strategy, the balanced scorecard approach has received high popularity and is used by a large number of organizations throughout the world. In the financial management profession, a lot of progress has been made in value-based management approaches, especially dealing with total shareholders' return. The focus on shareholder value and the stock markets has forced financial institutions around the world to improve their portfolio management practices. Another wave has been the spread of usage of activity-based costing, improving the way the resources of an organization are reflected in its product prices.

In information technology, the 1990s have witnessed an impressive improvement of service management practices within IT companies. However, this progress has been blurred by the dazzling speed of technological progress, forcing the IT departments to adapt their products and services almost constantly. The technological revolutions of the Internet and mobile telecommunication have been noticed and adopted by everyone. The end of the Internet hype and the economic downturn has forced organizations around the world to restructure. The main focus on the CIO agenda has shifted from maximizing business value out of information technology to short-term cost-cutting. But in the long run, both sides of the IT performance medal need equal management attention.

In this book several aspects of IT performance management are described. The way this management is executed and the techniques that should be used depend on the maturity of the relationship between the IT function and the lines of business of an organization. The foundation of our approach is based on the flow of money and related management objectives. To put it more bluntly: 'he who pays the piper, calls the tune'.

However, performance management is primarily based on perceptions. Therefore, this book introduces the IT value perception model. This model describes four separate levels of perception for the business value of IT. If the demand and the supply of IT do not share the same perception level, the balance is lost, which will lead to a lot of friction. For the different IT value perception levels, we have described a number of best practices and techniques. In this way, the book contains an overview of best practices and available thinking on the subject of IT cost and business value. Performance is always related to a target, a goal. So we will cover 'target setting' in a broad sense.

We need to state here that the concepts and principles in this book have not been researched in the academic field. They are lessons learned by professionals in the field, based on their experience with various organizations.

This book is not about what is good or what is bad. This book is about the 'what', the 'why' and to a limited extent the 'how' of managing the performance of IT. Therefore, the book finishes with a 'back-to-business' section in which a self-assessment checklist, a potential growth path and the next ten steps are provided. This enables the reader to start applying this book in his everyday working environment immediately. When you want to know more about the 'how' of IT performance management we would recommend another book in the Computer Weekly Series: Remenyi, Money and Sherwood-Smith (2000), *The Effective Measurement and Management of IT Cost and Benefits*.

1.2 IT as a business within a business

In the twenty-first century, IT has become a part of our economic society. There are industries that cannot exist anymore without IT: financial institutions, for example. The statement that IT is 'just another resource' that can be exchanged for people has become far too simple. Supported by IT, business can perform new activities that were unthinkable in the early days of automation. When used properly, this leads to far better service delivery to the customers.

In our view, the IT profession is young, but about to leap-frog into maturity. It is a profession that has suffered from various technology revolutions, which has led to numerous failures. The technology revolutions have led to a 'hype-led industry', where each new technology turned into a hype, which often led to broken promises. On the other hand, the success stories are numerous as well.

In order to help the thinking on the effectiveness of IT to a more mature level, we need to look at best practices in other professions and industries. Therefore, we regard IT as a business within a business. IT has its own place in the value chain of a company, but also has a value chain of its own. IT can help with the improvement of various key performance indicators of the balanced scorecard of the company, but also has a balanced scorecard of its own: the IT scorecard.

This metaphor of IT as a business within a business is a powerful tool to use widespread thinking on business strategy and financial management in the context of the IT department.

A business does not exist without a market. The IT functions within companies deliver products and services on the internal market. The demand for IT services is defined by the lines of business of the company. A complicating factor is that an internal market does not have free competition, which means that the demand and supply side of this market will not automatically be balanced by free competition.

Balancing demand and supply is a very important characteristic of IT performance management. In our experience with various organizations, we have come to the conclusion that the perception of IT services, its quality, its cost and its business value, are at the heart of discussion between the IT function and the lines of business. More often than not, the CIO is stuck in the middle.

1.3 The added value of IT

The IT value of a company depends on the strategic focus of the company and the level of perception of the IT services that are delivered to that company. Therefore, we want to introduce the IT value perception model (Figure 1.1).

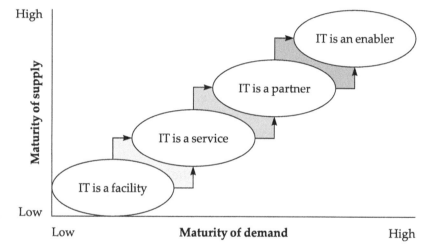

Figure 1.1
The IT value perception model

The IT value perception model shows two axes: the maturity of IT supply and the maturity of IT demand.

The maturity of IT supply deals with the professionalism and quality of the IT function in the organization. Maturity is measured in a number of different quality models, e.g. the Capability Maturity Model (CMM) for Software Engineering (CMM, 1995), or the IT Infrastructure Library (ITIL, 2002). These quality models describe guidelines on the processes that IT organizations can apply in order to improve their added value to the business. Although none of these quality models covers the IT function as a whole, the combination can give an indication to the overall maturity.

The CMM model can be adopted for the maturity of IT demand as well. This is about the self-awareness and self-consciousness of businesses to use and demand an appropriate level of quality from their IT supportive organizations. We can illustrate this maturity related to the ITIL process model. When IT is a facility, the business probably will not be aware of the existence of ITIL. When IT becomes a service, objective standards for service delivery will be started to be asked. At higher maturity, the business will demand an ITIL certification from the internal IT department, threatening to go to the external market.

The IT value perception describes the perception of the executive management of the added value that IT delivers to the company. There are four subsequent levels defined:

1 IT is a facility. Business has no overall view on IT, looks for solutions based on price. The IT department is regarded as a cost centre. They have to deliver what the business asks, at the lowest possible costs.
2 IT is a service. Business knows what service levels are required to run its processes. IT reduces the business IT costs and delivers quality service. Quality of service becomes more important than low cost. Starting to perceive the IT department as a service centre.
3 IT as a partner. Business manages its information requirements and has the capabilities to jointly create a business and IT plan. The IT department has adequate resources and capability to support the plan; it acts as an external service provider and becomes a profit centre, sometimes delivering services to other companies as well.
4 IT as an enabler. Business and IT jointly research IT solutions to achieve the strategic objectives and to develop new strategic objectives, resulting in a challenge for IT in implementing new technology and leveraging current technology. IT is perceived as an investment centre.

These four phases have been introduced as perspectives in Henderson and Venkatraman (1993) and were elaborated in internal IBM courses on IT cost and value (Rieger, 1995). It is important to note that IT departments will not 'walk through' the phases of IT value perception. A lot of IT departments will stay as cost centres, and for a lot of companies, where the usage of IT is not, and will not be, a strategic resource to reach the companies' objectives, this will work out fine. For other companies, the subsequent levels may be reached. However, these previous levels and responsibilities of the IT department will remain important, and in economic downturn, the IT value perception may 'fall back' to cost centre again. However, a mainstream growth path for an IT department will walk along these lines.

In most companies, IT is as a cost centre delivering services to the other business units. This means a natural focus on the cost effectiveness of IT.

As business units become more aware of IT possibilities, and IT services become more mature, IT departments are more and more pressed to prove their added value to the business. If IT is seen as a partner within the business strategy, this pressure becomes even more tense. The IT department will be forced to deliver market standard services. If they are self-conscious and mature, the IT department may start to deliver their IT services to the external market.

The ultimate business value of IT is delivered where the application of IT creates a new business model for the company; IT has become an enabler for the business strategy.

Now that companies implement their performance management strategies using balanced scorecard approaches and value-based management, IT business units need to jump on the bandwagon. The way to do this we call IT performance management.

In order to elaborate on the four levels of the IT value perception model, we will use four virtual IT departments. These departments do not exist in real life; they are used for illustrative purposes only. The descriptions are partly based on our working life experiences, both as employee from within, and as external consultants with clients. The other parts though are based on our imagination. The virtual IT departments will illustrate the IT value perception model in Chapter 10.

1.4 Reader's guide

The subject of the cost and value of IT is not easy and there are no magic solutions. Much of the value you will get out of this book depends on the energy you will spend in using the concepts, theories and techniques of this book in your day-to-day work.

Because our readers will not share the same reference framework when starting to read this book, the value that can be obtained from this book can vary a lot. This section is meant to guide our readers to read the book in a way that provides the best added value for them.

The book roughly consists of three parts:

1 Concepts of performance management, where basic thinking on services, cost and value will be explained (Chapters 2 to 5).
2 Performance management related to business strategy and sourcing strategy (Chapters 6 to 8).
3 Practical guidelines, hints and tips (Chapters 9 to 11).

Readers who have a thorough understanding of the IT performance management concepts will be able to skip large parts of Chapters 3 to 5 at their own convenience. We advise them, though, to read Chapter 2 in order to understand our frame of reference in this book.

For readers who do not need to have a thorough understanding of the details of performance management, but do need to quickly grab the basic messages of this book, we suggest reading Chapters 1, 2, 9, 10 and 11; additionally, they can read the introduction and summary of the other chapters.

What is IT performance management about?

2.1 Introduction

An important aspect of every form of communication is to be sure to have a common frame of reference. In our consulting engagements, we spend a lot of time talking to our clients to create this common view. However, in a book, interactive communication is not possible. Therefore, it is important for us to state the meaning of the words we use.

In this chapter we will briefly introduce the basic concepts of IT performance management. These are IT cost, IT value and the output of the IT organization: services. These services are supplied to match the demand for services as defined by the business units. The performance of the IT organization is measured in terms of quality of service, added value to the business and the costs of service providing.

Some other basic concepts of performance management to be introduced are investment, project, the planning and control cycle and measurements of performance indicators.

We will categorize the demand and supply of IT, resulting in the performance management grid. Additionally we will cover the concepts of IT portfolio management.

The last section of this chapter will cover the different phases of the IT value perception model, where the perception of cost and value, demand and supply shifts significantly.

2.2 Some basic concepts

2.2.1 Business and IT

In this book we will use the terms organization, business and IT. The organization is the entity that produces products, goods and/or services to external parties. It may be either a profit organization, or a non-profit organization.

Within the organization there can be multiple business units, which have a responsibility for producing and selling specific products. These business units are also called lines of business or LOB. In short, as an opposite of the IT department, we call these business units 'the business'.

Apart from the business units there is a unit that is responsible for the IT support of the business unit; we call this the IT function, or 'IT'. This IT function may be centralized in one department, or decentralized within the various business units.

So, when we speak of business/IT alignment we actually mean the collaboration and shared vision of the various business units in the organization and the IT function. The alignment is a responsibility of the board of the organization.

2.2.2 Service

The term service is commonly used and can have lots of meanings. A general definition is:

a business that does work or supplies goods for customers, but that doesn't make goods

We can distinguish two types of ingredients:

- 'Does work' is the competency, skills, process related.
- 'Supplies goods' is the product, architecture, assets related.

The two types are blended in an 'end-to-end' offering to the customer. IT services can be very different in character, structure, complexity, etc.

The term IT service is the most frequently used term in this book. It is key in our thinking on performance management. The IT department of an organization does not deliver products. It is an internal support organization, delivering services to the business departments. To understand and manage the performance of an IT organization, this service concept is crucial. The definition we use is:

IT service = 'an identifiable, measurable, orderable and chargeable unit of service from the customer view, that provides a required capability'. This can be, e.g., 'standard desktop service', 'application QQY support service', 'SAP consultancy service', etc.

Since we are dealing with performance management the 'identifiable, measurable, orderable and chargeable' part of the definition is key. It is good to note at this point that the term customer in this context is referring to the internal customers of the IT function: the business representatives. Chapter 3 addresses services and the structuring of services in detail.

2.2.3 Cost

Our definition of cost:

The amount of money needed to obtain and/or maintain something.

As we shall see, the concept of cost can also lead to a lot of confusion.

Let us be aware that there are two elements of cost:

1 The number, with the unit of measure that the number refers to.
2 The object that the number refers to.

A simple example:

● That bottle of milk costs €1.

The number is 1, the unit of measure is the Euro, the object is a bottle of milk. If you are in a shop, wanting to buy a bottle of milk, this is enough to know. However, if you are the controller of a milk factory, you will need to know a lot more.

Let's take a look at this statement:

● One FTE costs €90K per year.

In this statement the number itself is clear. The object of the cost, however, must be examined more closely:

● How many hours of work are included in one FTE?
● What are the cost objects of the FTE?
  – just the average salary of all employees?
  – or all secondary benefits also?
  – are the costs of the office buildings included?

And, finally, a statement from a real-life IT cost study:

● In 2002, we have spent 0.34 FTE on intranet maintenance.

In this statement, the unit of measure is unclear in itself, as we have seen in the previous example. The object is not clear either, unless 'intranet maintenance' has been strictly defined.

The object of a cost study must always be defined very carefully. Otherwise, all financial justifications and conclusions on IT investments are built on thin ice. The risk of comparing apples with pears is obvious.

Cost vs cash flow

It is important to understand the difference between cash flow and costs. Cash flows are actual flows of money that are spent or earned in a particular timeframe. When we read about the IT spending of organizations or the IT expenses, we should be careful to understand whether the spending relates to cost or to cash flows. Spending should refer to cash flows. Costs are associated with objects like product, services, activities, etc. An example where cash flows differ from costs is in large IT investments, particularly in hardware. Consider the acquisition by an engineering company of a new large database server. This piece of equipment is bought from an IT service firm for €50 000 in 2003. This will create a simple cash flow from the company to the IT services firm of €50 000. However, the company has a depreciation policy for long-term capital goods: they are depreciated in five years. This means that in the accounting manuals, the cost of the server will be equally spread in the years 2003–2007, which is equal in this situation to a yearly depreciation of €10 000.

Costs will be addressed in more detail in Chapter 4.

2.2.4 Value

The definitions of value are numerous. Our definition of value:

The worth attached by someone to something at a particular moment.

This definition shows one clear attribute of value: it is *subjective*. This is an important observation, as we shall see in this book. There is no such thing as an unambiguous, objective, measurable value: values are determined by a common set of rules that people agree upon at a certain point in time. The Generally Agreed Accounting Principles, for example, determine the value of a corporation in the USA, but in Europe there is a different set of rules, and the value of the company would be different. This will be the case at least until 2005, when the new International Accounting Standards will be implemented. Value is also subjective with respect to time. Take a look at the stock markets, and you'll know what we mean.

The business value of IT is subjective, too. It is about the perceived added value of IT to a business, based on a price/performance ratio. And (despite all quantified service levels that we will cover in this book) the perception of performance has a strong subconscious component. Trust between individual people is one of the things that is able to influence the perceived performance. And trust is hard to gain, but easy to lose.

We are aware of the subjectivity of business value and we do not have the ambition to provide a final answer, because we do not think there is one. We just have to deal with it. We are all human beings, and are allowed to make mistakes and do not always act rationally. The way we deal with it is to introduce the perception levels of IT value. These perception levels will be used throughout the book to illustrate the different issues that organizations with different IT value perception levels face.

With regard to the value of IT investments, the concept of time value is also important. Basically this concept concerns that the money that is in your pocket now is worth a lot more than the same amount of money that you will receive next year. It is one of the principles of the discounted cash flow technique, which we regard as the preferred way to justify IT investments. In service provisioning, timing can be important too, of course, and the added value of the service can depend a lot on the timing: think of just-in-time delivery where timing is mission critical for suppliers.

Being subjective, the business value of IT is subject to economic debate. The productivity paradox states that the enormous amount of money spent on IT has not been reflected in the productivity of labour. For us, it is clear that individual companies that are able to invest in IT to support their strategic goals are able to get true value for money. However, it is also very clear that companies that do not use IT with a clear goal in mind, and are not able to manage the performance of IT with respect to its intended use, have a fair chance to throw a lot of investment money 'down the drain'. There seems to be a risk/reward trade-off for IT investments.

By taking into account the risk aspects of IT investments, companies can be able to deal with this uncertainty. They deal with it in various ways, tackling various ways of the uncertainty that IT brings along, for example:

- Technology change: when do you hop on the bandwagon of another new IT technology? Leading edge may easily turn into bleeding edge, and has all the aspects of a high risk/high return profile; companies that always opt for 'proven technology' will have relatively low risks, but will not get much competitive advantage from their IT usage either.
- Lack of skills; outsourcing can lower this risk, but what will this mean for the innovative capability of your organization?

The business value of IT will be elaborated in Chapter 5, and the management dilemmas related to the optimization of this business value will be the subject of Chapters 6 through 8.

2.2.5 Investment and project

The terms investment and project in themselves are simple. In the field of IT investments, we have encountered hidden misperceptions, due to the fact that two worlds collide: the IT professionals and the financial professionals. This can easily lead to misunderstandings in the process of the validation of IT investments; that is why we want to explain this in a little more detail.

An investment is the application of resources (money in case of financial investment) in order to receive returns on this investment in the future. The financial controller perceives an investment project as the investment and its operational use: the full lifecycle of the investment is regarded (see Figure 2.1). When a new investment is considered, for example the procurement of

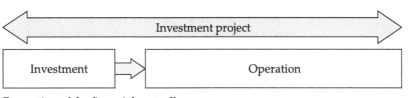

Figure 2.1
Investment perception of the financial controller

Perception of the financial controller

a new machine, the total lifecycle of this machine, say 15 years, is regarded. The procurement costs and initial costs in installing the machine are relatively unimportant.

For an IT professional, the term project is usually not related to the whole lifecycle of an IT investment (see Figure 2.2). The IT project usually refers to the project which develops and implements a new IT service. We will describe the process of new service introduction in detail in Chapter 3.

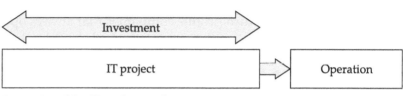

Figure 2.2
Investment perception
of the IT professional

Perception of the IT professional

After the project is finished, the IT service is in operation. A lot of IT professionals heavily involved in the development of new IT solutions regard the operational phase of the IT solution as relatively unimportant.

This does not mean, however, that the IT professional does not take operational costs into account when developing a business case for an IT project. But the focus is on the development, and there is a considerable chance that operational costs and benefits are underestimated. Fortunately, this chance is becoming smaller, because more and more professionals become aware of this situation.

As you can see, the terms that are used for investment and project are the same, but their explanation differs considerably.

In our opinion, IT professionals and decision makers who want to implement IT professional performance management in their organization should:

● Adopt the financial controller's full lifecycle view of IT investments.
● Instruct all IT project managers to use this view.
● Develop and use procedures and guidelines for IT investment appraisal that use the full lifecycle view of IT investments.

We will cover some examples of these kinds of procedures and guidelines in Chapter 5.

2.3 Performance management basics

In this section we will briefly introduce some basic concepts on how performance management should be executed.

2.3.1 Planning and control

Performance management concerns the way in which the performance of an organization or organizational unit is managed. Therefore, it is an important part of the management control cycle. This fundamental principle of management control is illustrated in Figure 2.3 derived from (Torgensen and Weinstock, 1972)

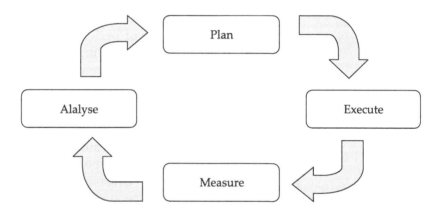

Figure 2.3
Planning and control cycle

Based on the goals and the objectives of the managed unit, the activities need to be planned. For the execution of this planning all kinds of resources are used. In order to know whether the execution of the activities develops according to plan, this execution needs to be measured. After the analysis of the measurements, the management can change the planning, add more resources, etc.

The questions of what to measure and how to measure are fundamental to performance management.

2.3.2 Metrics and measurements

Metrics play an important role in performance management. It is evident that without proper measuring of the performance, IT managers will not be able to control the IT activities. Metrics are the quantifiable objects that management needs to analyse in order to get feedback on the execution of their plans. These plans can be strategic, tactical or operational, resulting in strategic, tactical and operational metrics. Another widely used term for metrics is performance indicators. Examples of IT metrics are the availability of an application, number of helpdesk calls per month, total cost of ownership for a desktop. For each metric or performance indicator, multiple measurements need to be defined, implemented, measured and reported. These measurements can be automatically generated or may be gathered using extensive user surveys (for example, to measure client satisfaction).

There are a large number of performance indicators available for IT. We have decided not to give an overview of these performance indicators in this book. This is mainly because we think that more experience in IT performance management is needed to get a finite set of performance indicators that will be generally accepted as the most important. Here, we will give a short classification of IT performance indicators.

2.3.2.1 Key performance indicators

These are a set of strategic indicators that cover the performance of an IT organization. They are bundled in a balanced scorecard for IT and may cover diverse subjects such as customer satisfaction, total employee staff education days, percentage of projects delivered on plan, etc. We will examine the IT balanced Scorecard in depth in Chapter 5.

2.3.2.2 Financial indicators

These indicators are used for the financial management of the IT department. They are used by the controller for accounting purposes. Examples are IT budget and realization, hardware costs, maintenance costs, and personnel costs. We will cover the subject of IT costs in Chapter 4. Financial indicators are also part of an IT balanced scorecard.

2.3.2.3 Service levels

These are a set of criteria with which the quality of the service delivered can be measured. Service levels can be a part of the operational and client perspective of the IT balanced scorecard. In Chapter 3 service levels will be discussed in detail.

2.4 The IT performance management grid

The management object of IT performance management is the matching of IT demand and IT supply. To understand and control this matching, we introduce a framework called 'the IT performance management grid'. This grid will be our basis for discussing IT performance management in various chapters. In Chapter 3 we will discuss this grid in the context of IT services provisioning and new service introduction. In Chapter 5 we will cover the relationship with IT project portfolio management. In Chapter 6 we will use this grid extensively for explaining decision making on the services portfolio and in Chapter 8 this grid will be used to discuss IT sourcing.

2.4.1 IT supply: the IT value chain

Over the last 15 years IT service provisioning has evolved into a value chain with three distinct main areas for service provisioning (see Figure 2.4).

In day-to-day practice a wide range of IT services provisioning has developed. Nearly every service provider uses his own terminology, service structures, scope, service level elements, etc. In Chapter 7 we will address the market place for services. The IT value chain also applies to the internal service provisioning. The processes related to internal IT service provisioning (addressed in Chapter 3) are derived from this IT value chain.

Infrastructure services relate to keeping the IT up and running in the broadest sense. All activities are related to what we call:

- the technology-related/generic functionality of the middleware architecture, and
- the infrastructure architecture, such as desktop support, LAN support, WAN support, server/mainframe support, etc.

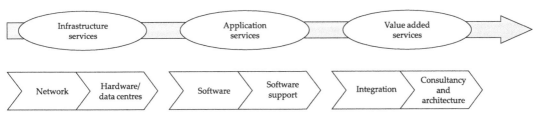

Figure 2.4 The IT services value chain

Application services relate to the development and maintenance of applications. All activities are related to what we call:

- the 'application architecture', and
- the business-related functionality of the middleware architecture.

Value added services relate to delivering value to the business in the broadest sense: consultancy, translating demand into supply, operational business/IT alignment, managing service provisioning, the service desk as a single point of contact for the users, etc.

We will use the three IT service types on the vertical axis in the IT performance management grid.

2.4.2 IT demand: the impact on business value creation

Looking at the demand for IT services we can distinguish three demand types based on the impact they have on business value creation. The IT services that accommodate these three demand types differ in the value that they bring. They also consequently differ in the capabilities that are needed to provide these services (see Figure 2.5).

Business support relates to the IT services that support processes like HR, finance, procurement, manufacturing, sales and marketing, etc. The key element here is that demand is defined from the perspective that a process needs to be supported, which results in required IT capabilities and delivered IT services that are subordinate to the value delivered by the process.

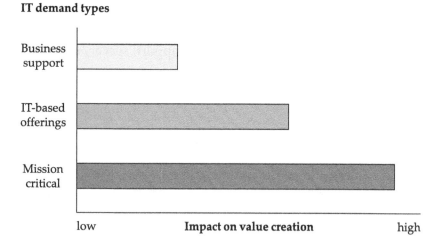

IT demand types

Figure 2.5
The IT demand types

IT-based offerings relate to IT services that are a 'component' of the end product in one or more product/market combinations of the business. The key element here is that demand is defined from the perspective of the customer of the business. This results in required IT capabilities and delivered IT services that are accelerating the customer value delivered by the business process. The IT capabilities needed to provide these services differ from the 'business support' type. The impact on the business results is much more direct and therefore higher.

Mission critical relates to IT services that are absolute key to /vital for the success of the business as a whole. In nature they can be 'business support' or 'IT-based offering' however, on top of the regular requirements, the 'senior management attention' involved puts additional constraints on the service levels delivered. This asks for the highest demand on the IT capabilities needed to provide these services. What is 'mission critical' today can be a normal service next year because of the changing environment of the business. We will deal with this issue in Chapter 6.

We will use the three IT demand types on the horizontal axis in the grid. Although we identified some relationships between the mission critical demand and the other two, the three types are not to be understood as a continuum.

2.4.3 Defining the IT performance management grid

The IT supply and IT demand dimensions provide for a grid that will be the basis for (strategic) decision making on IT. This is 'the IT performance management grid' (Figure 2.6).

The performance management of the IT portfolio is a balancing act of managing cost and managing value. The IT performance management grid will help understand where to focus:

● Cost is the main focus area along the IT supply axis:
  – the value added services and the application services have a dominant people-/competency-related cost orientation. It is the match between required and available competency that provides the quality of the IT service;
  – the application services have both a people-/competency-related cost orientation and a technology-related cost orientation. It is the match between required and available competencies regarding the application functionality that provides the quality of the IT service;

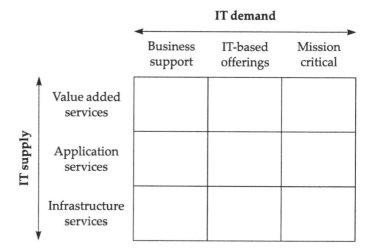

Figure 2.6
The IT performance
management grid

– the IT Infrastructure services have a dominant technology-related cost orientation. It is the match between required and available technical capabilities that provides the quality of the IT service.
- Value is the main focus area along the IT demand axis:
  – the mission critical IT services have a value orientation that is either risk or strategic opportunity related;
  – the IT-based offerings have a dominant customer value-related orientation;
  – the business support IT services have a dominant orientation for cost reduction in the business.
- The quality of service is the result of the matching of the demanded capabilities with the provided services in every cell of the grid. Neither a pure cost nor a pure value orientation is possible, because lowering cost = increasing value. The performance is the result of both cost and value. Performance indicators are always implicitly related to both, with one of the two being dominant.

2.5 The terminology used

In this section we describe the terminology that is basic to IT performance management. This section is based on the terminology introduced earlier in this chapter and will focus on the terminology used in matching demand and supply. We will start with the IT portfolio and work our way from there to the other terms.

2.5.1 IT portfolio

We define IT portfolio to be: 'the integral result of the matching of IT demand and IT supply, and as such the major object for IT performance management'.

There are a number of excellent books on portfolio management (e.g. Weill and Broadbent, 1998). In these books 'portfolio management' is approached from the perspective of 'capitalizing on investments'. We look at it more from a 'business in itself' perspective which focuses more on 'how to add value by providing service' than on 'how to leverage investments'.

The IT portfolio consists of two major areas that need to be managed:

● The IT services portfolio: the collection of IT services that is used in an enterprise and the means to provide these services. It is a complex of people, processes and technology, which is continuously changing based on the requirements in the business.
● The IT project portfolio: the collection of projects that designs, develops and implements new IT services.

Our definition of a project is: 'an organized set of activities to achieve a predefined objective at a planned moment in time'.

We introduced the IT performance management grid as a means to manage the IT portfolio and associated matching of IT demand and IT supply. At a given moment in time one can say that the IT services portfolio has a certain 'steady state' and the IT project portfolio contains the projects to provide for the next (planned) version of this IT services portfolio.

These projects realize the IT services and service provisioning that is needed for the IT demand which is expressed in required IT capabilities.

2.5.2 IT capability

An IT service offering is providing an IT capability that is needed from a business perspective. Some examples of IT capabilities are: CRM functionality, business intelligence, office automation toolset and support, 7×24 availability and support, consultancy on dedicated IT solutions, 155-Mbit transfer rate on a network connection, etc. From the examples you could conclude that anything goes. In a way that is correct as long as it is related to the provisioning of IT.

We consider an IT capability to be 'an integrated and internally coherent set of competencies + assets + processes' (CAP-ability). The ability, quality and power needed to achieve a capability are mainly based on the competencies. However, these competencies are highly influenced by the technology choices based on architectures that result in assets. Competencies and assets are brought together in processes that deliver the IT services that provide the required IT capability.

We will now zoom in on the ingredients of an IT capability, which are the basic means for providing and managing an IT service.

2.5.3 IT competency

The major ingredient of an IT capability is 'IT competency'.

In our definition competencies: 'comprise of "know-how" (=skills) + "know-what" (=knowledge) + "know-why" (=relevant experience) + "individual attitude" and will account for the quality of the results'. Some general characteristics:

- Competencies are 'people business'.
- Competencies always have a business relevance, an IT relevance or a mix of both.

The quality of the resulting service delivery will be highly influenced by both the people characteristics and the relevancy of the technology used. The management attention for IT competencies is focused on skills, knowledge and relevant experience of the IT architectures.

2.5.4 IT asset

The second ingredient of an IT capability is 'IT asset'.

We define IT assets to be: 'the technology that provides a defined functionality, which is owned by a company and which provides value'. Examples of IT assets are hardware (desktops, servers, network equipment, etc.) and software licences.

2.5.5 IT process

The third ingredient of an IT capability is 'IT process'. Competencies and assets are brought together in processes that deliver the IT services that provide the required IT capability.

Our definition of IT process is: 'a series of actions or tasks performed in order to provide one or more IT services or IT service components'.

In many cases the provided IT services support business processes, so for the purpose of understanding the relationships we distinguish between three process types in our terminology:

- Business processes, meaning the day-to-day activity to provide value to the external customer. These processes can be either primary (e.g. manufacturing, sales, etc.) or supportive (e.g. finance, HR, etc.) in nature, which doesn't make a difference here.
- IT service delivery processes, meaning the day-to-day activity to provide IT services to the (internal or external) customer (e.g. the IT helpdesk, the availability of the IT infrastructure, etc.).
- New IT service introduction processes, meaning the projects that design, develop and implement new or updated services or service components (e.g. SAP FiCo implementation, roll-out of a new desktop, etc.).

When we use the term 'IT service provisioning' we refer to both IT service delivery processes and new IT service introduction processes.

2.5.6 IT architecture

IT architecture is a result of strategic choices on technologies, the implementation of these choices are a set of assets. Architectural choices highly influence the ability to provide the required IT capabilities. In Chapter 6 we will focus on these strategic choices and the influence they have.

We deliberately avoid using the word 'system', because this turned out to mean anything that has a structure, function and result. For IT performance management the word 'system' has become useless.

We consider IT architecture to be: 'the underlying framework of technology, its structure, its limitations, its choices from the perspective of the technological capabilities and the way they are implemented/used in the enterprise. It is an abstract representation in terms of models/ frameworks of the technology that is or will be available to provide output of IT products.'

Within the scope of this book we only address IT architecture from a performance management perspective.

For the purpose of this book we limit ourselves to mentioning three architecture layers only:

- *The application architecture*, which is the most business-sensitive part of the IT architecture. This layer is the most visible to the user. It provides the functionality needed from an end user perspective. Several examples are: ERP, office automation tools, CAD/CAM tools, etc.
- *The middleware architecture*, which plays a key role in bridging the gap between business sensitivity and infrastructure sensitivity. This layer is in most cases not visible to the end user. It provides functionality to connect applications, transport information and 'translate' information to ensure integrity in data usage between applications. In case of 'groupware/workflow' application of this type of technology, it directly provides product output to the end user.
- *The infrastructure architecture*, which is the 'non-business-sensitive' part of the IT architecture. This layer contains all the technology that is basic to the other two layers, such as: mainframes, server parks, LAN, WAN, computer floor space, etc.

2.6 Balancing the demand and supply of IT

The business needs IT services for the realization of its business goals. These services can vary from a simple desktop for office automation to complex wireless solutions for a mobile workforce. The business need for IT services we call the IT demand. The IT services that are delivered to the business we call the IT supply. IT supply is performed by an IT service provider, which can be internal (ISP) or external (ESP), or both. We will cover IT sourcing in Chapter 8. The internal service providing role is usually performed by an organizational unit, which we call the IT department. Some organizational demand/supply models of IT services will be discussed in Chapter 9.

As Figure 2.7 points out, the IT department will be directing the IT supply. They will decide on the how to deliver the demanded service. They choose the hardware platforms that will be used, and the infrastructure of servers, desktops and network. They will also play an important role supporting the

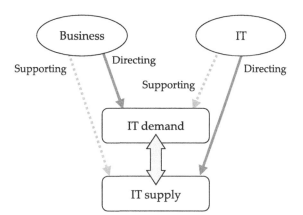

Figure 2.7
IT demand and IT supply

IT demand by identifying requirements and introducing new technologies.

The business will be directing the IT demand by expressing the business strategy and the capabilities that the organization will need to execute this strategy. The translation of these business capabilities into IT capabilities will be the main source for the demand of IT services. The business will support the IT supply by, for example, providing feedback on existing services. Increasingly, the business will initiate the usage of IT solutions themselves, because IT is more and more a natural part of their profession. In the past the IT department had to explain that it was possible to design a database for the collection of vendor data to support procurement. Nowadays, the procurement officer shows the IT department the proceedings of another management seminar on e-procurement and all the state-of-the-art solutions that were presented there. The demand for IT solutions has become proactive.

2.6.1 Communication between demand and supply

An important aspect of the alignment between the demand and the supply of IT is communication. Without a common language, mutual understanding is very difficult. The communication considering IT services and its components depends on several aspects:

- IT value perception level of the service requestor and service provider.

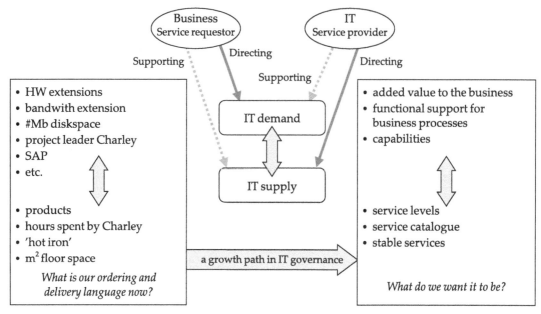

Figure 2.8 Demand/supply model: communication

- The maturity of the relationship between the requestor and provider of IT.
- Applications and technology involved.

At some point in time a specific demand/supply relationship will have to agree on the appropriate level at which demand and supply are matched. Looking at the specific roles in the demand/supply model, the proper level of expressing the supply of IT can be a well-defined growth path: see Figure 2.8.

2.6.2 Balancing demand and supply: IT alignment with the business

The optimal demand/supply model for IT will differ from organization to organization. There are a number of balancing acts that will affect this. We will mention only some of them. The balancing acts will influence the decision making on IT investments.

Each individual organization will have to find its own optimal balance. This optimum will depend on many things, the business strategy and the maturity of the organization to name just two. And, with fast changing environments and markets, this balance is not a static, all-time solution. The key to successful IT alignment with the business is the ability to change fast and easily, and adapt to changing market conditions.

2.6.2.1 Centralization vs decentralization

Many organizations struggle with the issue of centralized versus decentralized control. Which kind of responsibilities will a corporate IT department have, and which responsibilities will be delegated to the IT departments of the business units? An important argument for this discussion is cost optimization, which will be discussed in Chapter 4.

2.6.2.2 Insourcing vs outsourcing

Which tasks or processes do we regard as core competencies, which we will need to do ourselves, which can we do ourselves and which tasks may be done by third parties more efficiently? The question of outsourcing IT services and processes to external parties will be elaborated in Chapter 8.

2.6.2.3 Technology push vs demand pull

In a technology-focused company, new technologies will be pushed in the organization, and the IT department will be powerful. Other companies will have powerful business units that will not ask for any IT interference in their business, unless there is a very clear demand for a specific service. The subject of the management of the technology lifecycle will be discussed in Chapter 6 as a part of the portfolio management.

2.6.2.4 Consensus vs conflicting interests

Depending on organizational culture, the relationship between business and IT can vary in terms of (lack of) conflict. On one side, there is extreme consensus needed for any decision in a company. On the other side, there is a power struggle between the business and IT, which leads to lack of confidence and harsh contract negotiations on service level agreements.

In Figure 2.9 we combine the latter two balancing acts with the IT value perception model that was introduced in Chapter 1.

Between the diagonals, the maturity of demand and supply is balanced; you may call this the comfort zone. It is assumed that most decisions will be based on consensus. Outside of the comfort zone, conflicting interests and a lot more friction will

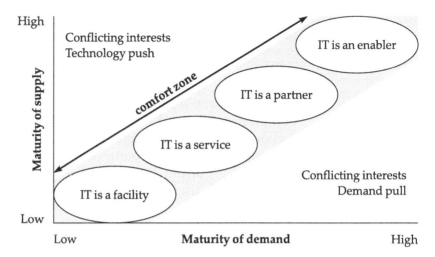

Figure 2.9
Balancing demand and supply

exist. When the maturity of IT demand is larger, a situation of demand pull will occur, and the IT department will be subject of a lot of criticism. In the opposite situation, IT supply will implement a technology push situation, and the alignment of IT with the business goals will be at risk.

An important part of IT performance management is to continuously monitor these balancing acts and to stay as close as possible to the optimum of the organization. A healthy relationship between business and IT will exist when demand and supply are balanced. The most important lesson is not to 'go into extremes'. Conflicting interests may lead to suboptimization, but can be healthy for an organization, when managed properly. An IT demand and supply model based on consensus, without any directions from both the demand and the supply side, in the long term will lead to an uncontrollable IT landscape, resulting in relatively high lifecycle costs and, in the worst case, chaos.

2.7 Demand and supply in the IT value perception model

The way in which the demand and the supply of IT will interact in organizations depends heavily on the IT value perception level of the organization. To illustrate the different IT value perception levels in Figure 2.10, we use the strategic alignment model of Henderson and Venkatraman (1993).

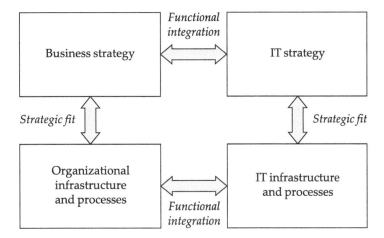

Figure 2.10
Business and IT
alignment

This model stresses that the functional integration between business and IT is as important as the strategic fit between strategy and its implementation using infrastructure and processes. In the different IT value phases, the decision-making process on the implementation of the business strategy is an important indicator of the IT value perception, illustrating the IT demand/supply characteristics of the organization.

IT value level one: IT is a facility

In the level one IT shop, there is not much management attention for IT. The IT manager reports to the financial director. IT is not regarded as crucial for the success of the organization. There is acknowledgement for the added value of IT, but this is not very different from the appreciation of the other facilities. The only thing that does matter for the financial director is the total IT costs. These must be as low as possible, but the IT requirements must be met as soon as possible. In these organizations you may expect simple package software, combined with smart home-grown applications. However, this is not always the case. The risk of this value level is summarized in the phrase 'penny-wise and pound-foolish' if the focus on low cost results in a focus on short term.

Using the Henderson model (Figure 2.11), we can illustrate the way IT investment and spending decisions will be taken: the business strategy will provide guidelines for the organizational infrastructure and related processes. The business managers will then turn to the IT manager with their requirements, and

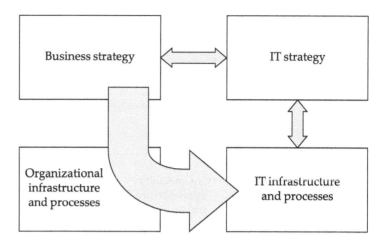

Figure 2.11
Business and IT
alignment level one

the IT manager will act accordingly. IT is regarded as administrative support; because of this view, there is no attention for strategic alignment. Because the IT function has a passive role here, there is no need for an IT strategy. The IT strategy can be summarized by the phrase 'your wish is my command' and the business is in charge. Without a proper counterpart in the IT department, this may lead to lack of standardization which may lead to chaos.

This level can be an end state for many organizations. But for other organizations it bears some inherent risks, which may also lead to a crisis. The most important risk is that the lack of IT strategy and standards will lead to a technological chaos, where multiple software and hardware platforms do not connect with each other. This will create manual interfaces or proprietary home-grown automated interfaces, both creating higher operational costs. As the complexity of the various systems and their interrelationships grows, the IT function needs to come into command, providing a healthy conflict between the wishes of the business units and the technological optimization. This will force the organization to adjust and change its IT strategy and processes, in order to move to the IT value perception level two.

IT value level two: IT is a service

Level two represents the self-assured IT department that has come to grip with its own processes and services. The IT service centre has done a good job in structuring its activities, adapting process reference models. The IT processes and organization have been reorganized following an IT strategy study, where technical standards and guidelines were set for the entire organization. This leads to a standardization and optimization of IT infrastructure, which lowers the IT costs significantly. These cost reductions improve the visibility of the IT department and its manager at board level.

Looking at the Henderson model (Figure 2.12), we see a clear (technical) IT strategy directing the IT organization and infrastructure. The IT standardization wave dictates the end users in a certain way to adapt to the changed IT service because of the higher objective of overall efficiency. The downside of this is that the end users will not always be pleased, especially when the quality of the service is perceived too low. 'You can have any colour of car, as long as it is black' worked very well for the automotive industry, but only temporarily.

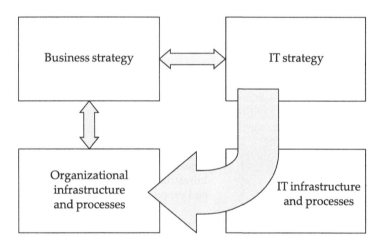

Figure 2.12
Business and IT
alignment level two

The implementation of this value perception level can deliver a lot of added value to organizations in terms of economies of scale and cost effectiveness. However, there is an important prerequisite for the successful ongoing level two state: a stable business strategy. Where business models are stable, IT is offered plenty of time to get control over its processes and infrastructure, without losing the business alignment that was created by the IT strategy study. When organizations are not able to cope with a stable business strategy, due to volatile market conditions, changing business models and industry value chains, there is need for the IT value perception level three.

IT value level three: IT is a partner

In IT value level three, the performance of IT is recognized as a critical success factor for the achievement of the goals and objectives of the organization. Business strategy is reconsidered in a proper control cycle, and the impact on IT strategy and IT investments is analysed automatically. In this way, the planning and control of IT investment is a direct consequence of the strategic business decisions. The business is clearly in the lead regarding the future of the organization; IT is a valuable business partner.

Looking at the Henderson model (Figure 2.13), we see the primary flow of decision making from business strategy to IT strategy, moving into the IT operations. Where IT solutions prove to be working very well, organizations with this IT value level might consider to market their IT solutions to third parties.

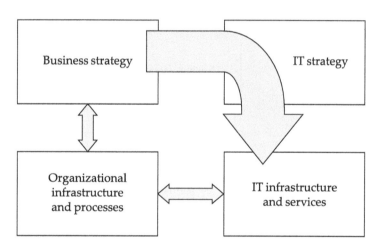

Figure 2.13
Business and IT
alignment level three

The main disadvantage of this value level is the somewhat passive role of IT in the development of business strategy. There are markets and organizations, where the impact of new IT technologies is crucial. In these cases, fast adoption of new technologies is important for survival; here, the IT department is expected to initiate research and development of the impact and possibilities of new technologies for the business strategy. This is IT value level four.

IT value level four: IT is an enabler

In value level four, IT is an important factor in the definition of and adjustments to the business strategy; probably, the business

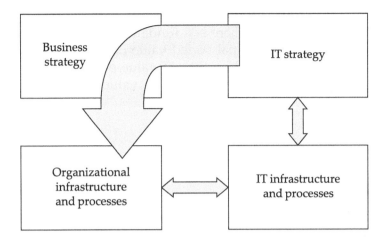

Figure 2.14
Business and IT
alignment level four

model would not be possible without intense usage of IT. These are the organizations where there is no division between business strategy and IT strategy: there is one business strategy, where IT plays a major part.

Looking at the Henderson model (Figure 2.14), we state that the distinction between business and IT has become irrelevant, and that there will be joint strategy definition sessions and joint strategy implementations plans. Although the business strategy will continue to impact the IT strategy, as in level three, the dominant question in level four will be: 'What can IT do for my business?'

2.8 Summary

In this chapter, we introduced the basic concepts of IT performance management. For the remainder of this book, it is important to keep in mind that we regard the IT function of an organization as an information service provider that can be managed as a business. The organization can be divided between the lines of business or business units on the demand side of IT, and the IT function on the supply side.

The concept of service is very important, because we regard the primary objective of the IT function in an organization as introducing and delivering the total of services that are supplied to the business. IT performance relates the quality of the service to the cost and the added value to the business. Quality of service also includes the mitigation of risk. Service, cost and value will be elaborated in Chapter 3 through 5 respectively.

The IT performance management will differ, because we believe that there is a fundamental distinction in the perception of the potential added value of IT between companies. Therefore, we introduced the IT value perception model. This model has four different levels of IT value perception:

1 IT is a facility.
2 IT is a service.
3 IT is a partner.
4 IT is an enabler.

These levels indicate the way the value of IT is perceived by the demand side and by the supply side. If this perception is not balanced, a lot of friction within the organization will be the result.

There is no such thing as the 'best' level. There is an optimal level for each organization, but for many organizations, this might be level one. A critical success factor for professional IT performance management is to be aware of your optimal IT value perception level, and act accordingly. Therefore, it is important to understand where your organization stands on the subject of IT value perception, and how this can be improved.

In Chapter 10 we will discuss the subjects of Chapters 3 through 9 within the context of the IT value perception levels. In Chapter 11, we will discuss the ways to assess the IT value perception level of your organization, and how to transform the performance management practices in order to improve the balance between the demand and supply of IT within your organization.

3 IT service and IT service provisioning

3.1 Introduction

The subject of this chapter is the IT service that is delivered to the business by the IT function. Performance management requires the IT function to provide value to the customer. To understand where to focus from a performance management perspective, an insight is needed into the structures and characteristics of the IT portfolio and the processes for IT service provisioning and new service introduction.

It has been argued before that IT service provisioning should be considered to be a business within a business. Sometimes this can become blurry, specifically when the word 'customer' is used. In this book we will distinguish between:

- 'external customer', being the 'end customer' which by definition is outside the company, being the entity that buys finished goods or services from the company;
- 'internal customer' being the entity that gets IT services supplied. A specific subset of the internal customer is referred to as the 'end user'. This is the person who is directly supported with IT; and
- 'customer' being either internal or external or both.

Additionally, a management approach to the processes for service delivery and new service introduction is described, along with the key management roles in IT service provisioning.

3.2 Structuring IT services

Managing a specific IT services portfolio requires a good understanding of the structures of services. Transparency in service delivery and related pricing structures is based on a common understanding of these structures.

The traditional way to structure goods and services is the 'bill of material'. The bill of material of a product consists of many 'raw materials' and 'components' in several defined layers. Every package of coffee, every car, every type of equipment is structured and described this way. Within a product line, multiple components can be used in a limited set of products.

The next step in the evolution of business economics is the idea of maximum reuse of standard components to generate multiple offerings from a limited number of products and services. In Boynton, Victor and Pine (1993a) this is referred to as 'mass customization'. By means of a 'configurator' a number of variants of offerings can be 'configured' out of a limited number of 'finished goods'/products, resulting in many 'end user service configurations'.

These general business economics can be applied for IT services as well.

3.2.1 The bill of material of IT services

A bill of material can be used to structure an IT service (see Figure 3.1). The starting point of this bill of material is the 'finished goods' level which we call the 'supported products' level. The lower layer service components are technical in nature; they involve respectively support and product components. These components converge into a finite set of supported

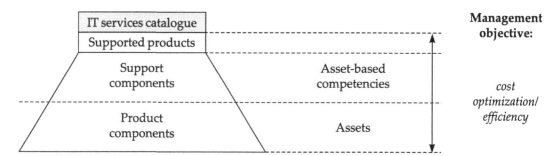

Figure 3.1 The bill of material structure for IT services

products, like 'PC' or 'Internet access' or 'application xyz'. These products will be part of the service catalogue; the components only exist below the surface. However, understanding the components and structure of the individual IT service is a prerequisite for the pricing of IT services.

The management objective is focused on 'efficiency' and 'cost optimization'. The assets, asset/product-based competencies and service delivery processes are the means to realize this.

The bottom-up structure of the 'supported product' (=the finished goods level in a traditional bill of material) consists of assets plus competencies to support the assets.

3.2.1.1 Product components

These are the asset-based layers in the service structure.

- Infrastructure architecture components with defined capabilities:
  - computer floor space;
  - WAN equipment and LAN equipment;
  - mainframe and server parks;
  - storage equipment/SAN;
  - generic software on the low end (OS, storage management SW, communications SW, etc.).
- Middleware architecture components with defined capabilities:
  - generic software on the middle layer (DBMS, object brokers, message-based service SW, etc.).
- Application architecture components:
  - application software with defined capabilities/ functionality;
  - generic software on the high end (browser, office tools, TP monitor, security SW, etc.) with defined capabilities.

In the layers we assume that the capabilities of the technology are defined. This is very relevant for understanding the competencies needed to support the technology.

3.2.1.2 Support components

These are the competencies-based layers in the service structure, where the required competencies are directly linked to the technology used.

- Infrastructure architecture components:
  - expertise on UPS/air-conditioning, etc.;
  - operational support services for:
    - WAN/LAN equipment;
    - mainframe and server parks;
    - storage equipment/SAN;
    - generic software on the low end (OS, storage management SW, communications SW, etc.).
- Middleware architecture components:
  - operational support services for generic software on the middle layer (DBMS, object brokers, message-based service SW, etc.).
- Application architecture components:
  - operational support services for:
    - application software;
    - generic software on the high end (browser, office tools, TP monitor, security SW, etc.).

3.2.2 The hourglass model for structuring IT services

The bill of material model has an important omission: the knowledge of the user/customer situation combined with knowledge of the 'supported product'. This will result in a service catalogue, which is technical supply oriented. In order to transform the IT services for mass customization a third set of components is needed.

3.2.2.1 Business knowledge-based components

These are the competencies-based layers in the service structure, where the required competencies are on the edge of business and IT.

- Application management and maintenance service component:
  - parameter setting;
  - authentication and authorization;
  - small changes/minor impact new functionality;
  - second line user support with access to third line support at the SW providers' organization
- Value added service components:
  - service configuration and assembly;
  - end user education;
  - 'key user' support/identifying requirements;
  - service level management.

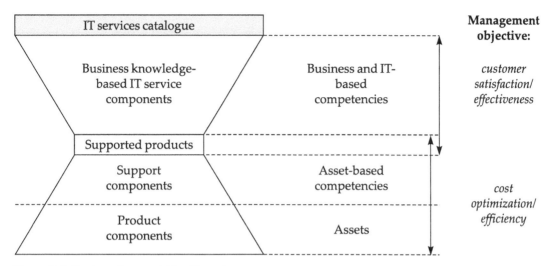

Figure 3.2 The hourglass model for IT service structures

The hourglass model (Figure 3.2) shows an end-to-end IT service structure, where products and services are combined into 'offerings' to the customer. On top of the supported products the (customer specific) business knowledge-based service components are added and combined into a consistent set of offerings that matches the specific customer demand. The number of mass customized offerings will be larger than the number of supported products, hence the hourglass shape of the model.

The result is one 'IT service' from and 'end-to-end' perspective, consisting of the three types of services components that are based on three different capabilities:

- *Assets* providing product-based service components.
- *Assets/product-based competencies* providing support service components.
- *Business-and IT-based competencies* providing knowledge-based service components.

Above the 'supported products' belt of the hourglass, the management objective is focused on 'effectiveness' and 'customer satisfaction', the business and IT-based competencies and service provisioning processes are the means to realize this.

Below the belt the management objective is focused on 'efficiency' and 'cost optimization'. The assets, asset-/product-based competencies and service delivery processes are the means to realize this.

Table 3.1 Example of a service structure

Service component type	Service component	Service element in this structure	Remarks
Value added services components			In the example these services are partly provided in the LOB using the application and partly by the internal service provider (ISP)
Knowledge based	Service level management	Management of the availability during office hours	Provided by the 'information management' department within the LOB
Knowledge based	'Key user' support	Support during office hours	Provided by the user department in the LOB
Support	Helpdesk/first line user support	Support during office hours	Provided by the ISP
Application services components			In the example these services are provided by the internal service provider (ISP)
Support	Second line user support with access to third line support at the SW provider's organization	Support during office hours	Provided by the ISP and escalated if needed to the helpdesk of SAP
Support	Corrective maintenance; small changes/minor impact new functionality; parameter setting	Support during office hours	Provided by the ISP on request by the head of the information management department of the LOB
Support	Application software with defined capabilities/ functionality and operational support services	SAP R/3 PLF booking transaction for stock updates in a warehouse	*Component of the application architecture:* operationally serviced by the ISP. This component has a client and a service software piece that together are providing the functionality
Product	Generic software on the high end	SAP Client on the desktop	*Component of the application architecture:* provides the basic SAP transaction functionality on the desktop
Product	Generic software on the middle layer	Internal SAP message bus concept based on ALE and iDocs	*Component of the application architecture:* the iDoc for the booking of this transaction has been made available for purposes of statistical analyses. The application for this is based on the SAS software package

Table 3.1 Continued

Service component type	Service component	Service element in this structure	Remarks
Infrastructure services components			In the example these services are provided by the internal service provider (ISP)
Support	Operational services	Desktop + server support during office hours + night shifts for batch and back-up recovery services	Provided by the ISP on the basis of an SLA
Support	Change and configuration management services	Support during office hours	Provided by the ISP on the basis of an SLA
Support	Operational services	LAN + WAN support during office hours + night shifts	Provided by the ISP on the basis of an SLA
Product	Generic software on the high end	SAP client on the desktop is used for authentication	*Component of the application architecture:* the SAP client has a link to the CMDB for user ID and password verification
Product	Generic software on the high end	Configuration management database for user ID password verification	*Component of the infrastructure architecture:* the CMDB is linked to the SAP HR application for synchronizing user IDs, user roles and user authorities
Product	Generic software on the high end	Browser functionality by means of MS Internet Explorer	*Component of the infrastructure architecture:* the browser is used as a standard user interface to search for non-structured data in external files that is required to do the SAP transaction
Product	Generic software on the high end	Desktop OS functionality of MS XP	*Component of the infrastructure architecture:* the standard OS for the desktop
Product	Generic software on the middle layer	TIBCO EAI capabilities	*Component of the middleware architecture:* the iDoc that is created by this transaction is made available to the SAS statistical application
Product	Generic software on the low end	HP UNIX	*Component of the infrastructure architecture:* the SAP application is running on an HP platform under the UNIX OS
Product	Storage equipment/SAN; mainframe and server parks; LAN equipment; WAN equipment; computer floor space	Availability during office hours + night shifts for batch and back-up recovery services	*Component of the infrastructure architecture:* provided by the ISP on the basis of an SLA

Over time, specific business knowledge-based components will become part of assets that can be obtained off-the-shelf. This will be elaborated in Chapter 7. The evolution of the IT services market place will cause sand grains to fall down the hourglass.

3.2.3 An example of an IT service structure

Table 3.1 illustrates the various levels in the hourglass model by means of the following example. A transaction to make a stock booking in the warehouse is supported by standard SAP functionality that is part of an SAP R/3 PLF implementation. The SAP application runs on an HP hardware platform and is serviced by the internal service provider (ISP). To be able to gather the input for the booking, MS Internet Explorer is used to browse unstructured data in files. This transaction is also input to a statistical analysis tool called SAS, the linkage is based on internal SAP middleware capabilities plus the use of TIBCO EAI software to integrate these applications.

3.3 Defining and describing services and service structures

When matching IT demand and IT supply, required IT capabilities need to result in provided IT services. The description of IT services and service structures in an IT services catalogue is the basis for this match.

3.3.1 The criteria for describing IT services

When building an IT services catalogue with service descriptions there are some general criteria that need to be taken into account. In Table 3.2 we describe the quality criteria for service descriptions and service level agreements.

3.3.2 The structure of IT service descriptions

This section describes a structure for IT service descriptions (see Figure 3.3).

This structure consists of the following objects:

IT service = an identifiable, measurable, orderable and chargeable unit of service from the customer's view, which provides a required IT capability. This can be, e.g., 'standard desktop service',

Table 3.2 Criteria for describing services.

Criterion	Remarks
To be influenced by the user	The quality and quantity of the delivered service needs to be related to a specified demand. The specification of the demand has a content aspect and a volume aspect. The content aspect is part of the definition of the requirements; the volume aspect is influenced during service delivery
Recognizable and repeatable results	The delivered result of an IT service must be observable, recognizable and repeatable
Unambiguous description (including structure)	An IT service must have a clear, unambiguous structure/construction. Service components can take part in more than one service; however, the eventually delivered service still must be unambiguous
Market conformity	An IT service is the unit that is being traded on a (internal) market where demand and supply are continuously matched in a negotiation process. Only when there are multiple suppliers of the service can there be 'market conformity'. In order to achieve this the pricing of the service needs to enable a comparison
Measurable	An IT service needs to be orderable, forecastable, deliverable and chargeable. The related quantity must be derivable from a defined demand of the user

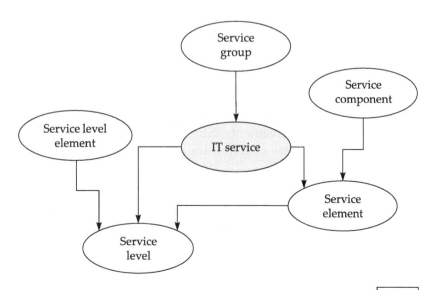

Figure 3.3
The structure for IT service descriptions

43

'application QQY support service', 'SAP consultancy service', etc.

Service group	=	category of services which identifies a specific group of offerings by the service provisioning organization. This can be, e.g., 'value added services', 'infrastructure services', 'professional services', etc.
Service component	=	an identifiable and measurable unit of service from the provider's view, which can take part in one or more services. This can be, e.g., 'first-line support', 'HW usage', 'SW license fee', 'operational support', etc.
Service element	=	a discrete part of a service with a defined number of units of the related service component. This can be, e.g., the average amount of 'HW usage' expressed in the unit of measure as defined in the service component 'HW usage' or the normative number of hours support for 'operational support', etc.
Service level element	=	an identifiable, measurable, orderable and chargeable unit of the level of service from the customer view. This can be, e.g., 'availability', 'service desk window', 'back-up frequency', 'information access authority levels', etc.
Service level	=	a defined level of service for a particular service or service element expressed in the unit of measure of the service level element. This can be, e.g., 'the agreed level of availability of SAP maintenance and support', 'the agreed service desk window for the desktop services', etc.

All the above-mentioned terminology will be used when describing a service catalogue. However, the service level descriptions in a service catalogue are limited to describing the boundaries of those levels to be agreed upon. The actual service levels will always be described in specific 'service level agreements (SLAs)' which are part of the contract between the service requestor and the service provider. In Chapter 8 we will address the structure of service level agreements.

3.3.3 An example of the way to structure an IT services catalogue

To illustrate how IT services can be grouped in an IT services catalogue, this section shows an example of our day-to-day practice. This example is from an internal service provider of a company that has an IT Value perception level two: 'IT is a service'.

The content of this catalogue is based on four questions:

- What is being delivered?
- How is the service being delivered?
- How is the service charged?
- How do we track this in our books?

The first question will be addressed here. The second, third and fourth questions will be addressed in Chapter 7.

3.3.3.1 What is being delivered?

This question will be answered in three levels:

(a) Based on the accountability of the provider.
(b) Standard versus tailored results.
(c) The actually available standard services.

(a) What is being delivered and what is the IT service provider accountable for?

The top level of the defined service groups is based on a mix of the accountability from a provider's view and the type of activity involved.

IT services consist of:

- Professional services = the availability of qualified know-how/ expertise with the obligation to deliver the required effort.
- Operating services and application development and main-tenance (ADM) services = the availability of functionality to the end user with the obligation to deliver defined results.

For operating and ADM services the provider is accountable for timely delivery of the defined result at the agreed service/ quality level. For professional services the provider is account-able for a proper match of requested know-how and delivered know-how, as well as for the timely delivery of the required effort.

Professional services are delivered by individual craftsmen, their know-how/expertise is defined along two angles:

- The 'professional type', such as project leader, consultant, operator, SAP engineer, etc.
- the level of experience, such as junior, mid, senior.

(b) Standard versus tailored results

The next level of the service groups defined is based on the distinction between standard and tailored services.

IT services consist of:

- Professional services: always tailored results.
- Operating services and application development and maintenance services: tailored services are delivered based on a case-by-case, upfront agreed result of a specific process.
- Operating services: standard services are delivered with a standard result of a standard process.

The tailored services can be any type of activity with a defined result and service level. Essential to delivery of tailored services is that the agreement on the result and the service level is made upfront. Usually the delivery process is as much tailor-made as the delivered service itself. The process can be based on a method or a process blueprint which is tailored for delivering the specific service.

By definition standard services are the result of a standard process. The result is predictable and repeatable, identical regardless of time and place of delivery with the same quality level. The delivery comes in two different formats:

- The continuous availability of functionality.
- One-time results on request by means of a service request (SR).

(c) What services are available?

Standard services can be delivered as:

- *Desktop services*, which provide every end user with a basic IT tool set which consists of the company-wide standard for: office tools, desktop/laptop HW/OS, e-mail capabilities, Internet/intranet access, LAN/WAN connectivity and services, security services, single log-on.
- *Application services*, which provide authorized end users with the defined 'end-to-end' application functionality to be able to be a specific actor in a specific business process.

Professional services can be delivered in two ways:

- Based on a request for a specific professional type and level of experience, a qualified individual will be assigned by the service provider to the tasks for an agreed period of time.
- Based on a request for a defined number of hours day/week/ month the availability of a specified professional type and level of experience is agreed. The individual performing the task can differ based on the availability. Again the service provider is responsible/accountable for assigning an individual.

In summary the catalogue grouping structure looks like Figure 3.4.

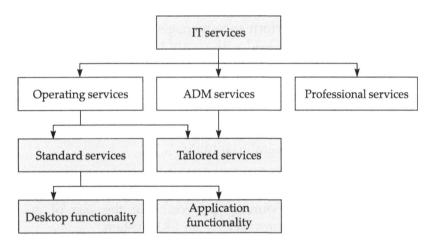

Figure 3.4
Service grouping in an IT services catalogue

This figure will be extended with the charging options for the various groups of services in Chapter 7.

3.4 The introduction of new IT services

When the term 'portfolio management' is used with regard to IT, usually this is referring to a process of decision making on IT projects. We prefer to use the term 'IT project portfolio management' for that purpose.

However big an effort a project may be and however big an impact the project may have, it still is by definition a 'one-time event' delivering new or upgraded IT services or components of IT services.

The IT project portfolio is the vehicle for realizing the planned next version of the IT services portfolio. In fact we are assuming a continuous process of 'IT service refresh' based on IT service lifecycle principles. This is discussed in detail in Chapter 7. We will address decision making on the IT project portfolio in Chapter 5. For now we limit ourselves to the better understanding of the types of IT projects we can distinguish and their impact on the IT portfolio. All of these project types belong to what we call 'new IT service introduction'.

3.4.1 Integrated service provisioning projects

The first group of projects deals with the 'end-to-end' delivery of IT services. The impact involved is in all service component layers and as such in the complete IT supply axis of the IT performance management grid. The business is completely in the lead with regard to the implementation. The impact on IT is significant and very complex. Projects and their impact are hard to control.

The difficulty is in the complexity of the newly defined service, service components and required service levels.

Several examples:

- Business re-engineering/business restructuring projects, like the implementation of an ERP system.
- Sourcing projects, like the use of an application service provider for an ERP system.

These projects are fancy/highly visible which leads to a potential friction between the management attention these projects receive versus the management attention that is available for the project types.

3.4.2 Application portfolio-related projects

This group of projects deals with 'business sensitive IT'. This implicates that the business will always be the prime stakeholder and will take a major part in the project. But IT can be in the lead as well as a business manager. These projects always have an impact on the IT infrastructure services as well. The impact of these projects on the IT portfolio is complex and hard to control, but the overall complexity is less than the first group of projects.

Several examples:

- Functionality upgrade/refresh projects, such as the implementation of an SAP module, the introduction of a new version with additional functionality, the restructuring of a part of the business with a large IT-related effort.
- Application development and maintenance (ADM) optimization projects.
- Sourcing projects, like out-tasking maintenance of legacy environments.

3.4.3 Infrastructure-related projects

These projects deal with 'non-business-sensitive IT'. This implicates that this is usually an IT internal project that is focused on realizing cost efficiencies, economies of scale, process improvement, etc. The impact is relatively easily controllable from a managerial perspective. The scope of these projects is completely within the infrastructure services in the IT performance management grid.

Several examples:

- Technology upgrade/refresh projects, such as the replacement of a server park, the implementation of NAS/SAN technology, etc.
- IT infrastructure optimization projects, such as data centre consolidation, server consolidation, etc.
- IT process optimization projects.
- Sourcing projects, like out-tasking the workplace environment services.

3.5 Performance management of IT service provisioning

Most of the available books on managing service provisioning are focused on processes and/or assets. A very good overview and in-depth series are the IT Infrastructure Library guides (ITIL, 2002) on processes and related best practices.

In this book a high level managerial perspective is used to describe the performance management principles that relate to the IT service provisioning. This perspective focuses on the flow of money and related management objectives. To put it more bluntly: 'he who pays the piper calls the tune'.

Using this perspective, some key statements can be formulated:

- Implementation of 'price/performance' ratios for IT services is a prerequisite for controlling IT. Every service level of a particular IT service has a price tag attached to it.
- Standardization of IT services and service components leads to optimization of the IT service delivery which helps controlling cost levels.
- Selling 'NO' for non-standard services is not acceptable, a 'YES, HOWEVER ...' with a higher price for non-standard services helps influence IT services demand towards standard services.

In the main, in practice these statements have not turned into reality:

- In how many service delivery organizations are senior management decisions focused on the IT services portfolio rather than the project portfolio?
- How many service delivery organizations within the internal service providers (ISP) are leading in the service definition and new service introduction process?
- How many service delivery organizations are even involved in the early design stages?

Some basic principles for performance management in IT service delivery will be explained using an IT management model. This model was effectively used in the 1990s during the internal restructuring of the IBM data centres and is referred to as 'the IBM Geo-plex model'. The model has been successfully implemented by many other companies.

3.5.1 Stable IT services and new IT services

The IT portfolio contains three areas that need to be managed differently.

1 The services portfolio, containing two areas:
   - stable IT services, which are reviewed on a regular basis for further optimization of the price/performance ratio. For these services the service levels have become definable, measurable and controllable. Service level agreements (SLA) are agreed upon between the service provider and the service requestor;

- new IT services, which are delivered based on a 'dedicated solutions' approach. The agreement on the level of service can only be based on a 'best effort', because there is still a lot of effort to go into optimization and stabilization of the service delivery. This additional effort needs to be financed by a margin on the price.

2 The IT project portfolio containing:
  - the new IT service introduction area, which contains projects addressed in section 3.4.

The main drivers for the management of the IT services portfolio are customer satisfaction, operational efficiency and cost optimization. Customer satisfaction is achieved by mass customization of IT services. Operational efficiency and cost optimization can only be achieved by delivering standard IT service components by using stable standard processes. Any deviation from standard IT service components leads to disturbance of the operational efficiency and cost optimization goals.

The main driver for the management of the introduction of new IT services is speed needed in the business of new IT functionality/products and services to the customer. Other drivers can be efficiency and effectiveness improvements.

These drivers cause different choices by the responsible managers. By definition the management goals are conflicting, this results in a continuous friction between the stable service delivery organization and the new services introduction organizations. The 'speed needed in the business' objective of the latter can result in uncontrolled growth of server parks or the load in the data centre (causing performance issues), exotic technologies and a great deal of management hassle.

To manage this conflict of interest, the model that we introduce here, isolates the areas that have a different management focus into:

- Stable IT service delivery with:
  - 'service delivery front offices' that have a customer focus for the delivery of stable IT services;
  - 'supported product back offices' that have an operational efficiency objective for the stable IT services.
- New IT service delivery with:
  - 'service delivery projects' that provide the new IT services from an isolated 'quarantine' or 'tuning' zone and that have a 'learn and improve' objective for the new IT services;

- 'new IT service introduction projects' that have a 'speed needed in the business' objective.

An overview of the model is shown in Figure 3.5.

3.5.2 The management of stable IT service delivery

We will start with the target situation of providing uninterrupted/steady state IT services at a defined service level with a defined price. In this situation continuous IT optimization is taking place, formal processes are implemented and a defined level of control is achieved.

The financial control involves two management areas:

- 'Service delivery front offices' with a customer satisfaction focus.
- 'Supported product back offices' with an operational efficiency focus.

The control over the flow of money is used to handle the intrinsic conflict between the focus of these management areas.

3.5.2.1 Service delivery front offices

The 'service delivery front offices' provide the 'end-to-end' IT service or group of services to the business.

The key management role is the 'service delivery manager', who is responsible for the end-to-end service delivery to his customer. His management objective is 'customer satisfaction' and the means he has available are competencies and processes. His business is 'people business'. In this area of the service provisioning model the assets/technology plays a minor role.

The service delivery manager will negotiate service levels and associated (internal) pricing. In many cases this negotiation is with a counter part on the IT demand side, which is usually organized in the business. The roles related to managing IT demand are called 'service manager' or 'service level manager'. The IT demand side is always in the lead and the result of the negotiation is reflected in service level agreements (SLAs).

The service delivery manager has control over the available funding for his part of the IT services portfolio. He provides for the funding of all processes, assets and competencies involved in the end-to-end service delivery. This means that he assigns portions of his available funding to the activities that he manages and to the managers of the supported product back offices.

3.5.2.2 Supported product back offices

The 'supported product back offices' have an operational efficiency objective. They provide the application services and infrastructure services or service components. The most common layers are:

- Product support, where all the technology-related competencies reside.
- Operations, where the operational support activities take place.
- Assets and facilities, where the technology resides.

Every back office has one or more 'operations managers', who have an operational efficiency and cost reduction target. The means available to achieve his targets are: the assets (=the available technology and the effectiveness of its usage), the processes and the competencies to support the products. His business is 'technology business'.

The operations manager gets portions of the total budget assigned by all service delivery managers which provides for his funding. Thus, a UNIX platform operations manager will receive funding from multiple service delivery managers who have applications in their portfolio, which happen to run on the UNIX platform.

By organizing the responsibilities this way, it becomes clear that the total funding available through all SLAs is the limitation for all activities that need funding. Technology refresh in the back offices needs to be funded from that single source of funds.

3.5.3 The management of new IT service delivery

Once the stable service delivery has been established, every new IT service or service component that has been developed and implemented will create disruptions in the stable service delivery. Therefore new service delivery should be isolated from the stable service delivery. New IT service delivery is based on two management areas:

- 'Service development and implementation projects' that have a 'speed needed in the business' objective.
- 'Service delivery projects' that provide the new IT services from an isolated 'quarantine' or 'tuning' zone and that have a 'learn and improve' objective for the new IT services.

3.5.3.1 Service development and implementation projects

The new IT service introduction area contains the wide variety of projects that we mentioned earlier in section 3.4. The management objective of a programme or project manager focuses on 'timely delivery' of the project deliverables. There are many methods and best practices for project and programme management available. In our day-to-day practice we still observe a tendency to focus on projects instead of IT service delivery. We want to emphasize that a project delivers 'just another version' of an IT service or service component. Planning the next version of the IT services portfolio should be the basis for the project portfolio.

3.5.3.2 Service delivery projects

The service delivery projects provide the delivery to customers of new IT services. The friction between the stable service delivery process and the new service introduction can be resolved by a two-step approach.

Step 1 Isolation and tuning

First the new IT service delivery is isolated in a 'quarantine' zone or more positively phrased 'tuning zone', or 'service nurturing and transition area'. The new IT service is isolated from the stable service delivery for a limited period. In this period the focus of the service delivery team will be on 'tuning'/ 'learning and improving' the service delivery, stabilizing it, improving price/performance ratios, etc.

Step 2 Transitioning

The next step is increasing the service level and the price/ performance ratio by step-by-step transitioning service components out of the tuning zone activity into the stable environment. Alternatively the new services can be outsourced or out-tasked to external service providers (ESP).

A project manager for service delivery is heading the service delivery project. During the life of this service delivery project, the project manager is the single responsible manager of the service delivery, directly dealing with the customer and managing the related budget. The project manager is responsible for the complete life cycle of the service delivery project including both steps mentioned above.

3.5.4 The complete picture and the management roles

The approach to performance management in IT services provisioning is summarized in Figure 3.5. The exact organizational structure only slightly influences the responsibilities mentioned here. Therefore, do not consider this to be an organizational model.

The programme or project manager manages a service development and implementation project. He has the responsibility to deliver the defined project deliverables in a timely manner and to transfer control of the project results to the project manager for service delivery.

The project manager for service delivery has the end-to-end responsibility for delivering a new IT service or service group

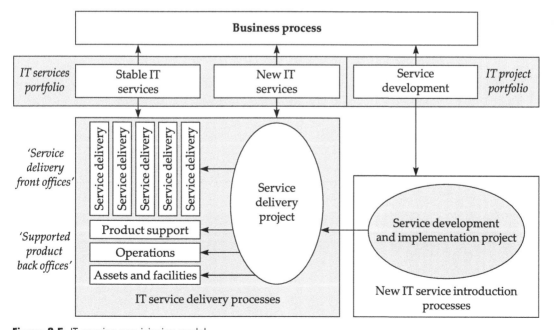

Figure 3.5 IT service provisioning model

from a tuning zone. The project manager for service delivery also manages the optimization, stabilization and transition of the new IT service to the stable IT service delivery environment.

The service delivery manager negotiates the match of IT demand and IT supply with the business IT representative: the service manager. The service delivery manager is responsible for the end-to-end service delivery and provides for the buckets of funding to the operations managers. The operations managers manage the availability of stable IT services.

3.6 Summary

In this chapter the basics regarding IT services and IT service provisioning have been introduced. From a performance management point of view the structures of IT services were explained. The structure for describing IT services and an example of a way to structure a services catalogue were described as well.

The second theme in this chapter was the performance management of IT services provisioning. A model for managing stable standardized service delivery was introduced. This model explained how to deal with the disruptions caused by the introduction of unstable new services. In this model the flow of money and the control of this flow by a limited number of key management roles was explained.

4.1 Introduction

In this chapter we will address cost as one of the two drivers for IT performance. In Chapter 5 value will be addressed as the second driver. Current practice in most organizations is a focus on managing, say optimizing, the costs of IT. The authors want to emphasize that optimizing the cost of IT always has to be seen in combination with the improvement of the value of IT.

In this chapter the terminology of IT cost will be explained. Although the term 'cost of IT' is regularly used in several books by consultant firms, etc., most people have different definitions. In the first section we will explain different views of IT costs. After the introduction on IT costs, two IT accounting models will be introduced. These models give insight into IT costs and structure and section 4.3 will describe how they can be used. Following the introduction of the two models, the control of IT costs will be explained in section 4.4. Finally, the techniques for IT optimization will be described.

4.2 Cost of IT

IT costs can be interpreted in many ways. IT product and service vendors use terms such as decrease overall TCO or decrease cost to market their products. What does this mean? The next question should always be which cost or which cost model? In this chapter an overview of the main stream models on IT costs is given and the terminology used is explained. But let us start with some definitions to better understand the scope and context of costs.

4.2.1 Regular and one-time costs

Regular costs are costs which will occur over a period of time, they can be fixed or variable, and are incurred by repeating activity or by merely the elapsing of time (depreciation). When regular costs are related to receiving a service, these costs are called fees. One-time costs will occur only once based on a specific activity; they can be fixed or variable.

When looking at costs, the lifecycle of the related product or service can be used. In buying a new server, for example, the activity 'buying' will lead to the initial cost of the price of the server. This initial cost is a one-time cost. In the following years a maintenance contract will lead to regular costs. Finally, the phasing out of the server will lead to some costs for ending the maintenance contract, transport the server, etc. Although in some cases the server can be sold, leading to 'negative' ending costs, these ending costs are one-time costs.

One-time costs can be interchanged for regular costs. For example, when a server is leased instead of bought the starting one-time cost will be minimized, the regular cost will increase. The one-time costs at the end of the lifecycle will normally be low or marginal. Ending a contract before the end date will lead to much higher costs, these costs are described in the contract terms and are called ending costs.

For employees the lifecycle of costs is similar – starting with the hiring and training of the new employee (one-time cost), paying his salary (regular cost) until his pension (one-time costs are zero) or firing (separation package = one-time cost).

4.2.2 Costs vs spending

In determining the IT costs we often use information from budgets, financial overviews and financial accounting. To make better use of these information sources it is important to understand the difference between cost and spending.

Spending is the real expenditure performed; costs reflect that spending in the financial accounts. In other words spending should reflect the cash flow (see section 2.2.3). For example, when a mainframe is bought, this will be reflected in the financial accounting as follows:

- Investment mainframe: €300 k (spending).
- Depreciation: €100 k per year (regular costs).

When the same mainframe is leased, this will be reflected in the financial accounting as follows:

- Lease costs mainframe: €110 k per year (spending and regular costs).

In some countries/companies software may not be written off, when a software package of €300 k is bought, this will be reflected in the financial accounting as follows:

- (Investment) software package: €300 k (spending and one-time cost).

While performing a cost study, we will always look at the costs. In optimization studies and especially in the creation of business cases, the financing should also be taken into account. Choosing buying, leasing or other financial constructions can influence the business case enormously. In Chapter 5, business cases and financing will be discussed in more detail.

4.2.3 Direct vs indirect costs

In financial accounting the terms direct and indirect costs are used.

- Direct costs: costs which can directly be assigned to a product or activity (the organization's results). For example: dedicated servers for applications, software, consultants.
- Indirect costs: overhead costs, which are not directly assignable to a product or activity. For example: management, communications, HR, etc.

In its TCO models, Gartner uses another definition for direct and indirect, see section 4.3.2.

4.2.4 Hidden costs

Some (benchmark) organizations use the term hidden costs. These costs are related to IT but are not visible in the (IT) budget or investment/business cases. Examples are peer support, self-education, etc. These hidden costs are difficult to measure; they are supposed/assumed costs.

4.3 Understanding IT cost

Controlling the cost of IT is an important part of performance management. Control starts with understanding the IT costs and its structure. This understanding is achieved by introducing IT accounting models to the organization. These models can be used to perform cost studies or introduce continuous IT cost accounting.

Introducing such models to an organization creates an extensive insight in the IT costs of the organization. In controlling the cost an IT accounting model should be used. Two groups of models are commonly used:

- The ABC model which is based on activities and cost drivers.
- The cost model which is based on cost categories and cost elements.

In this chapter both models are introduced including an explanation of how they should be used.

4.3.1 Activity-based costing

'An ABC model is an economic map of the organization's expenses and profitability based on organization activities' (Kaplan, 1998). This map can help to gain a better insight into the costs and cost drivers of an organization. The ABC model can be used for three objectives:

- Cost optimization, which activities/tasks can be more effective and/or efficient. In some situations this will lead to out-tasking or even eliminating the specific task (see Chapters 4 and 8).
- Service analysis, profit and loss, cost transparency, pricing, viability of a product, business growth (see Chapter 7).
- Performance indicators – most organizations use mostly financial measures as performance indicators. The cost factors of ABC enrich the set of performance indicators of an organization (see Chapter 5).

An ABC system is based on cost drivers, the drivers or factors which influence the results of the production process. In other words the cost drivers are the basis for the cost of the product or service. Before the introduction of the ABC model, most cost management systems were only based on direct materials and direct labour. The amount needed and the cost of these materials

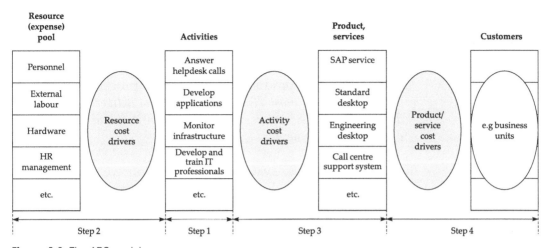

Figure 4.1 The ABC model

and labour led to the price of a product. When using the ABC model, the more indirect costs (sometimes called non-variable costs) such as sales force, purchase department, marketing, etc. can be related to cost objects: products, services and customers. This is described in Figure 4.1. The steps in this figure will be described below.

Can ABC be used to control the costs of IT? Yes, in two ways:

● Using ABC to manage the costs within the IT organization, the IT organization is seen as a separate services company, offering services to its customers (see Chapter 3).
● Including IT as resources in a general ABC system, IT is seen as a resource performing indirect or supportive activities.

Kaplan and Cooper (1998) give two rules for useful situations for applying activity-based cost systems:

● The Willie Sutton[1] rule: Look for areas with large expenses in indirect and support resources, especially when these expenses have been growing. *This rule applies clearly to an implementation of a general ABC system including IT. Most*

---

[1] Willie Sutton was a successful US bank robber during the 1950s. Willie, who was eventually captured at his home not far from a local police station, was asked during his initial interrogation, 'Why do you rob banks?' Willy replied, with the wisdom that made him successful for many years, 'That's where the money is!' (Kaplan, 1998)

organizations see IT as indirect and/or as a support function. Above that in most organizations the IT costs are perceived as too high, leading to a strong focus on IT cost cutting.

• The high-diversity rule: Look for a situation where there is a large variety of products, customers or processes. *This rule applies clearly to most IT organizations who deliver a large set of different products/services, in different quantities and to a large set of different customers.*

But what is an ABC system? In this section we will give the example of the development of an ABC system for an IT organization. These steps are based on the work of Kaplan and Cooper (1998) in the area of ABC systems and related to IT organizations. More detailed information on how to create and use ABC systems can be found in Kaplan and Cooper's book, and for some examples see Pryor (1995) and Cokins (1996).

4.3.1.1 Step 1 Create an inventory of activities (see Figure 4.1)

Setting up an ABC system starts with the creation of an activity inventory or dictionary. Activities are the central part of the ABC system and resemble the difference between traditional cost systems (relating resource expenses directly to end products) and ABC systems.

Describe the activities performed by the IT organization. Each activity is described by a verb and an associate object, for example answer helpdesk calls, develop applications, roll out new applications, monitor infrastructure, perform changes, solve incidents, develop and train IT professionals, create management information, etc. The best way to create this inventory or dictionary is by looking at each department and the activities performed in this department. This includes both production departments (e.g. operations, helpdesk, and application management department) and support departments (service level management department, quality and process department, HR). The activities therefore can be divided into two groups: IT operating processes and IT management and support processes.

To finalize this step and validate the information a cross-check can be made with the organization's process model if this is available, also reference models for IT processes such as ITIL (ITIL, 2002) or IBM's ITPM (ITPM, 2000) can be used for such a cross-check.

4.3.1.2 Step 2 Relate resources to activities

The relationship between resource expenses and activities is made by so-called resource cost drivers. Examples are shown in Table 4.1.

Table 4.1 Resource pools and cost drivers

Resource pool	Resource cost driver
Personnel	Hours
	Percentage of FTE
Office space	Square metres
HR	Number of employees per IT department

Several mechanisms exist to charge the resources to activities, based on measurements or estimates.

For the assigning of personnel to activities an employee survey may be used. This survey reflects the activity inventory which is created in step 1. Employees (or groups of employees with similar jobs) will mark the activities which they perform and estimate the percentage of their working time to each activity. As rule of thumb a minimum percentage of 5 per cent per activity is often used, although in optimization and process improvement studies it is interesting to see the total number of activities which people perform. By making the estimation the employees are more involved in the developed ABC system and will be less reluctant to accept the system and actions based on the analysis.

Another possibility to relate the resources to activities is a time and motion study; such a study can be performed in an isolated (demo) environment or a real-life study. These studies are performed by external people. While the employees are performing their job, the researchers are registering the time spent on the activities, or taking a sample test in which for each hour (or part of an hour), the activity the employee is working on is determined.

Another source can be the time registration used in most organizations; the timesheets describe the activities performed by each employee. For non-personnel resource expenses both measurements and estimates using percentages may be used.

For most studies a combination of the different mechanisms will be used, it is important to understand the balance between the cost of measurement and the cost of errors in this context (see Section 4.4.4).

The activities also have attributes. Attributes can help in structuring the activity inventory (especially important when these inventories are large) and in the analysis of the results of the ABC study. Examples of these attributes are found in Kaplan (1998):

- *Business processes*, activities are related to business processes, for example using ITIL or ITPM.
- *Variability*, activities can be indexed on the level of variability in the activity cost, for example the hiring of external consultants based on time and material is very flexible while the labour costs of regular employees are fixed. Activities which are primarily performed by external consultants will have a variable character, and activities performed by internal personnel have a fixed character. This will enable managers to understand their possibilities for short-term cost reduction.
- *Activity cost hierarchy*, this attribute is often used for operational processes. An activity cost hierarchy divides the activities on unit level, batch level, product-sustaining level and customer-sustaining level. See Figure 4.1 for an example of this hierarchy for an IT organization.
- *Location*, activities are categorized related to the locations in which they are performed; this method is very useful in process improvement studies and situations in which the organization is grown from mergers and acquisitions.

4.3.1.3 Step 3 Relate activities to services and offerings

The third step in creating an ABC system is relating the activities to products, services or offerings. The right side (see Figure 4.1) of this relationship can differ, depending on the use of the system or study. In some situations the (existing) services portfolio can be used. For IT organizations performing on the external market the portfolio of offerings may be used.

The relation between the activities and the products, services or offerings is based on so-called activity cost drivers. The determination of activity cost drivers can be very time consuming, because the activity cost drivers may differ for each combination of activity and product, services or offering. Three different types of activity cost drivers exist: transaction, duration and intensity/direct charging, where the cost of measurement increases in relation to the complexity of the cost driver.

- *Transaction*, examples for IT organizations are the number of lines of code, number of problems, number of calls, etc. The risk of using these simple cost drivers is that there may be a difference in the amount of activity needed per result. For example, some helpdesk calls use only a few seconds of the helpdesk personnel, for other calls minutes may be needed.
- *Duration*, examples are number of calls × duration, number of changes × hours spent. These drivers incorporate the difference in amount of activity, but not the difference in resources used to perform the activity, for example specific personnel, or equipment.
- *Intensity/direct charging*, in this situation the resources are directly charged to the product. These drivers are very cost intensive and should only be used in extreme situations (see section 4.4.4).

In combination with the drivers an index can be used; where the complexity of the output (high, medium, low) is taken into account.

4.3.1.4 Step 4 Relate products, services and offerings to customers

The last step in creating an ABC system is relating the products, services and offerings of the IT organizations to its customers. Customers can be divided into market segments or their internal equivalent business units. In other situations internal and external customers are combined.

In some situations available information makes it easy to relate to products, services or offerings to customers. Especially in situations were cost charging is based on the services and in situations with external customers. In these situations an analysis based on product/service cost drivers should only be performed to validate the available information. An analysis based on product/service cost drivers is similar to the activities performed in step 3.

4.3.1.5 Concluding

Creating an ABC system is too expensive to be a one-time isolated activity. Additional activities may be required. Using the system for continuous measurement, service analysis or as part of a balanced scorecard requires incorporation of the ABC system in the financial accounting. This way the ABC system will be kept alive and less additional costs will be made. The ABC system gives insight into the costs and its structure; section 4.4 describes what can be learned from this insight and how this insight can be used to control the costs. Section 4.5 will continue with how to optimize the IT costs.

4.3.2 Cost model

4.3.2.1 Cost categories

The simplest division of IT costs is to use six categories (see Figure 4.2). In most cost models these categories can be easily mapped.

Although these categories are simple and straightforward, when we take a closer look discussions will arise. Let us take the example of an organization which has outsourced their desktop environment including LAN servers, helpdesk support, etc. All these costs will be made visible under the category external service provider. This makes it impossible to compare its cost model with the cost model of an organization

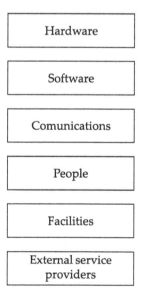

Figure 4.2

Cost model: general IT cost categories

Hardware	Cost elements	Discussional cost elements	Alternative cost category
	Mainframe Servers Storage	Desktops Printers	Employee cost Employee cost or facilities (non-IT) cost
		Servers with specific functional (back-up domain controllers)	Communications
		Maintenance fees	External IT service provider

Figure 4.3
Distribution of cost category hardware

that has not outsourced any of its activities. The cost model of the latter has divided the costs of their desktop environment over four categories: hardware, software, communications and people.

Cost categories are the highest level of a cost model; these cost categories are further detailed using cost elements. The partition of a cost category in cost elements should be based on the goals of the costs model/study and the available data. In Figure 4.3 the category hardware is given as an example. Some cost elements are easily determined: mainframe, servers, storage. Other cost elements will lead to some discussion and alternative cost categories are given in the right part of the figure.

Because of these discussions it is important to determine the cost model upfront with all stakeholders before starting a cost study.

4.3.2.2 Interaction between cost categories

Costs which occur in one category are related to the costs in other categories. These relationships are important to recognize when trying to reduce or optimize the costs of IT, but also in starting new projects and evaluating their business cases. Take the example in Figure 4.4.

The project of implementing automated software distribution will influence almost all cost categories:

- Hardware will be needed to create an infrastructure which can support automated software distribution (increasing the hardware costs).
- In the software category increase can be expected, software is needed to distribute the software, for end users to determine

Figure 4.4
Description of
improvement project
(example)

> **Technology improvement:** Automated software distribution
> **Description:** Automated software distribution enables an organization to install software on each separate workplace without any physical activity.
> **Two techniques exist:**
>
> • Push (the servers drive the upgrades).
> • Pull (the end user drives the upgrade, an installation script is run from a centralized server).
>
> **Advantage:** Automated software distribution as part of a consistent change management process reduces the effort of software changes significantly.

which software is needed, etc. In addition some software may be upgraded or new versions are needed to operate in an environment with automated software distribution (increasing software costs). Software licensing is also influenced by this project. Some producers of software require different licence systems which may increase costs. In contrast to this the introduction of automated software distribution can lead to more standardization of software and/or its versions; this can lower the software licence costs. These costs can be found under software or under external service provider.

● The introduction of automated software distribution will lead to decreasing costs in the area of supporting end users and manual distribution of software. This will in general decrease the costs in the personnel category. However, it must be recognized that extra work is needed in the area of the application catalogue and the maintenance and support of the automated software distribution system.

● The costs of communications will increase: the network will now be used to distribute software, increasing the load on the network in contrast to local copies by the helpdesk or the use of CDs. Some organizations combine this system with the loading of applications to the desktop each morning; this will further increase the load on the network.

This example (shown in Figure 4.5) clearly shows that the statement that automated software distribution will lower costs or decrease the TCO is too simple. You also ought to keep in mind that in this example we only looked at the costs within the IT department, but the influence on end users is not taken into account – extra training, support, time spent on unneeded applications, etc. Using a clear and accepted cost model in

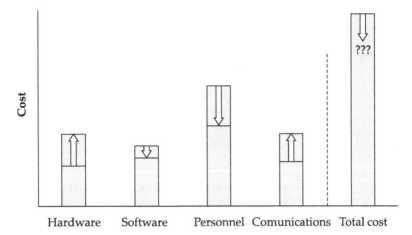

Figure 4.5
Interaction between
cost categories
(example)

making the business case for this project or discussing such a
system with a producer will help in creating the real picture.

4.3.2.3 TCO, example of a cost model

A commonly used cost model is total cost of ownership (TCO),
which the Gartner Group started to use at the end of the 1980s.
The TCO model's primary use was supporting organizations in
making decisions on infrastructure investments while using the
total costs of computing associated with their current and future
infrastructures. Since that moment the Gartner Group has
expanded their model, including the increasing complexity of
infrastructures (distributed computing, netcomputing, etc.)

Total cost of ownership can by defined as all costs associated
with the owning, operation, usage and disposal of a computer
through its lifecycle. A computer is seen as a PC or terminal, in
other words the total cost of ownership per end user or seat.
These costs are mostly calculated as seat costs per year.

In current TCO models both direct as indirect costs are
incorporated. Gartner has defined direct and indirect costs
differently from the more general accounting definition as
described in section 4.1:

● Direct costs are the budgeted costs and represent the
  expenditures on IT by an organization (capital, labour, service
  fees), they are represented in an IT budget plan.
● Indirect costs are unbudgeted costs, resulting from the usage
  of IT and represent the delivery of IT to end users.

The TCO model is based on cost blocks (comparable with the cost categories as introduced in section 4.3.2.1) and cost elements. For a description of the TCO model see Redman (1998). The TCO model as described by Gartner is extensive and can be flexibly adapted to the needs of the organization. Nevertheless, it is important in the case of benchmark studies (see section 4.4.1) to base all studies on the same model and/or clearly identify adaptations to the basic model.

The TCO model is created with an end user view in mind. Results of the TCO model show the TCO per end user and pie charts on the distribution of the costs per cost block. Comparisons can be made with benchmark data of organizations with a similar character. Gartner gives the information to derive TCOs for comparable organizations based on their benchmark data and a set of organization drivers. In additional analysis alternative TCOs can be derived, reflecting change in the infrastructure, the number or complexity of the platform, and the introduction of new management practices.

Although the TCO model organizations enable to benchmark their seat costs against benchmark data, industry averages, etc. and can recover in which cost blocks these differences originate, extra analysis is needed to uncover possibilities for cost reduction and optimization especially in the more central parts of the IT infrastructure.

Another disadvantage of the model is the Gartner interpretation of indirect costs. They see indirect costs as costs that reflect the inefficiency of IT when used by end users. The cost category for indirect costs is then called productivity loss, for example peer and self-support, education, planned and unplanned downtimes.

Although these all represent costs related to IT, they shouldn't be all seen as a negative form represented by 'productivity loss'. In some situations the total IT costs will decrease by using forms of peer support or self-support (using supportive help systems). Another cost element, education, in itself will lead to less productivity because of the used working time which is needed to educate. However, the education enables end users to improve the use of the supporting technology, resulting in higher productivity, less inefficiencies, less need for (peer) support, etc.

A better term for Gartner's indirect costs is hidden costs, costs which are not made visible in the IT budget, but are related to IT. Several consultancy firms set objectives and introduce customer projects to decrease hidden costs. It is important to understand that these costs are difficult to measure. Influencing these hidden costs may lead to increased IT costs in other categories and is therefore difficult to measure and control.

4.3.2.4 How to perform a cost study

Performing cost studies is time intensive, and requires in-depth knowledge of IT, finance and the specifics of the organization. These skills should all be available in the team that performs the cost study, consisting of finance experts, IT architects and (external) IT cost consultants.

The preparation and performing of a study can be described in five steps. The first two steps can be seen as the preparation of the cost study (in which a simple cost determination model can help for planning) and structuring the study. The third step is data gathering, in which a structured, self-explaining spread-sheet should be used, including a sheet which captures information on the acquired data. The last two steps can be seen as analysing, conclusions and follow-on.

1 The first step in a study is the creation or adoption of a cost model. The selection of such a model can be based on the need or requirements of the cost study. For example, if there is a need to benchmark the organization against industry average a standard TCO model will be used. In cases where an organization is in the process of acquiring a new organization, the TCO or cost model of the acquiring organization will be used. In other situations there is a need to get an insight into the possibilities of centralization of the IT activities, get a more general insight into the IT costs within the organization, etc. In this situation the cost determination model of Table 4.2 can be used to facilitate this step.
2 In the second step the study will be further structured and planned. In this step the cost determination model is essential to quickly assess the possible ways to determine the costs for all cost elements. The cost determination model gives the team a structure for their activities, recording the origin of the data or the estimations and the way of working. This is necessary to perform a cost study which is traceable and repeatable, important criteria for a cost study, especially in situations where the case study is used for benchmark purposes or for future references. See Table 4.2 on cost determination model for more details.

71

3 The third step is actually performing the cost study, gathering the data based on the cost determination model. It is important in this step to work very precisely in describing the origin of the data in the cost model. Table 4.3 sets out which information should be recorded for the data.

4 In the fourth step the gathered data will be analysed. Depending on the objective of the cost study different analysis techniques will apply. In some cases benchmark data will be used to draw conclusions. In other analysis a set of hypotheses or issues determined at the start of the study will be validated.

5 When the cost study is used as a base case, the results can be used to determine the effects of project plans and investments (see Chapter 6 on portfolio management and Chapter 5 on decisions on investments). When the cost study is seen as the 'zero-state' of a future cost management system, the cost model including the way of working should be described intensively to use in a periodic process.

Cost determination model

The cost determination model can be used in the creation of the cost model. It also supports the planning of a cost study. It structures the development of the cost model by asking specific questions to determine the cost categories and cost elements.

Table 4.2 Cost determination model

Aspect	Description
Organizational scope	Select a distribution of cost categories and elements which supports both the objective of the cost study and the execution of the cost study (gathering of data) ● On which organizational level do we want to make comparisons? ● Are there important imbalances in the organizational structure? ● On which organizational level is relevant data available? ● How is the financial accounting structured?
Cost categories and/ or elements	A start can be made from the general cost categories as described earlier in this chapter, or based on a cost model.
Part of cost model Y/N	The scope of the study can be determined upfront and reflected in the cost model. In that situation this question can clarify to the team and the rest of the organization: what's in scope and what's not? In other situations this selection will be the result of the first step, in which is decided which cost categories and/or elements will be part of the cost model, based on the objectives of the study and the possibilities to gather the data.

Table 4.2 Continued

Aspect	Description
Data available Y/N	Is the data available or in other words is the data described formally or informally within the organization?
Data source	What is the source of the data (a document or a person)?
How to collect data	Which steps are needed to collect the data? • Data available and source known: describes the steps needed to acquire the data. Sometimes permission is needed, or only a specific person can acquire the data. In other situations the data should be retrieved from a system. • Data available, source unknown: Which steps are needed to find the source. • Data not available: see next steps
Costs measurable Y/N	When data is not available, it may be possible to measure the costs. This can be determined by people from the organization together with experienced IT cost consultants. Criteria are resources, time, costs and value of the measured data.
How to measure costs	Which steps are needed to measure the data?
How to estimate costs	Which steps are needed to estimate the data? Can we use external information, which basic data is needed to perform this estimation. An estimation should be based both on volume and price, e.g. number of pc's and cost of the pc.
Estimate (volume)	What is the basis for the volume estimation?
Estimate (pricing)	What is the basis for the pricing/cost estimation?
Part of budget Y/N	When data is based on the budget this should be accounted for and additional information is required.
Charged or measured?	When costs are based on a budget it should be clearly identified whether the data in the budget is measured or based on a charged rate.
Manageable by department Y/N	Budgets, costs and volumes can be imposed by central organizations or the 'customers' of the organization. This is important to recognize because: • It can cover up inefficiencies in the organization. • It may prevent you from doing recommendations or executing the recommendations. • It can lead to unexpected reactions when performing changes, investments, etc.

Information gathering sheet

The information gathering sheet is used when data gathering is performed. It describes the attributes of the data which should be registered to create traceability and controllability of the data. This is especially important when the cost study will be repeated over a period of time.

Table 4.3 Information gathering sheet

Data attribute	Remarks/details
Source	What is the source of the data (document, system, etc.), including date, page number?
Fixed figure, measured, assumption, estimate	Is the figure based on another source, measured, is it an assumption or an estimate?
Actual/budget/ planned/year-to-date	For financial figures it is important to recognize if they are actuals, budgets, plans and year-to-date.
Assumptions	What is the basis for the assumption, sometimes assumptions are based on information from other sources, or other organizations, locations, etc?
Estimate basis (volume/price)	What is the basis for the estimate, give both the volume and the price if available? For example, cost of office space: bases are the number of (estimated) square metres and the (estimated) price per square metres.
Benchmark data	Relevant benchmark data may be noted already.

4.4 Controlling the cost of IT

The IT account models introduced in the preceding paragraph can be used to control the IT costs. The insight can be used for several purposes as explained in the first part of this chapter. To control the IT costs a cost management system should be used. Controlling the cost will lead to costs, in other words performing cost studies and especially introducing continuous cost management systems will lead to new (increasing) costs for the IT organization. In the last part of this section the factors that influence this cost of costing and how this should be balanced will be explained.

4.4.1 What can we learn from our costs?

Organizations have several reasons for performing cost studies:

- They want to benchmark their IT costs.
- They want to control their IT costs or better optimize them, (see Section 4.5).
- The IT costs can be used to support decision making on new investments, acquisitions, outsourcing, etc. (see Chapter 6).

Cost studies can be very useful in these situations, but it should always be kept in mind that each figure can be given with a correct synthesis beneath it and each conclusion can be made. To support the conclusions of a benchmark study it is therefore necessary that facts and assumptions are clearly marked and that sources, calculations, etc. are noted (see the information gathering sheet, Table 4.3).

4.4.1.1 Benchmarking

A large part of the cost studies is performed using the gathered information for a benchmark of the IT costs. Organizations use these benchmarks to:

- Analyse the operations of the organization.

It makes it possible to assess their strengths and weaknesses in combination with opportunities for improvement:

- Learn from the business best practices or other organizations (parts).

The frontrunners in their business can use processes/approaches which may be applied to their own organization, it's important to understand why these best practices lead to better results.

- Determine the competitiveness of the organization.

Organizations have a need to determine their competitive position on the internal or external market. For example, in the case of a merger or when the organization wants to deliver service to the external market.

Section 4.3 explains how cost studies should be performed based on an ABC model and a cost model. When an ABC model is used the next step is analysis; when a cost model is used the fourth step in a cost study is analysis. Benchmarking may be (a part of) this activity.

Although benchmarking is often performed, it is a tricky activity. Benchmarking may lead to false conclusions because of incomparable situations and unreachable targets. Before starting a benchmark some questions should be asked, these questions help in realizing the risks of benchmarking:

- Do I want to prove a point and is there a relatively objective and reliable reference available?
- Can I prove my point without influencing the result upfront?
- Would it really help in managing perception and or business/ IT alignment when I benchmark?
- How comparable/how different to the outside world do we want to be?
- Do I want to benchmark to support realistic target setting?
- Can I do realistic target setting without benchmarking?
- Do I want to do internal benchmarking, e.g. business unit by business unit only, or do I want to use external reference data?
- Is my internally available data reliable, consistent in definition and comparable to the external sources?
- Am I into the 'snapshot' accounting realm or do I have continuous tracking of performance indicators?

The answers to these questions will help you decide on:

- Benchmarking yes or no?
- Internal only or internal and external?
- For what purpose?
- To what level?

Performing a benchmark asks for a five-step approach. The first two steps may be performed in parallel with the other activities of the cost study. But the cost study results should be available before starting step 3 otherwise the results of the cost study may be influenced by the benchmark.

Step 1 Identify what is to be benchmarked

After setting clear objectives for the benchmark the benchmark data topics should be determined, including their level:

- Costs.
- Value.
- Performance.
- Other: services, products, etc.

The benchmark topics are influenced by other internal and external factors or characteristics of the organization. These cost influencers will be discussed in more detail in section 4.4.3. For this step it is important to understand that some information on the organization is needed to fully utilize the possibilities of a benchmark. Information which should be taken into the comparison are especially:

- IT environment/process maturity for cost considerations.
- Organization aspects (size, structure, etc.) related to cost.
- Service quality and customer satisfaction for cost considerations.

Use the cost model (see section 4.3) as a reference for this step.

Step 2 Select and engage sources

Benchmark data can be used from different sources:

- Internal (with zero-state or past results).
- Internal (comparison between different organization parts).
- Research sources: CIO online, IDC, other external service providers.
- Benchmark partners: Gartner Group, Meta Group, peer organizations.

The source should be in line with the objective of the benchmark and should provide comparable information.

Step 3 Data normalization

A valid comparison of data requires that the data is of the same type and level. Examples are comparing data with a different unit; for example, different currencies or Mbytes with bytes. Therefore all data should be normalized before the benchmark is performed. It is also important to understand which normalization is performed by the benchmark data source.

Comparable data is data with:

- Same type; the unit which is used.
- Same level; the elements included.

Normalization should be performed on the following aspects:

- The cost (and value model). Examples of comparable level are:
  - personnel costs: education, workplace, other facilities; are overhead costs included, etc.?
  - data centre costs: includes the square metre price, also facilities like airconditioning, generator, etc.;
  - external IT service providers: seat prices including improvement projects, helpdesk support, etc.
- The cost (and value model). Examples of comparable type are:
  - is the same currency used?
  - is the unit equal: service time, working time?
  - financial accounting aspects: depreciation periods, tax rates.
- Cost and value influencing/enabling factors. Examples are:
  - services, processes, etc.; are the same definitions used?
  - service levels, even 99 per cent service time can be interpreted differently; in service hours the service is available 99 per cent or the service is available for 99 per cent.

Although normalization is necessary, some data may be difficult to normalize. This should always be noted because this may lead to significant differences in the benchmark.

Step 4 Perform benchmark

After the normalization the benchmark can be performed. It is important in a benchmark to compare the same measures. Comparison of the complete data centre costs of a benchmark source with the data centre costs for only one business unit may lead to incorrect conclusions because they are different measures.

In addition to taking the IT environment into account for cost interpretation the benchmark can also be used to compare IT environments and IT management best practices. The information on differences should not only be noted but also the reasoning behind it. For example, the costs for workplaces may differ enormously because in the reference company a B brand is used or because all workplaces have flat screens.

Step 5 Communicate findings and conclusions

Communication of the findings and conclusions seems to be easy, but it is one of the trickiest parts of benchmarking. In the beginning we described that benchmarking may easily lead to unreachable targets and false conclusions.

Therefore it's important to communicate all findings and conclusions with the necessary reasoning. Target setting should not be a part of this step, only the direction should be given. Some information on optimization possibilities, best practices and innovative approaches may support the findings and conclusions.

4.4.2 Cost management systems

Controlling the costs of IT requires a cost management system. Detailed information on cost management systems can be found in ITIL's cost management (ITIL, 2002) or in more general financial accounting books. We give here only some general considerations for IT cost management systems.

- IT cost management systems should be a part of the financial accounting of the IT organization, this decreases the costs and stimulates continuity.
- IT cost management systems should reflect the overall organization's principles on cost management. Preferably they are part of the general cost management system.
- Continuous management versus periodic measurement, this choice should depend on the organization's objectives and the cost of costing should be taken into account.
- Level of the cost management system, take the cost of costing into account when the level of detail is determined.
- The cost management system should reflect the organization; changes in the structure of the organization and its management may lead to revisions in the cost management system.
- Cost management systems should be aligned with IT portfolio management (see Chapter 6).

4.4.3 When do you have an optimal cost level?

As described earlier in this chapter the scope and level of detail of a cost study should depend on the objective of the cost study. Organizations may start with a first objective of getting insight into their IT costs. Experience shows that sponsors of such studies create a need during the study to relate their figures to some kind of benchmark. Earlier in this chapter we described the pitfalls with benchmarking. And although it can give an organization a better vision on their situation, extra analysis is needed to determine the optimal cost level for an organization.

The total costs of an IT organization are influenced by different aspects of IT, the business organization and the external environment. The characteristics and choices made in these areas have an impact on the total cost level. Although the described cost influences may be seen as the most important we do not claim to give a complete view.

Nearly all decisions that are made in an organization have an impact on the cost drivers. The following is an overview of the most important cost influencers (in arbitrary order):

- General IT adoption of the industry.
- Complexity of the business.
- Centralization of the business.
- Strategic technology choices in the organization.
- Complexity of IT infrastructure.
- Level of centralization in the IT organization.
- Level of automation in the IT organization.
- Level of concentration in the IT organization.
- IT competencies within the IT organization and on the external market.

What are the factors that should be taken into account in such an analysis of the optimum cost level?

- Strategy of the organization; some organizations want to be frontrunners in the area of technology, or want to minimize manual labour, etc.
- Relation between total operational costs and the IT costs; these figures may also be available in benchmark databases. This relationship can identify the character of the organization: labour oriented or technology oriented (see also Section 4.3.2.2 on interaction between cost categories to understand the mechanism of the cost balloon).
- Specific situations such as location, history of mergers and acquisitions, etc.; these specific situations can lead to incomparable benchmark figures.

The result of these analyses may be that extra investments in IT are needed, or can create competitive advantages. But in most situations this is merely the starting point for IT optimization activities.

4.4.4 Cost of costing

Performing a cost study and continuous cost management are expensive activities. Before starting such an expensive activity, these costs should be balanced with the benefits. The costs of these studies are influenced by the factors shown in Table 4.4.

In case of continuous cost management, in addition to the factors above, the factors found in Table 4.5 play a role for the setting up of such a system.

In cost studies and the implementation of cost management systems we always search for a balance between the level of detail or accuracy and the costs related to getting this level of detail or accuracy. Principles such as the 80 per cent to 20 per cent rule and 'good is good enough' apply here; it is the balance between accuracy/detail and cost (see also Figure 4.6). The cost system or cost study should find an optimum in which the impact of errors is minimized and the value of measurement is maximized. For an ABC-based cost system a number of 30–50 activities is seen as an optimum, ignoring activities using less than 5 per cent of the time of an individual or resource pool. It is important to base the level of detail on the object of the study or system. When the objective of the system is determination of product or customer costs 10–30 activities is an optimum. In comparison, when the object is process improvement a cost model based on hundreds of activities might be needed.

This cost balance model can be understood by looking at the following example. An IT organization wanted to perform

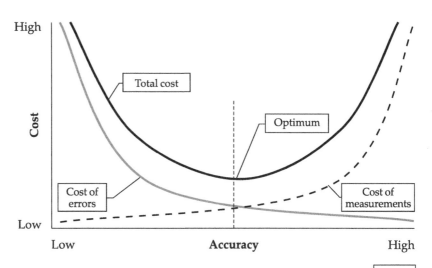

Figure 4.6
Cost balance model

Table 4.4 Factors influencing the costs of a cost study

Factor	Low cost	Medium cost	High cost
Scope/detail of the study	Direct IT costs	IT costs including project costs, developments costs.	Including IT costs within in the business.
		Costs are medium, extra time is needed to get a clear understanding on costs made by business and costs made by IT, time is needed to have an understanding on terminology used.	*Costs are high because of extra work, higher chance of double counting, more time needed to have an understanding on the terminology used.*
Size of the organization	Local organization with several departments or business units on one or a small number of locations.	National organization with several business units, several to large locations.	International organizations. Different business units.
Complexity of the organization	Organization with a central IT organization.	Organizations with a combination of decentralized IT organizations and a strong central IT organization or CIO function which plays a governance role.	Organizations with decentralized IT organizations, or combinations of decentralized IT organizations and central IT organizations.
	Costs are low because one set of terminology is used and one organization has the necessary data sources.	*Costs are medium because information sources will be part of the central organization, terminology will be more formal, although for detailed information sources from the decentral organization are needed*	*Costs are high because of the high number of information sources, the differences between terminology.*
Maturity of the (IT) organization	Small organization, family enterprises. Organizations that don't have to report to external parties.	Public enterprise.	Mature public enterprises are not only obliged to have clear figures on costs, spendings etc. but also use standard ways of working and are controlled by external accountants.
Quality of the data sources	Data sources are complete and available.	Data sources exist, consistence checks and additions are necessary.	Data sources are incomplete, fragmented and/or inconsistent.
	For example, an automated CMDB or asset management database.	*A CMDB exists but is outdated.*	*No CMDB exists.*

Table 4.5 Factors for costs of continuous cost management

Factor	Low cost	Medium cost	High cost
Measurement period	One-time.	Quarterly.	Weekly.
	Yearly.	Monthly.	Daily or even continuous.
	Although the costs for structuring the model and planning are a large part of the total costs.		*Costs are high because of the need for automation to analyse the large set of data.*
Automation/ manually	Manually, if possible based on available information in management systems.	Semi-automated, using export/input functionality or other connections.	Automated.
			Although this is a necessity when the measurement period is small or the scope very large.

chargeback on their PC and workstation-related activities based on the number of employees per business unit. The information of the HR department should form the base for this chargeback. This resulted in a lot of resistance of the business unit directors based on two arguments:

- The number given by HR was out of date.
- The number of employees was higher than the number of workplaces (because of part-timers and flexible workplaces).

The IT department didn't accept the method because the number of employees was more than 20 per cent lower than the number of registered workplaces in their helpdesk system (which was expected to be less than the total number of workplaces).

The IT department proposed to implement an automatic asset management system which registered all workplaces (workstation/desktops and laptops) via the network. The implementation of such a system for the complete organization would not only have a long implementation period but also a large investment.

The organization has reached its optimum by performing a half-year 'wall-to-wall inventory' of the workplaces by a group of students (one week's work) and a simple asset management system for all laptops.

4.5 Focus of IT optimization

Recent years have shown a focus on IT optimization, mostly because there is a need to reduce the IT cost. This need can be the result of the economic situation and organization-wide cost-cutting programmes. Another reason can be found in situations where the business is not satisfied with the value for the cost of IT.

IT optimization is finding an optimum for the IT costs of an organization. As described in section 4.4.3 an optimum is organization specific, depending on internal (level of automation, age of automation, number of employees, standardized infrastructure, etc.) and external factors (competition, type of business, etc.) and must be seen in relation to the value of IT (Chapter 5). Most of the time IT optimization is seen as a cost reduction exercise, although examples can be found where IT optimization means increasing IT spending. All IT optimization initiatives will lead to a shift in IT costs.

- An IT optimization initiative may result (as part of a complete set of changes) in refocusing on activities around new technology and outsourcing cost-extensive activities like legacy maintenance and operations. This will lead to a shift in the cost distribution on the cost categories' external service provider, personnel, and slightly on the cost categories' communications and facilities, and probably (in the long term) to an overall cost reduction.
- An ABC study can discover that a large amount of the costs are made for the maintenance and operations of self-made applications; this can lead to a change in strategy towards package-based applications, which will lead to a shift from the cost category personnel towards especially software (licences, etc.).

In the remainder of this chapter IT optimization will be seen as cost reduction, although the described techniques can also be used in situations where optimization may lead to increasing IT costs.

4.5.1 IT optimization techniques

Different techniques can be used to reduce IT costs: standardization, consolidation, concentration, centralization, outsourcing (including out-tasking) and cost cutting. These are the most commonly used techniques.

Cost cutting is seen as a technique which focuses on the decreasing of IT costs. The targets are mostly short term, and focused internally on the IT organization. The effects on the value of IT and the business are not taken into account. Examples (real life) are:

- Decrease of IT budget for the following year of 15 per cent.
- Decrease of IT personnel of 10 per cent.
- No external personnel for the rest of the year.

Cost cutting will lead to both decreasing quality of service and fewer services. In some situations this can lead to increasing total costs. Although cost cutting can be used to decrease IT costs, it is not seen as a real optimization technique because of its short-term view and internal IT focus.

Outsourcing is not a cost saving initiative in itself, but more a lever for the realization of standardization and optimization. We will address outsourcing and variants like out-tasking in Chapter 8.

The following optimization techniques will be described using the remaining six areas: hardware, software, communications, facilities, processes and organization (parts). These correspond mainly with the cost categories introduced earlier in this chapter. Instead of the cost category personnel, the area's processes and organization are used. The cost category external IT service providers will not be discussed, for more information on the management of external service providers see Chapter 8, where the possibilities and effects for using the technique for each area will be described.

4.5.1.1 Centralization

Centralization is seen to create a situation where someone or something is under the control of one central authority, but does not include locations of people or assets. In IT optimization situations centralization can be used to centralize:

- Organizations, for example one central helpdesk instead of local helpdesks.
- Processes, for example one central incident management process instead of local incident management handling.

In most situations the overall quality of service will improve and the business will value IT more because they will better able to meet expectations. In other words: the differences between organizations, employees, services and users will be reduced and may lead to an overall improvement. Cost reductions can be found in the area of personnel; through standard processes personnel will be more effective and efficient and less management is required.

Centralization of hardware, software, communications and facilities will only lead to changes in the control and management. In other words the effect will be especially in the organizational area.

4.5.1.2 Consolidation

Consolidation can be best described as the uniting of things which results in an improvement. Consolidation is sometimes divided into logical and physical, but this division will not be used here. In IT optimization situations consolidation can be used to consolidate:

- Organizations, for example helpdesks, operations.
- Physical environments, for example data centres and research centres.

Consolidation is in these situations not just combining these organizations but also improving these organizations (second part of the definition). The quality of the new organization or (in case of physical consolidation) data centre or research centre should lead to improved quality of service. Cost reductions might be expected in the areas of facilities and personnel (more effective use of personnel, less management).

4.5.1.3 Standardization

Standardization is changing something to conform to a fixed standard, type or form. In IT optimization situations standardization can be used for hardware, software and communications. Standardization simplifies the IT environment. Because specialties no longer exist, fewer interfaces are needed, fewer system images are needed, etc. Additionally less specific knowledge and skills are needed. Cost reductions may be found in the area of personnel (less specific personnel needed, more efficient use of personnel, less education), external service provider (less specific knowledge needed), software and hardware (fewer maintenance contracts and lower licence fees). Moving from one-of-a-kind to packages will increase licence fees. In case standardization means one service for one requirement (instead of multiple solutions) the licence fees decrease due to economy of scale.

When standardization is used for facilities corresponding cost reduction may be achieved because the devices are standardized and maintenance contracts may be simplified. For example, all data centres have the same type of airconditioning, network, power generator, etc. In addition people will make fewer errors because all facilities are equal.

Standardization of processes and procedures can be based on generally accepted models such as ITIL, IBM's ITPM and CMM. In this area standardization is the first step towards central-ization in which one process exits for the whole organization. In addition to cost reductions in the area of personnel, standardiza-tion of processes will lead to better quality of service. End users can better understand the way of working of the IT organization when this is similar in the whole organization; this will lead to a higher (average) customer satisfaction.

Standardization of organizations is only an improvement when it is combined with other optimization techniques such as concentration or centralization.

4.5.1.4 Concentration

Concentration is the gathering of people or things in one location. In IT optimization situations concentration is used for organizations (personnel) and hardware (facilities). Concentra-tion has a minor effect on the quality of service. Cost reductions will be especially in the area of facilities and personnel (less travelling). Concentration of hardware will result in different requirements for data communication, depending on the chang-ing communication flows between servers and between servers and end users. In the hardware area concentration is a prerequisite for consolidation.

Concentration won't apply to communications, processes and software.

4.5.1.5 Centralization vs concentration

Centralization and concentration are often mixed up. It is important to understand that centralization/decentralization is about responsibilities and authorities. Concentrated/local is about geography; concentrated is in one place, deconcentrated or local is in many places. This terminology can be used for different aspects of IT in the organization, for example for the information systems, data centres, organizations, etc. A specific example of a centralized organization, which is not concentrated, is a virtual organization. Virtual organizations are often used for international merged organizations and organization parts with specific (country or language-based) skills. Examples are:

- A helpdesk with local language support, which operates as one helpdesk, with one telephone number, but where the employees work in their home country and are supported by extensive information systems and communications.
- A virtual engineering organization, which is managed as one organization, with one management team, the engineer will stay working in their home country using network and system management tools to perform their jobs.

4.5.1.6 Centralization vs consolidation

Centralization and consolidation are two closely related terms which often lead to discussions. Consolidation is about uniting things or people leading to an improvement, where centralization is about responsibilities and authorities. The following combinations occur:

- Centralized and consolidated. Assets or people are united, and under the control of one central authority.
- Centralized and not consolidated. Assets or people are not united and under the control of one central authority.
- Decentralized and not consolidated. Assets or people are not united and each unit has its own decentral authority.

4.5.1.7 Consolidation vs concentration

Consolidation and concentration are also often mixed up. The difference lies in the fact that concentration is about location, the placement of assets or people in one location. Consolidation is about uniting, leading to an improvement. For example, the improvement of a helpdesk organization with three distinctive operating helpdesks towards three helpdesks operating in a same way, closely interacting and exchanging information would be consolidation. Where locating these three helpdesks in one location would be concentration. The combination of these two improvement techniques would lead to one new helpdesk.

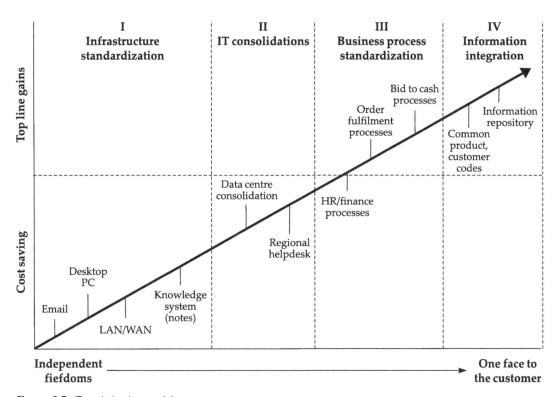

Figure 4.7 IT optimization model

4.5.2 Stages of IT optimization

The authors of this book have experience in different programmes for IT optimization. And although each situation is
different a general order can be given on which optimization
programmes should be based. The Working Council for CIOs, a
best practices research firm, has created a model based on the
experience of many of its member organizations (WCCIO, 2000).
We have used the model shown in Figure 4.7 often in customer
situations and have validated its content often.

4.5.2.1 Stage I Standardization of the infrastructure

In this stage organizations standardize infrastructure parts; this
can be hardware, network or software standardization efforts.
The software has an infrastructure character, for example office
applications, email, knowledge systems. The hardware is the
more user-related part of the infrastructure, PCs, desktops,
terminals, networked computers, etc. All these parts of the
infrastructure have two important things in common:

- Changes in these parts are non-threatening for managers in the IT organization and the business.
- These infrastructure parts are relatively isolated. Changes have a minor impact on the other parts of the infrastructure, the way of working and the business processes.

This makes standardization of these parts relatively easy. The benefits of these standardization activities can be enormous depending on the organization's situation and complexity of the infrastructure.

An example is a worldwide organization which used more than 50 different types of email systems (this can even be multiplied by the number of versions of each type). In about 18 months this organization standardized towards one email system with three different versions and local language support inside. Leading towards enormous cost reductions in software licence fees, standardized underlying hardware, less supportive personnel, less administrative personnel, fewer people involved in interface development, etc.

In addition the quality of the infrastructure improved by having easy communications between business units and countries, fewer problems with storage and retrieving old data, better supporting changes in business units and movements of employees.

4.5.2.2. Stage II IT consolidation

In this stage organizations consolidate IT on both IT organizational and infrastructural levels. Examples are helpdesk consolidation and data centre consolidation. Consolidation projects have a large impact especially on the IT organization, for the business (end users) the impact will be less although their contact points with IT may change. This large impact on the IT organization is caused by breaking through the old management systems, ways of working, hierarchies, etc. In addition IT consolidation is combined with standardizing the underlying infrastructure. In that way IT consolidation is sometimes an enabler for infrastructure standardization. For data centre consolidation this implies not only consolidating the organization and the data centre but also standardization and consolidation of the hardware in these centres, standardization of the way of working, standardization and consolidation of storage. In the case of helpdesk consolidation the organization will be consolidated and processes and tooling will be standardized.

These activities lead to cost reduction mostly in the area of people and facilities; additional cost reductions can be made in the area of hardware and system tooling. In most situations the cost of communications will increase. Additionally quality improvements may be expected from the standardized processes. A business case should determine whether the activities are leading to a positive end result.

An example in this area is a worldwide organization consolidating their more than 150 data centres worldwide to five large data centres, leading to enormous cost reductions in the area of people and facilities; as a result the organizations worked more efficiently and at a high level of quality leading to better appreciation by the business. These projects are not only feasible or interesting for worldwide organizations. For national organizations with a merger history profitable business cases are also created and executed.

4.5.2.3 Stage III Business process standardization

In this stage the business processes within the organizations are standardized including underlying systems and tooling. Examples are a single consolidated order fulfilment process and a single HR/finance process for the entire organization. It is important to understand that not only in organizations with different business units and locations in different countries are processes not standardized, even in small national organizations operating in two locations different processes exist.

Standardization of business processes has a large impact on the business organization; large groups of people have to change their way of working, use new and different tooling, have to be educated and sometimes a reduction of employees may be implied. For IT this will be one of the largest projects, resulting in new technologies and infrastructure, and a large migration effort.

For more information on this stage, see Chapter 6.

4.5.2.4 Stage IV Information integration

The last stage is the integration of information through the complete organization based on information repositories and sometimes even aligning information with outside parties. The result will be a complete one-face to the customer.

For more information on this stage, see Chapter 6.

4.5.2.5 Order of IT optimization

The order of these stages is based on two aspects:

- Time in which cost savings will be achieved.
- Influence on end-users in the business environment.

It is important to understand that experience shows that the highest cost reductions will be achieved by reducing the number of employees needed to perform the IT services. Changes in other cost categories will almost always influence the personnel category. For example:

- Standardization of hardware will lead to less support, and therefore fewer personnel.
- Automated software distribution will lead to fewer personnel needed for software distribution.
- Centralization of hardware facilities (data centre consolidation) will lead to more efficient personnel planning and therefore fewer personnel.

However, the loss of personnel needed does not necessarily mean that jobs will be lost. It is important to recognize that decreases in the need for IT services personnel can be used to enable growth without the need for more people, to improve the quality of service or by decreasing the number of contractors.

Each model has always some side marks. Most importantly each organization should always do a short assessment (e.g. workshop with key players) to understand the key cost drivers in the organization, the obvious cost reduction opportunities, etc. This should be the basis for adjusting the model into a specific programme or approach for the organization.

Additionally focus should be on creating a clear shared view of the goals of the IT optimization; in doing this a power sponsor should also be identified. This power sponsor needs to support the optimization goals and the focus of the optimization activities.

4.6 Summary

In this chapter we covered the cost of IT and described the different types of costs. Similar to value even cost can be seen as a perception; it all depends on which costs are included.

We showed that there are two main stream accounting models: ABC and a cost model, which can be used to understand and control the IT costs in the organization. Controlling and managing the IT costs requires an optimum level. A benchmark study only can give direction about the optimum level, but can never be used for real target setting. Targets depend on an almost infinite set of internal and external factors on the area of the organization, the business and the IT environment. Although understanding IT costs is very important there are costs involved and these costs should be weighed out to the needed accuracy.

To optimize the IT costs in an organization different techniques exist. These techniques can be used for the different areas of IT (hardware, software, personnel, facilities, communication, etc.). In most situations a combination of different techniques is needed to achieve the required target. A very common order for optimization is given; this order starts from standardization initiatives, to IT consolidation (IT organization-focused initiatives), to business process improvement and finally information integration.

5 Measuring the added value of IT

5.1 Introduction

In this chapter we will cover the added business value of IT and describe many ways and techniques that can be used to quantify and measure this business value.

We will start with an explanation of the context of IT value, which of course has an impact on the things to measure and the ways to measure them.

After explaining the different contexts, we will describe ways to quantify value. We will do this by narrowing the scope, starting from the value of a company to the value of an individual IT investment proposal. Halfway along this track, the ways of using scorecards to measure the added value of IT departments will be discussed.

We need to keep in mind, though, that although the value of IT can be measured in many ways, value itself is subject to the perception of the individual observer. This perception may be false, blurred and irrational; in real life, one has to deal with it. The good work of many people working in the IT department delivering high quality service to all business units can become spoiled in one hour, when a single computer virus damages part of the email file of the CEO.

5.2 Context of value

What is the business value of a company? The answers is, of course, 'it depends'.

For shareholders, the business value of a company equals the current stock price, multiplied by the number of stocks outstanding. This shareholders' value is an important indicator for public-owned companies. The financial analysts of Wall Street investment banks strongly influence the stock prices. For them, the business value of a company is a mixture of a number of financial indicators regarding both the past and the future. They regard both the company itself and the economy as a whole. These financial indicators and the economy influence the stock price which is a perceived value.

For marketing managers, the value that the customers perceive, the customer value, is the most important indicator. Another indicator is stakeholder value, which is the value that the company brings to each of its stakeholders, e.g. shareholders, employees, government, neighbours, clients and suppliers.

Where the concept of business value itself is discussed, the business value of IT is discussed even more. A lot of effort has been made to define this business value of IT, with mixed success. The 'productivity paradox' states that despite all the investments in IT, the productivity of the average employee has not improved. However, as with the business value for the company, the business value of IT can be perceived in a number of ways, not necessarily financial or by productivity:

- Enabling mass customization of products and services.
- Enabling very high quality mass production.
- Enabling high quality error detection.
- Enabling low risk testing by the use of simulation.
- Enabling the introduction of new products and services via the Internet.
- Performing fundamental scientific research (astronomy, human genome project of DNA).
- Enabling true globalization of companies.

This kind of business value was not possible before advanced usage of IT. More than once, the usage of IT has opened new business frontiers, new markets and new chances for companies to create value for customers that simply did not exist before.

However, within each company, the business value of IT stays an important issue. There are a number of values of IT that need to be distinguished. In this chapter we will repeatedly change the scope to discover the various ways of looking at the business value of IT.

1 The business value of the organization (section 5.3).
2 The business value of the IT department (section 5.4).
3 The business value of IT investment proposals (sections 5.5 and 5.6).

The business value of the IT services portfolio will be discussed in Chapter 6.

5.3 The business value of the organization

5.3.1 Value-based management

In financial management literature, traditionally a lot of focus has been on the subject of business value. Scientists a long time ago accepted the fact that accounting figures do not give an accurate view on the value of an organization.

The net profit of an organization is the result of the way all activities are financially accounted for. This means that the principles of accounting that are used influence the net profit. In the annual reports, a number of pages have to be dedicated to the explanation of these accounting and valuation principles. Additionally, often non-structural events such as provisions, net results of the buying and selling of business units and other extraordinary events will add to the confusion. To put it bluntly, showing profit is a choice.

To relate the profit of a company with the assets that are needed to generate that profit, other financial metrics were created such as the return on net assets (RONA), which is derived by dividing the operating profit by the total invested capital, or the return on investment (ROI).

The ROI is calculated by dividing the accounting profit by the total of investments needed. Although first used as a measurement for companies as a whole, the ROI has become a very popular measurement for individual investments as well. Particularly in the IT industry, the ROI is a very common way to express the value of an individual investment.

Another recent wave in financial management practices is called value-based management and includes another aspect in the business value of an organization: the cost of capital. The cost of capital is dependent of the inherent risk. This leads to a more accurate business value indicator: the Economic Value Add (EVA™). The theoretical basis of this indicator was laid in the term 'residual income' in the 1950s, which was improved to create EVA by Rappaport (1986) and Stewart (1991). Although not easy to calculate, the impact of EVA is very simple:

- If the EVA is positive, the organization creates value.
- If the EVA is negative, the organization destroys value.

Another important aspect of value-based management is the concept of value drivers (Urff, 2000). Value drivers are performance indicators that have an impact on the enterprise value of an organization.

Seven generic value drivers have been identified:

- Sales growth
- Operating margin
- Working capital
- Cost of capital
- Growth duration
- Tax rate
- Fixed assets

Additional value drivers will depend on the organization and its strategy. These value drivers can then be visualized in a value driver tree (or DuPont formula). Figure 5.1 shows an example of a part of such a tree.

It is easy to understand that with such a tree at hand, the value-based management of all levels of the organization will improve, because all individual contributions to the overall value of the company are transparent.

The value drivers contribute to the shareholder value of an organization. However, the sensitivity of the value drivers can vary considerably: some of them have hardly any impact at all, where little differences in other value drivers may have a large impact. This sensitivity of value drivers is company specific. The analysis of the value drivers of an organization can lead to a prioritization of investment opportunities; if the organization wants to maximize its shareholder value, it can invest in those projects that influence the value drivers with the largest impact.

5.3.2 The balanced scorecard

In a similar search to combine the different perceptions of value, Kaplan and Norton introduced the balanced scorecard (Kaplan and Norton, 1992). This scorecard combines four perspectives:

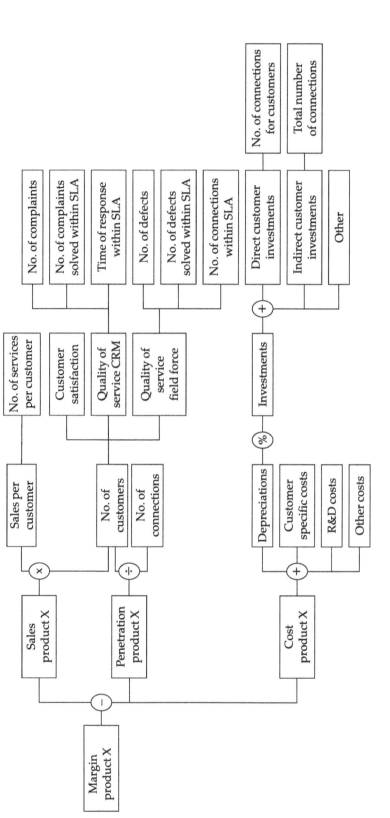

Figure 5.1 Example of value driver tree

1 The *Learning & Growth* perspective directs attention to the organization's people and infrastructure. Adequate investment in these areas is critical to all long-term success.

2 The development of a true learning organization supports success in the next balanced scorecard perspective, the *Internal* perspective. The Internal perspective focuses attention on the performance of the key internal processes that drive the business.

3 In order to translate better processes into financial success, companies must first please their customers. The *Customer* perspective considers the business through the eyes of a customer, so that the organization retains a careful focus on customer needs and satisfaction.

4 The *Financial* perspective measures the ultimate results that the business provides to its shareholders.

Together, these four perspectives provide a balanced view of the present and future performance of the business (derived from Kaplan and Norton, 1992; see Figure 5.2).

In each of the four perspectives, a number of measurements can be defined, which are regarded as the key performance indicators (KPIs). These indicators will give the executive management of a company a bird's eye view of the current performance of the company.

The balanced scorecard has proven to be a popular management concept, and a lot of companies have implemented their own version of a scorecard, with their own organization-specific KPIs. When the company has a balanced scorecard in place, with KPIs and its measurements, there is a large opportunity to link the added value of a proposed IT investment to the impact on the KPIs of the balanced scorecard. If the impact on those

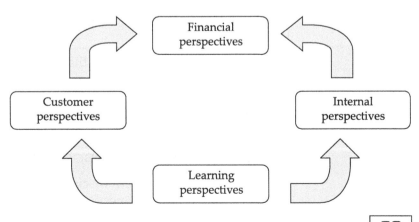

Figure 5.2
The balanced scorecard perspectives

business KPIs is part of the business case, the IT department and the business will share a common language to describe the added value of IT.

KPIs will be part of the value driver trees as shown in Figure 5.1. This combination is an overall business management tool for the understanding of business value, expressing the benefits of IT investments in terms of impact to KPIs and, consequently, the value drivers will deliver a mutual understanding of the business value of IT for both business and IT.

Whether or not these top-down value measurement instruments can be used for IT investment appraisal depends on the maturity of the value-based management practices of the organization. The CFO or the financial department will have the lead in the implementation of such instruments, and the IT department will be a follower.

Anyway, it is highly recommended for IT management to understand the current financial management practices of the organization, especially with regard to value-based management and link the IT initiatives with these practices.

If there are no management instruments such as value trees or balanced scorecards implemented, the search for IT value of individual IT investments must be done bottom-up. This bottom-up value analysis is explained in sections 5.5 and 5.6.

5.4 The business value of the IT department

5.4.1 The IT scorecard

The balanced scorecard is a performance management tool that can be used for a company as a whole, but also for departments within a company. Especially when a department perceives itself as a service organization, delivering services to its internal clients, the scorecard can be implemented at a departmental level.

Therefore, it is no surprise, that apart from the business balanced scorecard, departmental scorecards have been developed, e.g. the HRM scorecard, the sales scorecard and the IT scorecard. Let us take a closer look at a typical IT scorecard.

5.4.1.1 Learning perspective

IT is a technology-driven discipline. The knowledge of IT professionals is outdated very quickly. It is crucial for each IT department to keep investing in its own people by education and adopting new technology. It is not a good thing to have a large number of legacy applications, but having 'legacy people' is worse.

5.4.1.2 Internal perspective

The performance indicators for the internal perspective are related to the IT processes as described in standard process models. Most of them have an impact on the service levels that are negotiated with the customers of the IT organization. The negotiated service level cannot be higher (more ambitious) than the achieved internal performance indicators that relate to them.

5.4.1.3 Customer perspective

Customer satisfaction is one of the main KPIs for each and every IT organization. This satisfaction is determined by the customer as the relationship between the perceived quality of service and the expected quality of service; the expected quality of service will be the level of quality the customer and the IT department have agreed upon in the service level agreement (SLA). Very high customer satisfaction can only be achieved when the customers' expectations are exceeded. Managing the expectations of the customer is important to prevent the expectations becoming irrational.

5.4.1.4 Financial perspective

The PIs for the financial perspective of an IT organization will differ depending on the IT value perception level and the accompanying financial management practices involved.

If the IT organization is regarded a cost centre, performance indicators will be derived from the cost effectiveness point of view. If it has a profit/loss responsibility, there will be one or more profit-related performance indicators.

5.4.2 The scorecard process

The initial process of the development of a scorecard can be a large top-down project with a lot of specialized help, providing a very sophisticated scorecard. Starting with the creation of a vision and a mission statement, the business goals and strategy are defined. The critical success factors of that strategy are identified, and the objectives are derived for the goals and the critical success factors. In order to measure the objectives, key performance indicators are defined and the result is a balanced scorecard.

Another way to implement this is the pragmatic, bottom-up approach. This approach starts with the measurements that are part of the operational work today. These measurements are collected and analysed. The department manager then has to wonder why these measurements are in place and how they contribute to operational, tactical or even strategic goals. At the same time, he has to discard those measurements that do not contribute at all. In this way, each department manager will create his own 'performance indicator tree'. This will create the need for additional performance indicators and accompanying measurements. The top of that tree consists of performance indicators that can be shared within the management team. The management team then discusses the key performance indicators that will be part of the organization or line of business (LOB) scorecard. At this point, a check with the company's existing business goals and strategy is performed to prevent a lack of alignment.

Once the initial scorecard has been agreed upon, it is necessary that the scorecard is part of the routine of the organization. We need a scorecard management process.

5.4.2.1 The scorecard management process

The scorecard management process consists of five processes that interact between the operational process ('operations') and the management process ('management'). See Figure 5.3.

- Collecting measurements:
  - collection of measurement data (from operation to measurement).
- Reporting process:
  - reporting of operational performance to management (from measurement to IT scorecard).
- Defining initiatives:
  - analysis of the performance in order to define improvement opportunities and describing those opportunities into initiatives.

- Implementation process:
  - steering, changing and/or re-engineering of operations with the help of initiatives.
- IT scorecard management process:
  - extension (criteria for making additions);
  - deletion (procedure to make deletions);
  - change (of measurement methods, desired results, key performance indicators, etc.).

For each of the five processes, the triggers, the roles involved and the results of that particular process are recorded. The IT scorecard will be used for the IT supply organization within a company; the ownership of the scorecard therefore lies with the director of IT, or the CIO. The CIO may delegate this responsibility to the QA manager within IT, who in practice will carry out the necessary actions.

As shown in Figure 5.3, there is an improvement cycle for the IT services organization, triggered by the results of the IT scorecard. These results lead to initiatives to improve the performance of the organization. Additionally, there can be improvement initiatives without the authority of an IT scorecard result. These initiatives will be triggered by day-to-day operations. When adopted by the management, the IT scorecard will incorporate those additional initiatives as well, defining metrics or performance indicators, in order to measure the success of those initiatives.

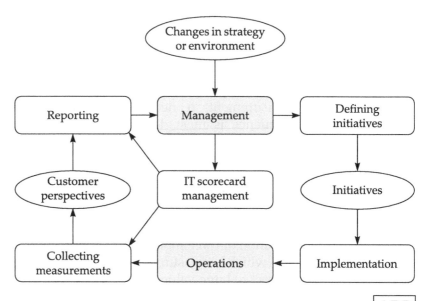

Figure 5.3
The IT scorecard management process

If the organization changes and improves its operations without the reflection of those initiatives on the IT scorecard, the IT scorecard will lose its role as an organizational management instrument.

5.4.2.2 Collecting measurements

The process for collection of measurement data consists of periodic collection of measurements to fill in the IT scorecard.

A clear distinction needs to be made between the terms 'periodic' and 'frequency' for the purpose of this process. The periodic collection of measurement data points to the fact that this is a regularly recurring activity. During this activity, the measurement data is transformed into information for the IT scorecard. Frequency is related to how often a particular measurement is carried out and this frequency may vary per measurement.

The periodic compilation of the IT scorecard is purposefully not the same as the periodic assessment of business. For some parts of the organization, it is of supreme importance to have a higher frequency of measurement than just once a month for the purposes of internal reporting. For example, the availability of a service may be measured continuously; however, it is a periodic measurement that takes place for the purposes of the IT scorecard. This final result is delivered in the measurement process as described above. In these cases, an average or a chart of the time period results can be used.

On the other hand, there are areas where the contrary may be the case and all too frequent measurements may be redundant, e.g. it makes little sense to measure on a monthly basis to what extent employees satisfy their developments targets which are compiled for the duration of a year.

For each perspective, unit and subunit and even for each measurement, it needs to be carefully investigated which frequency is most desirable for the IT scorecard. Again, the measurement frequency desired for the IT scorecard may vary from that of a particular organizational subcomponent. It is important to realize which consequences there are when the measurement frequency of a particular KPI is less than once per month. A KPI measured once per quarter and which indicates 'red' on one month will therefore be in the 'red' position for the duration of three months. Something similar is also valid for the KPI which is measured once a month for the IT scorecard, but is subject to large value fluctuations during the time period. Thus, careful consideration needs to be given to each measurement with regard to the frequency with which that measurement is to take place.

5.4.2.3 Reporting

Performance measurement and its publication within the IT scorecard is not a goal in itself. This section, however, treats the process of compiling a report separately from the framework of control: it describes the way in which the IT scorecard is set up periodically and which organizational roles are important for that purpose. The following paragraph investigates more closely how the IT scorecard can make a major contribution to the process of improvement.

The reporting process combines the activities of setting up the IT scorecard based on the measurements. The following steps need to be executed:

1 Compare the measured values of the various metrics with the previously established norm; this will classify the outcome as desirable, critical or unacceptable.
2 Combine the outcomes of the various metrics into perform-ance indicator scores following predefined classification rules (e.g. one metric scores unacceptable: this means the perform-ance indicator scores unacceptable).
3 Publish the key performance indicators in the scorecard.

5.4.2.4 Defining initiatives and implementation

The steering of the organization takes places at the periodic meetings of the CIO management team where initiatives are designed to undertake actions for improvement on the basis of the IT scorecard. The IT scorecard thus becomes a driver for improvement.

KPIs can attain a score that is desirable, unacceptable or critical. For KPIs that do not score 'desired', the causes of undesirable performance need to be investigated. The responsibility of this task lies with the owner (responsible manager) of the KPI. In the ideal situation, each KPI that needs to be reported as 'critical' or 'unacceptable' needs to have a plan for improvement. This plan for improvement will preferably consider the objective of the KPI, and not the KPI or its measurement itself. However, it is possible that a critical or unacceptable score for a KPI becomes 'desired' after a redefinition of the norm scores for that KPI.

The CIO management team is responsible for the target realization of the IT department. Therefore, the results of the IT scorecard are assessed by this team. At the same time, this team also evaluates the initiatives for performance improvement.

5.4.3 The IT scorecard management process

Improvement and adjustment of the IT scorecard is subject to two different aspects:

1 The improvement of the IT scorecard by means of adjustment of the metrics and their relative weight in the reporting model.
2 The improvement of the IT scorecard by means of the measurements contributing to the IT scorecard.

5.4.3.1 Improving the reporting model

The improvement of the model is an important process in order to align the scorecard with the business periodically. The model needs adjustments as a reply to changing market conditions, new service introductions, and new strategy directions from the business. This might lead to the adding, deleting and/or changing of KPIs.

Another type of adjustment can be the change in priority for KPIs, resulting in changes in the weighting of KPIs in the scorecard.

The targets for each KPI can be subject to adjustment as well. Process improvement programmes within the IT department itself may lead to more ambitious norms for the internal perspective. Budget cuts will affect the financial perspective.

Therefore, a scorecard reporting model is supposed to be a living document. The reporting model for the IT scorecard needs to be reviewed regularly whether or not it still satisfies the requirements set against it. Setting these requirements is part of the IT strategy implementation process. Twice a year would be an appropriate frequency to do this.

5.4.3.2 Improving the measurements

We have described above how the reporting model can be adjusted (e.g. by adding, deleting or changing certain KPIs) in order to improve the IT scorecard, or adjust it to changing circumstances. Another aspect for improvement of the IT scorecard is the area of measurements. The improvement process for measurements takes place periodically in connection with the adjustment process of the reporting model. This needs to take place regularly for the efficacy of the IT scorecard.

Similar to the trigger for the adjustment process of the reporting model, the trigger for this improvement process of measurements is periodic. It needs to be evaluated on a periodic basis whether measurements satisfy the requirements that are set against them. Setting these requirements is part of the adjustment process of the reporting model.

5.5 The business value of IT investments

Now that we have discussed the business value of the organization and the IT department, we will focus on the business value of IT investments.

In the literature, more than 150 IT investment appraisal methodologies have been described. For a, probably not exhaustive, list of references, see Renkema (2000). The large amount of methodologies leads us to a number of observations:

- The problem of IT investment appraisal is tough.
- There is no magic bullet solution.

At the heart of the problem is the quantification of business value. The concept of business value is very company specific, and this is one of the reasons why, in our opinion, there is no such thing as 'one best way to appraise IT investments'.

In the literature (see, for example, the IT value continuum in EIU, 1999) four areas of increasing business value creation by means of IT are mentioned:

- Technological/infrastructure value is experienced by users when the integration of hardware, software and architectures is provided in a seamless array of basic IT capabilities and services. The main performance management goal in this category is efficiency. Examples of benefits achieved: increased productivity, increased functionality, user satisfaction, improved application development process, reduced costs, improved systems integration, quality services and products.

- Organizational/process value is achieved through departmental or business capabilities that are unleashed by leveraging an IT investment, such as improved decision making and increased flexibility. The main performance management goal in this category is effectiveness. Benefits achieved: increased profits, business speed, increased revenue, collaboration, internal integration, responsiveness, empowerment, customer satisfaction and loyalty.
- Extended reach value is the strategic integration of information technologies through a company's value chain, to suppliers, partners and consumers. Benefits achieved: customer image/perception, customer satisfaction, globalization, integrated partnerships, growth in exports, integration across value chains, market penetration and leverage, cross-functional integration.
- Competitive value is achieved in a breakthrough use of IT. This breakthrough may change the nature of competition or the structure of the industry by enabling a new business vision. Benefits achieved: new revenue, substitutes, innovation, new businesses, strategic advantage, new markets, restructured industry.

Each area requires additional capabilities on top of the previous one and is harder to reach and harder to measure.

An underlying assumption of (IT) investment appraisal methodologies is that decision makers in companies act completely rationally. Well, this is not always the case.

In a joint worldwide study of the Economist Intelligence Unit and IBM Global Services (EIU, 1999), 350 senior executives were questioned on the strategic value of IT. The executives were asked which methods they were using to measure the value of IT investment proposals; multiple answers were possible. The survey indicates that executives are blending non-financial measures of value with financial measures (see Table 5.1).

Another observation is that the number of different value measurement methods that are widely used is limited. Nevertheless, these senior executives have a lot of different perspectives on the business value of IT. One out of three senior executives uses his instinct, which is irrational by default.

The blending of financial and non-financial measures illustrates the fundamental difference between the subjective and objective definitions of value. Both are needed in the discussions between the line-of-business managers and the IT manager of a company.

Table 5.1 Usage of value measurement methods

Value measurement method	% used
Gains in operating speed	54
Gains in quality	52
Gains in capacity	41
Cost displacement/cost avoidance	40
Return On Investment (ROI)	37
Instinct	33
Internal user surveys	32
Net Present Value (NPV)	24
Economic Value Added (EVA™)	23
Internal Rate of Return (IRR)	21
Breakeven analysis	20
Supplier surveys	4

It is therefore important to keep in mind that a business case plays an important role in investment decision making, but it is not the one and only basis for decision making.

The way decisions on investment are taken is dependent on leadership style and, again, on the perception of IT value within the company. In different phases of IT value perception, there will be different ways to decide on IT investment proposals and business cases. This will be elaborated in the last chapters of this book.

The term 'business case' is broadly accepted as the justification of a project proposal. All IT investments need funding, and the way to get access to that funding varies a great deal. Most companies have some sort of process to decide on IT investment. In order to prepare the executives' decisions, a rational method for IT investment justification and selection is recommended.

The process of selecting the most valuable investment proposals must be well defined within a company. The IT investment proposals need to be supported from idea to realization in order to get a rational selection process. This pipeline management process (Figure 5.4) is well known from business disciplines. For instance, the sales process, where many leads will turn into a bunch of proposals and where only a few sales will be closed. Most project management methodologies offer such a pipeline process.

The key to a structured pipeline process is the definition of common, structured deliverables for each phase which will be evaluated in a standard way. Each step in the process will

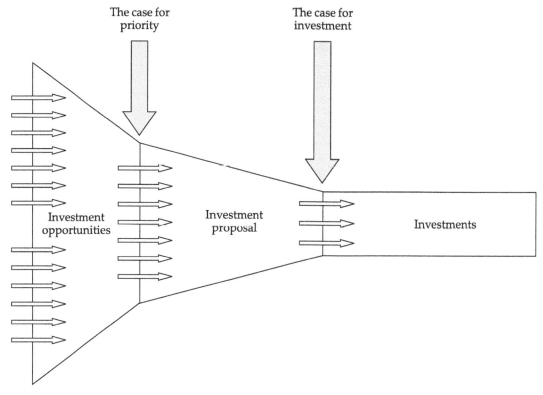

Figure 5.4 The pipeline management process

deliver a more detailed description of the optional investment, with fewer assumptions and more facts. The amount of resources spent on each investment proposal will increase as well. It is therefore important that with each 'filter', a number of investment proposals will fail to pass. This way, the amount of time spent on unjustifiable proposals will be minimal.

For the same reason, it should be kept in mind that this procedure will have more benefit in an organization if the investment proposals have a substantial scope. It is easier to prioritize 20–50 medium and large-sized investments than 300 small ones.

We distinguish between two kinds of 'business case': the case for priority (section 5.5.1) and the case for investment (section 5.5.2). The overall investment justification is done using a pipeline management process.

In larger companies, the pipeline process may have more phases (Figure 5.5). The first phase will be the internal business unit process, which will deliver a set of IT investment proposals that

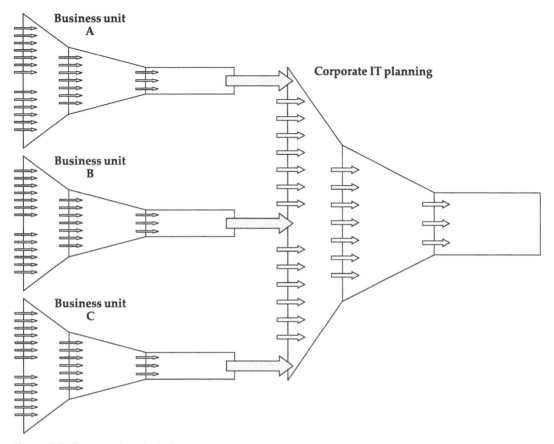

Figure 5.5 The two-phased pipeline management process

will be input for the pipeline process at corporate level. In this second phase, the corporate IT department will bundle the input of the various business units; some proposals may be combined in order to achieve economies of scale for a corporate IT solution; other proposals will not be accepted due to corporate priorities. These priorities, for example, may be based on a shareholder value analysis indicating that investing in business unit A may be far more rewarding than investing in business unit B. Another reason to reject business unit investment proposals at a corporate level (or to put it on hold) may be the finding that it is not feasible for the organization to start too many organizational change projects at the same time.

5.5.1 The case for priority

The case for priority is about the selection of IT investments out of all proposed project plans. Most of the companies have more investment proposals than budget; therefore, a selection is needed. How to prioritize those IT investment proposals? What criteria need to be used? By intuition, the obvious answer is to select those proposals that:

- Deliver the most 'value for money'.
- Support strategic business goals.

However, looking and justifying investment proposals one by one holds a dangerous risk of suboptimization. Therefore, the context of the proposals must be carefully looked at.

5.5.1.1 Prioritization models

One of the first broadly acknowledged methods for investment appraisal and selection was introduced by Parker and Benson in their book *Information Economics*, as early as 1988. The name of the book became a synonym for the research field of economic appraisal of IT investment. The Parker–Benson method introduces a scorecard with a number of financial and non-financial criteria, where values can be scored and weighted. The non-financial criteria are divided into business-specific and technology-specific criteria. This type of analysis, also known as multi-criteria selection, is a nice way to rationalize the costs and benefits of the various investment proposals, enabling the organization to make an objective judgement. Detailed descriptions of the technique can be found in Parker (1988).

At present the relevancy of most of the Parker–Benson criteria is beyond discussion. The multi-criteria evaluation method is a good way to compare various alternative IT investments. The criterion 'strategic match', for example, could be easily detailed into various business objectives, where the project proposal could be scored against each objective. Techniques that can be used to perform these evaluations are panel discussions, workshops and/or interviews; these will depend on the common way of decision making in the organization.

To determine which criteria are important for an investment appraisal, the Parker–Benson method provides a good start. However, as we have seen in the previous chapter, IT investments are not one of a kind. By introducing portfolio management, a classification of IT investments will emerge, each group stressing its own priority indicators.

Weill, Broadbent (1998) offer such a categorization. They stress the fact that the objective of IT investments is not only to provide business value by implementing current strategies, but also to use the technology to enable new strategies. The latter goal is an important objective of those IT investments that never get enough attention: the IT infrastructure.

The categorization is based on the type of management objectives that organizations have with the IT investments. Weill and Broadbent propose four categories:

Category	Management objectives
Infrastructure	Business integration Business flexibility and agility Reduced marginal cost of business unit's IT Reduced IT costs over time Standardization
Transactional	Cut costs Increased throughput
Informational	Increased control Better information Better integration Improved quality
Strategic	Increased sales Competitive advantage Competitive necessity Market positioning Innovative services

This classification is used for benchmarking purposes, where the shares of the four classes of investment can be compared between companies.

However, this classification, in our opinion, has a number of shortcomings:

- There is no connection with the IT value chain as discussed in section 2.4.
- It is hard to distinguish between informational and transactional investments, because nowadays most off-the-shelf transactional application packages do have management information capabilities.

113

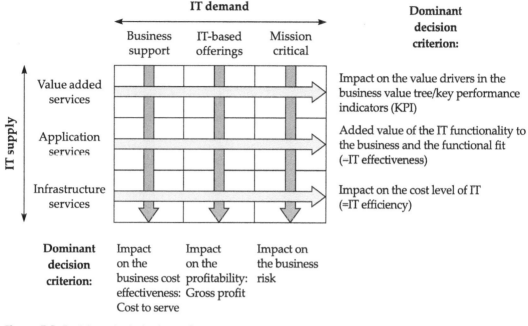

Figure 5.6 Decision criteria in the performance management grid

- Infrastructural, transactional and informational investments will always have underlying strategic objectives.

Another way to provide context for the investment proposal is to categorize it in the IT performance management grid we have introduced in the previous chapters. The IT performance management grid helps to focus on the dominant decision criteria, regardless of the quality of the process.

Every row and column in the grid has one dominant decision criterion (Figure 5.6). This results in two criteria per cell that need to be judged in their mutual influence.

By categorizing the proposed investments in one (or more) of the cells of the matrix, the management objectives that have to be important in the justification and the prioritization of the investment proposals become evident.

Along the axis of the IT supply

Infrastructure services: investments are judged on the *impact on the cost level of IT*. This is the area where IT infrastructure standardization and 'economies of scale' bear most fruit for the business. In general we are speaking of *IT efficiency*. Key to managing this IT efficiency is the level of control we have on the generic infrastructure and middleware components in the IT architecture. It is vital to be in control to being able to continuously 'clean up and optimize the machine room'.

Application services: investments are judged based on the IT functionality that is delivered to the business. *'Functional fit'* is a term that is used to measure the impact of the service on the business capabilities. In general we are speaking of *IT effectiveness*. Here information and application standardization are critical success factors. However, extreme standardization, as in the implementation of an ERP application with the scope of a 'huge E', can become an obstacle for the flexibility of the business.

The architectural solutions need to be ironed out carefully to provide for the flexibility needed. An intelligent implementation of middleware architectures is the basis for success.

Value added services: investments should be judged on the *impact* they have *on the value driver trees of the business*. Key to becoming successful is the awareness of the need to learn and the measures taken to learn quickly. Success can be measured only if the organization has implemented some sort of scorecard based on key performance indicators.

The difficulty here is that in many businesses distinct value driver trees are not available. On top of that, these services are usually performed internally and the maturity of the services themselves and the measurement systems are relatively low. In fact, decision making is mostly based on 'we cannot afford to do without'.

Along the axis of the IT demand

Business support: investments are judged on the *impact on the cost level of the business*. Industry-specific levels of the *'cost to serve'* provide for the targets. Key to success is the business and IT alignment in achieving these targets. When IT is still considered to be a burden and cost savings in IT are considered more important than cost savings in the business, alignment is still a long way off. Optimization along this axis is usually only beneficial from an ERP perspective with a well-defined limited scope of the E. Smaller organizational levels for optimization lead to scattered IT infrastructures and a wagon load of management hassle.

IT-based offering: investments are judged on the *impact on business profitability*. The 'bottom line impact' is the key here. IT capabilities needed to provide these services differ from the business support category in that the services are a component in a service of a higher order. With that the 'cost per unit' of the IT service/service component is influenced by the required IT capabilities and the IT service delivery process. Simple common practice 'standard cost price calculation' also goes for these types of end products/offerings, no matter how complex the offering is. Optimization along this axis is usually only beneficial when the services of a higher order can eventually be positioned outside the company in a separate business that takes part in the value chain. We will address this in Chapter 8.

Mission critical IT: investments are judged based on the *business risk* involved. These services are a critical success factor of the business as a whole. One can even ask whether making a business case makes any sense since 'not doing it' is not an option. Optimization along this axis is usually beneficial to minimize risk.

The management challenge is that every cell in this grid has two dominant criteria that need to be judged in their mutual influence. Sometimes these criteria support each other, sometimes they are conflicting. Choices are not easy and are influenced by expected change over time, planning horizons of the business and the business partners.

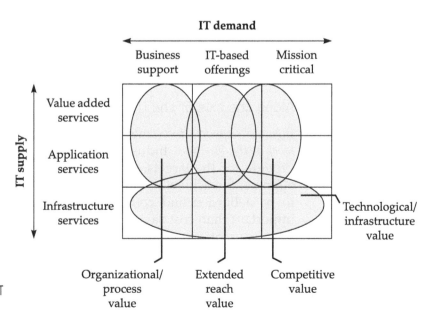

Figure 5.7
The business value of IT
services

When we project the value areas we introduced at the start of section 4.5 on the IT performance management grid, we have an indication of where to look for which added value (Figure 5.7).

It will not be possible to measure all value effects in every case, but being aware of the types of value creation helps in understanding the IT portfolio decision-making process.

5.5.1.2 An approach for the case for priority

Using one or more of the theoretical models in the previous section, a structured approach to the case of priority can be defined. A suggested approach is the subject of this section.

1. Inventory of project ideas

The first step is the collection of all plans, ideas, proposals that exist within the organization considering the deployment of an IT solution. For each idea, a limited set of data needs to be available to enable the first screening.

Some examples of the data that needs to be provided are:

- Who is the business sponsor of the investment?
- Why does the investment need to take place?
- What will happen if the investment is not made?
- First rough indication of the costs and needed resources of the investment.
- First indication of identified savings and additional business value.
- Expected lead time for change realization.
- Etc.

It is important not to spend too much time investigating each project idea; otherwise, too much time and money will be wasted on rejected project ideas. For this purpose, it is efficient to standardize the case for priority by using standard prior-itization criteria, for example (a subset of) the criteria of Parker–Benson. When standardized, the investment proposal form can be standardized as well, which will create a clear picture of the data that needs to be collected for each project idea.

The size of the investment will guide the remainder of the investment justification procedure. It is very common to distinguish investments into small, medium and large: the larger the investments become, the higher the organizational level to decide on these decisions. Often, the corporate control department has defined hurdle rates for the investments that need board approval.

2. First filter of project ideas

The first filter will be a 'showstopper list'. This can either be a list of minimal data that needs to be available for the project idea (for example, the idea must have a business sponsor) or a list of current corporate programmes that can be used here to stop elaborating on project ideas that basically are reinventing the wheel ('we are developing a project management tool in business unit K next month' when 14 different project management tools are already being used). The remaining project ideas will be filtered by using a multi-criteria analysis. This step will gain effectiveness when the criteria are standardized, along with their relevancy rating. This will deliver individual scores, which will automatically show the priority of each project idea.

If the criteria are split between financial criteria and criteria regarding strategic contribution, a matrix can be drawn to illustrate the scores of the various individual investment proposals (Figure 5.8).

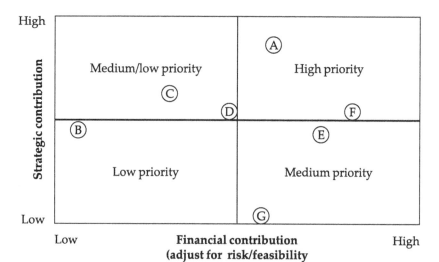

Figure 5.8
Portfolio management matrix

3. Elaboration of project ideas

In this step, the project ideas that are approved by the first filter need to be elaborated into cases for investment. This means that two deliverables need to be created for each proposed investment:

- A business case (subject of the next section).
- A portfolio evaluation.

The portfolio evaluation consists of the positioning of the proposed investment in the portfolio model that is used by the organization (for example, Weill–Broadbent or the performance management grid). This information will be needed when the individual investment proposals have been financially justified, but have to be screened against the total IT portfolio of the organization.

4. Second filter: IT investment validation

This filter will approve business cases that provide all relevant information on the cost, value and risks of the investment. The financial justification will be an IRR or an NPV above the hurdle rate. These concepts will be explained in the next section.

When Weill and Broadbent are used within the organization, there will be a definition of the to-be division of IT investments among the four investment classifications (strategic, informational, transactional, infrastructure). When the portfolio is out of balance, investments that enlarge this imbalance will have a lower chance to get approval. For example, if an organization spends 42 per cent on IT infrastructure, and a benchmark study has shown that the peer organization spend 35 per cent on IT infrastructure, a large IT infrastructure project will only have a fair chance if its business case states that the future IT infrastructure spend will significantly drop as a result of the proposed investment.

When using the performance management grid, it is obvious that the decision criteria will differ for investments in different cells of the grid. Figure 5.6 shows the primary decision criteria for each cell and column. Infrastructure investments for business support functions will be justified in a totally different way than mission critical applications. Although this might be obvious, and at some length will be common practice within current organizations, we have yet to see such a detailed portfolio management-based approach on IT investment justification.

5.5.2 The case for investment

This is the individual cost–benefit analysis of an IT investment. Of course, all remarks made on decision criteria in comparing and prioritizing various alternative investments are valid in the case of a single investment. When the initial appraisements are positive, and the investment does have priority, a detailed business case for the investment needs to be created. In order to elaborate on the high level case several indicators need to be determined or calculated in more detail. The most important indicators are financial.

The most commonly used financial indicator for the added value of an IT investment is the return on investment or ROI. The ROI is calculated as the sum of the benefits of the investment (the cumulative savings) divided by the investment itself. This simple calculation has made the ROI very popular in the IT industry. However, from a financial management perspective, ROI is an unacceptable indicator, because it does not account for the time value of money.

Another popular financial indicator for IT investment appraisal is the break-even period. This method determines the moment in time where the positive cash flows will equal the negative cash flows of the initial investment. At break-even time, the ROI of the investment will be 100 per cent. The power of the break-even indicator is its scale: time is something to be understood by everybody and answers the simple question: 'When will I start to earn from my investment?' Another advantage of this indicator is that it can be applied when using the concept of time value of money as well.

The concept of time value of money is caused by the fact that investment money needs to be financed. This capital is not free, because it can be used for other purposes than the proposed investment. These alternative purposes will yield money as well. In order to make a fair comparison, companies use a discount factor. The discount factor is a virtual interest rate, at which the future cash flows of the investment need to be discounted. The rate is dependent on the cost of capital for the organization. The discount factor is based on three elements: the interest rate, inflation and risk.

5.5.2.1 The interest rate

The investment money can be used as an alternative to buy stocks or it can be put away in a savings account. This would give a return on investment as well, by raising stock prices, dividend or received interest. Therefore, an amount of money will grow over the years by an average interest rate.

5.5.2.2 Inflation

A second element that will cause the value of money to change over time is inflation. Inflation causes money to depreciate in value of time, due to rising prices and wages.

5.5.2.3 Risk

The risk factor expresses the chance that investors will not gain from their investment, but will lose money instead. In an investment portfolio, there will always be investments that do not yield money as expected. In order to compensate for these losses, all investments need to yield a little more. The risk of an investment can be analysed in many ways. Investment bankers give credit ratings to individual companies based on these risk analyses. This is an important factor in the cost of capital for the individual companies. The discount factor for investments will normally be decided by the Corporate Controller. It will vary from company to company, and from year to year.

Using a discount factor means that positive and negative cash flows of an investment today will be valued differently than the same cash flows in four years' time. Therefore, the future cash flows need to be discounted by the discount rate in order to obtain the virtual 'present value'.

Two financial indicators use the time value of money to validate an investment proposal:

- The net present value (NPV) is the sum of the discounted positive and negative cash flows that relate to the investment, given a discount rate; the net present value of the investment should be positive.
- The internal rate of return (IRR) is the discount rate at which the net present value is zero. The IRR should be larger than the internal discount rate used.

As you can see, the two indicators are like twins; if one indicator has been calculated, so has the other. In order to use the NPV or IRR, an organization needs to set their standard discount rate for their investments.

Although these definitions and calculations seem to be complex, it is good to know that the mainstream spreadsheet software packages support these financial indicators as standard functions, which no longer require the user to make the calculations himself.

5.6 The investment proposal: the business case

The decision process of IT investments needs to be facilitated as much as possible by the use of standard procedures, formats and templates. The use of a standard template for business cases is a good example. The business case is developed for individual investment proposals, but will support the investment decision process as a whole. In the case for prioritization, only a high level business case will be needed; for the case for investment a detailed business case as described in this section is recommended.

5.6.1 Content and objectives

In Chapter 2 we have shown the differences in perception between the financial controllers and the IT professionals. The scope of a business case should be the whole lifecycle of an IT investment and cover the changes between the current operations and the operation after the development project has been finished successfully (Figure 5.9).

The business case is the business justification that supports the commitment of time, resources and funding for the proposed investment initially and ongoing. It is created together with the project plan and will be mandatory for the go/no go decision of significant investments. It consists of:

- A report which describes:
  - the current (as-is) situation, and the need for the investment;

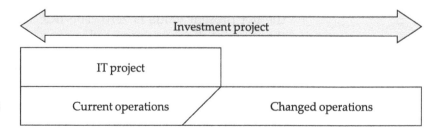

Figure 5.9
Scope of the business case

- the investment and its costs;
- the deliverables of the investment, and the projected value;
- the financial analysis, derived from the spreadsheet model;
- alternative solutions, and why the preferred alternative was chosen;
- risk analysis of the investment.
- A financial spreadsheet model, containing:
  - a self-documenting cost estimation model with a substantial time horizon, showing:
    - current costs and future estimated costs without the investment (base case);
    - costs and derived benefits of the investment, accompanied by inherent risks;
  - the model is parameterized, which enables fast what-if analyses.
- Presentation to communicate the alternatives developed, the assumptions made creating the model and the results.

The primary objective of the business case is justifying the investment. However, as a facilitator in the investment decision process its use and added value will be a lot more. For example:

- Creating an improved and common view of the proposed investment, using the same financial criteria, enabling to compare various investment proposals easily.
- The uncertainty in the investment can be shown by using estimated ranges instead of point estimates; when over time the uncertainty diminishes, the ranges will become smaller.
- The discussion on assumptions will create a platform for discussion on the consequences of the investment; these discussions will be further facilitated by the use of what-if analyses using the spreadsheet model.
- The assumptions in the model can be evaluated after the investment has been made as well, thus resulting in a control tool for the project and the investment as a whole.

5.6.2 The impact of IT portfolio management

Portfolio management provides context to the individual business cases of an organization. The impact of portfolio management should influence business cases in two ways:

1 The value categories that will be analysed in order to find business benefits of the investment. A tough question that keeps managers and consultants busy is the justification of IT infrastructure investments. This is no different from other infrastructure investments. The business value of these investments can only be measured indirectly. On its own, these investments do not create business value, but for the company to create business value, IT infrastructure investments are a prerequisite.

One way to retrieve measured business value from an IT infrastructure investment is as follows. The business value of the infrastructure is translated into the impact on the IT applications that depend on this infrastructure. These applications impact the added value of business units, whose operational value impacts the financial value of the company itself. We admit that this is a very indirect way to quantify the business value of these non-business-sensitive IT investments.

Another, more direct way, to assess the business value of IT infrastructure investments is to focus on efficiency and effectiveness value of the IT organization (see Section 4.5, Optimization).

2 The decision criteria of the investment. In section 5.5.1 we have shown the dominant decision criteria for IT portfolio decision making along the business value added axis of the performance management grid. The lesson here is that the subject of the investment must be very clear: is the investment business support, offering or mission critical? The focus in the business cases must be very different. For a mission critical investment, for example, much more emphasis must be on risk management and risk mitigation.

5.6.3 An approach for the development of a business case

To develop a business case, a structured approach is recommended. Business cases for large investments will usually be created by small multidisciplinary teams typically involving a project manager, a controller, an IT solution architect and an end user. The business case will be developed simultaneously with the project plan. The project plan describes how the initial investment will be used to implement the requested change, and contains a thorough estimation of the initial one-time expenses.

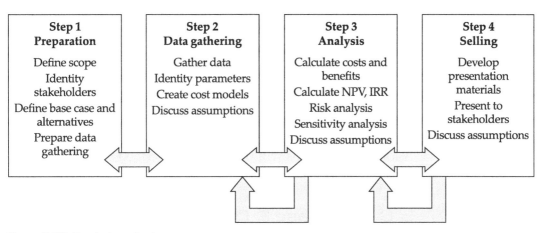

Figure 5.10 Developing a business case

The structured approach consists of four steps: preparation, data gathering, analysis and selling (Figure 5.10).

5.6.3.1 Phase 1 Preparation

The preparation phase starts with a context analysis for the need of a business case analysis and its scope. A lot of questions need to be answered, for example:

- What is the scope of the investment? Which activities are included and which are not?
- Who is the sponsor of the investment and who are the stakeholders?
- What are the current and future business objectives that this investment is helping to achieve?
- What data is available on the current situation (the base case)?
- What data is available already and has been collected in the studies that already have been done on the subject?
- What is available on the 'don't do it' option?
- What is the business risk involved when the proposed investment will not be done?

It is also very important to understand the need for change, and how the sponsor wants to justify this. There may be alternative solutions that need to be evaluated.

To make a first draft of the financial spreadsheet model, the following items need to be clarified:

- Specification of the alternative solutions to be investigated.
- Standard investment justification method used.
- Currency of all financial data; if applicable, the currency rate used.
- Time scale (week, month, quarter, year) and time horizon.
- Management accounting practices available (depreciation practices, discount rate, taxation rules, etc.).

A lot of these issues will usually be prescribed by the corporate controller's department.

5.6.3.2 Phase 2 Data gathering

The data gathering phase is used to collect as much relevant data as possible for the business case. This normally includes the current situation, the future situation and the one-time investment cost. In order to know what data is relevant for the business case, it is necessary to get a grip on the expected business value.

The most convenient and widely used way to do this is a bottom-up impact analysis of the IT investment. This is a simple but effective way to brainstorm the possible business value of the investment. Just as with costs, it is possible to make a checklist of benefits that may be the result of the investment: more customers, higher customer retention, higher cross-sales, etc.

A technique developed by the Knowledge Network for IT cost and value of IBM, which can help to organize your thinking, is called Operational Value Analysis. This technique uses a matrix of the source of the value vs the impact focus. The source of the value is divided into:

1 The individual role.
2 The department.
3 The company.
4 The value chain of the products that are delivered by the company (the extended enterprise).

The impact focus defines:

1 Technology: the description of the impact of the new capability that is a result of the proposed investment.
2 Business process: definition of the performance indicator that can be used to measure the impact.

3 Economic benefit: calculated benefit from the new capability.

The next step is to quantify the economic benefits found and include them in the business case.

For the gathering of data on the current situation, hard cost data is normally available with the controllers of the organization. The investments can be obtained from the resource plan of the project manager and various data from external parties (proposals of IT service providers and hardware and software vendors). To be able to get financial data for the future situation assumptions will have to be made.

Assumptions can be based on end user surveys, interviews of key stakeholders or workshops with subject matter experts. It is important to document the assumptions and the sources that were used to make the assumptions.

The initial (one-time) costs of the investment may be influenced by different options to finance the investment. This is elaborated in section 5.7.

5.6.3.3 Phase 3 Analysis

In this phase the data gathered will be used to build the spreadsheet model, where all future cash flows will be documented, based on either hard facts or assumptions. With this data the net present value (NPV), internal rate of return (IRR) and 'discounted' break-even can be calculated.

Additionally, two analyses may be performed.

A sensitivity analysis will show the impact of various assumptions. For example, if the assumption has been made that the sales of company X will grow 10 per cent as a result of the investment, the sensitivity analysis will show the alternative NPV with growth percentages of 8 per cent and 12 per cent. This will enable the decision makers to get a better grip on the uncertainty of the assumptions and its impact. Alternative assumptions of multiple indicators may be combined into an alternative scenario. It is not uncommon to create four alternatives: an optimistic, a pessimistic, a high probability and a 'what happens if we don't do it' scenario.

When a risk analysis is required as part of the case for investment, the risks can impact the business case in two ways:

1 Risk = Damage × Probability per cent: the impact of the risk is calculated by multiplying the possible damage of the risk with the probability. If there is a 10 per cent chance of a US $5 m damage, the cost of the risk will be US $500,000.
2 Cost of risk mitigating measures, e.g. restoring the delivery of IT services after serious calamities.

Beware that the mitigating measures are intended to minimize the probability of the risk; therefore, the two elements should be aligned in the model.

When risk is taken into account in the business case model, the risks of the as-is situation should not be forgotten. Usually, risk mitigating measures are taken as a result of higher risk awareness. This will mean that current IT expenditures regarding these risks will be low. In this situation there will never be a positive financial business case for the risk mitigating measures, unless the current risk has been quantified.

On the other hand, risk mitigating measures will often not need a business case, because they are required either by law or the corporate risk manager.

5.6.3.4 Phase 4 Selling

Sometimes, after the analysis, it seems that the business case will not lead to a positive NPV. If this is the case, there are a few options left:

● Get more data and use it instead of assumptions in the model.
● If your sponsor agrees, change assumptions, but make sure that the assumptions remain realistic and that the key stakeholders approve.

If these options will not deliver better results, the conclusion has to be drawn that in the given circumstances the proposed investment cannot be justified. We strongly advise you not to put unrealistic figures in the model, or manipulate the model strongly towards a positive conclusion. Sooner or later, this will backfire on you. Be aware of and cautious for 'local politics' or any other kind of power game effects of one or more stakeholders.

If the business case model is ready and the optimal alternative has been calculated, the investment proposal is ready to get a positive decision. The way this decision has to be reached will differ for each organization, and depend on the height of the investment. You should concentrate the selling focus on customer and stakeholder needs.

Usually, above a certain limit, board approval is necessary. In these cases, the sponsor of the investment may need to prepare an executive presentation in order to gain approval for his proposal. For the executives, the presentation needs to start with the proposed investment. Immediately after that, a clear picture with a simple message needs to be shown. Yes, it is feasible: economically, business-wise, technically and time-wise. This picture should show either costs going down, or savings up. A payback period chart, for example, is a very communicative picture.

These few slides with clear messages of course need to be supported with all the spreadsheet figures and details, but do not bother the key decision makers with these details; if the business case creation has gone correctly, these details have been discussed with the key advisors and influencers of the board, so that the presentation will show no surprises to the board members.

5.7 Financing the investments

IT departments spend a lot of time defining and calculating the IT investment in order to create a business case. From a financial point of view, however, this is only a part of the story: the IT investment explains where the money has to be spent and why, but where does the money come from? The answer is financing.

The financial aspects of the operations of an organization are volume (of sales), price and costs. This results in an operating profit (or loss). The profit is used to pay taxes, dividend to shareholders and interest to banks. The remainder is called retained earnings, which is the basis for the funding potential of the organization, of which new investments can be done. Thus, each organization has a funding potential to invest. This funding potential might be increased by lending more money or selling more shares on the stock exchange. The funding potential can be used in multiple ways, of which IT is only one possibility. A simple alternative is to put this money in a savings account and gain interest from it. This is why the cost of capital needs to be taken into account in the discount factor for the evaluation of IT investments.

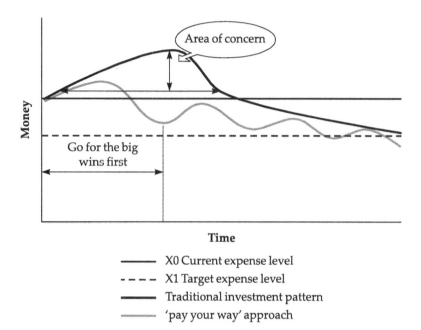

Figure 5.11
The pay your way
approach

Time

——— X0 Current expense level
- - - - X1 Target expense level
——— Traditional investment pattern
════ 'pay your way' approach

There are ways that financing options can be used to improve an existing business case. We will describe three examples.

The first example considers the financing of a cost reduction programme by using the realized savings of quick wins to finance consecutive projects. This is called the 'pay your way' approach. Figure 5.11 illustrates the way 'the area of concern,' i.e. the upfront investment for the programme, is decreased.

The second example is to use financing in order to smooth the cash flows that are involved with the proposed investment. For example, a hardware investment of €2 m can be paid at once, or the hardware might be leased using monthly payments during the next three years. This will add extra costs for financing, but probably will improve the NPV of the investment.

The third example considers a delayed payment schedule, which may be part of the terms and conditions in a deal with an external service provider. This is done in case of large IT optimization projects, for example network upgrades.

5.8 Summary

In this chapter we covered the subject of business value of IT investments. We saw that value is a subjective phenomenon, which always has to be analysed in its context.

The value of organizations is often measured in terms of shareholder value. Various techniques of value-based management are applied here.

Another popular technique that can be used to measure the performance of both organizations and departments is the balanced scorecard. This technique uses financial and non-financial performance indicators to measure and control the performance of an organizational unit in four perspectives: the learning (or capability) perspective, the internal (or processes) perspective, the external or client perspective and the financial perspective.

We showed that the balanced scorecard can be used for the IT department as well, delivering an IT scorecard.

The measurement of business value for IT portfolios is important to prioritize the IT investment proposals for the organization. The organization needs a pipeline process to prioritize the proposals, each step requiring more data and analysis of the individual proposals.

A detailed justification of an IT investment is called a business case for investment. This business case contains a detailed analysis of cost, value and risks; where data is not available, assumptions need to be formulated and validated. The financial justification of the business case preferably uses a discounted cash flow technique such as net present value or internal rate of return, calculated using the organization's internal discount rate and compared with a hurdle rate.

The portfolio management techniques can add more variation and flexibility to the investment appraisal, stating that different kinds of investments need to be justified differently. This introduces business case variants, related to the portfolio management classification.

There are multiple options to influence the outcome of a business case by considering various alternatives regarding the financing of the investment.

Managing the IT portfolio

6.1 Introduction

Managing the IT portfolio is a complex activity that nevertheless has to be executed by many CIOs and IT department managers all over the world. In this chapter we will address this complex activity top-down to a level that becomes actionable. To give you a good understanding of the complexity and the way to deal with it, a distinction is made between 'managing the content of IT' and 'managing the performance of IT'. One cannot say anything about the performance of IT without taking into account the content.

The first part of this chapter will discuss the content of IT and the IT portfolio. It will focus on the fit between IT demand and IT supply that is also referred to as 'business and IT alignment'. We start with the question: 'what is there to align?' taking it from strategy/strategic choices to 'The Architectures' and architectural choices. We will introduce the role of architecture in IT portfolio management, which will help us understand where to focus from a performance management perspective.

In the second part of this chapter we will return to the IT performance management grid that was introduced in Chapter 2. Here the performance management issues of all rows and columns mentioned in the grid will be dealt with. A description of the performance management activities concludes this second part.

At the end of this chapter the planning and control of the IT portfolio and the key roles in IT portfolio management are addressed.

6.2 Strategy and strategic alignment

There are a lot of good publications on strategy and strategic alignment. Only some essentials that we think are vital for IT performance management will be covered here. Our approach is based on four major lines of thinking:

Outside-in strategy influences on the IT portfolio:

- Ansoff (1977) and the related Boston Consulting Group thinking on 'corporate strategy', 'portfolio management' and 'growth/share matrix' (Hedley, 1977).
- Porter (1980) on 'strategy', 'five forces model', 'value creation web'.

Inside-out strategy influences on the IT portfolio:

- Treacy and Wiersema (1995) on 'the discipline of market leaders'.
- Boynton, Victor and Pine (1993) on 'dynamic stability'.

6.2.1 Outside-in strategy influences

This first category deals with the way that the environment influences strategic choices with regard both to the business and to IT.

6.2.1.1 The business portfolio, value creation and the value chain

The origins for our thinking lie in publications in the 1970s and 1980s. In these publications the concepts of deliberate choices on 'product/market combinations' (also called 'portfolio management') were launched successfully.

The BCG growth/share matrix was the dominant framework for portfolio management.

The value-based approach originates from several publications of Michael Porter and has since then been the major 'school' in business strategy. To put it simply: a company has to understand the environment and the forces in and from the environment to be able to make strategic choices on the business.

Recently we have become aware that access to the market by means of a deliberate choice of the 'channel(s)' also plays a key role in the required capabilities to do business. The value creation-based thinking of Michael Porter can help us in understanding strategic choices and their relative importance for the IT portfolio.

The relevant strategic choices can be summarized as decisions on:

- Positioning = choosing products, markets and channels.
- Price/performance = choosing where to play a role in creating customer advantage.

6.2.1.2 New technologies

The influence of new technologies on value-based approaches is becoming increasingly important. With the maturing of the use of the Internet the options of what is sometimes called the 'real time enterprise' for creating new offerings have rapidly grown. This technology can be used as a new channel in existing product market combinations, but it also has:

- Increased the likelihood of substitutes.
- Lowered the barriers for new entrants.
- Increased the options for complementors.
- Increased the competition.

After the 'dot.com' hype, the usage of this mature technology leaves us with tremendous opportunities that have become economically justified. Traditional IT outsourcing has matured into strategic sourcing because of the development of technology. In Chapter 8 we will focus on this subject. This situation doesn't apply to the Internet alone. In fact the relevance of planned continuous 'technology watch' activity has increased. The business strategy is highly influenced and sometimes even driven by new IT technologies.

6.2.2 Inside-out strategy influences

The second category of strategy schools of thought deals with the deliberate strategic choices that a company can make itself.

The relevant strategic choices can be summarized as decisions on:

- Value propositions to the customer = choosing what value to bring.
- Capabilities = choosing how to bring this value.

There are two strategy schools of thought that highly influence these choices.

6.2.2.1 The discipline of market leaders

The publication of Michael Treacy and Fred Wiersema on *The Discipline of Market Leaders* is often quoted, sometimes even without the awareness of quoting!

This publication describes the need for a focus strategy. Different customers ask for different value propositions; however, a company cannot be equally good at everything, so to become a market leader companies have to focus. Deliberate choices on a development direction for the company's value proposition help position company identity and the associated business portfolio.

In essence there are three distinct value propositions:

1 Best in class cost level: 'operational excellence':
  'providing customers with reliable products or services at competitive prices, delivered with minimal difficulty or inconvenience'.
2 The best product/service: 'product leadership':
  'providing products that continually redefine the state of the art'.
3 The best end-to-end solution for the customer: 'customer intimacy':
  'selling the customer a total solution, not just a product or a service'.

6.2.2.2 The dynamic stability model

The second school of thought is usually referred to as *mass customization* thinking. In the 1990s new competitive strategies were defined by Boynton, Victor and Pine in their publications on 'dynamic stability'. Their analysis and theory is based on the relationship between product change and process change (Figure 6.1).

The major breakthrough in this thinking lies in the focus of organizations on one of the two diagonals in this matrix:

● *Industrial revolution strategies* are based on the invention/mass production diagonal going back as far as the industrial revolution.

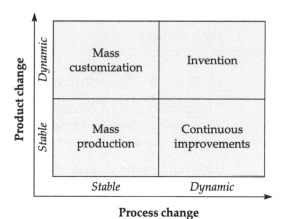

Figure 6.1
The dynamic stability
model

- *Dynamic stability strategies* are based on the continuous improvement/mass customization diagonal resulting in new competitive strategies.

Organizations usually consist of a mix of strategies, depending on the products/services that are being produced/rendered.

6.2.3 The relevancy of strategic choices regarding IT performance management

The combination of all strategy schools mentioned and the impact of new technologies has an extensive impact on IT portfolio management:

- Business capabilities are derived from the value propositions and the focus strategy. From there, the IT capabilities are derived from business capabilities.
- An operational excellence focus strategy leads to a cost level focused IT strategy.
- A product leadership focus strategy leads to an IT strategy that is focused on technology innovation and related competencies.
- A customer intimacy focus strategy leads to a decentralized customer knowledge centric IT strategy.
- When the end product contains a dominant IT component, IT and business capabilities become one and the same. The adoption of the mass customization thinking is key for success here.
- Choosing a traditional strategy (invention + mass production) leads to a cost level/integrated solution (ERP) focused IT strategy.

- Choosing a dynamic stability strategy (continuous improvement + mass customization) leads to a 'component-based'/ middleware focused IT strategy.
- New IT capabilities such as the Internet provide for a new channel with a revolutionary impact on the companies' offerings and processes. This can create an immediate reversed impact on earlier choices of business strategies.
- Traditional cost saving-based outsourcing suddenly becomes really 'strategic' sourcing when complete IT services provisioning becomes a new player in the value system.

All of these are key to new company business strategies and can only be achieved based on a consistent IT strategy, IT architecture and IT portfolio management. In the second part of this chapter we will return to these topics.

6.2.4 What is (IT) strategy about?

We take it as a given that the line between a traditional business strategy and an IT strategy is becoming thinner and thinner, even to the level of a complete fusion. In this respect the understanding of the IT value perception level of the company becomes a strategic issue. The maturity of IT demand and IT supply becomes crucial in the ability to achieve new strategic goals. It is this matching of IT demand and IT supply that becomes a key differentiator for the business.

Every deliberate choice on products, markets and channels has impact on this delicate balance of IT demand and IT supply. So all IT strategy definition work starts with analysing the IT value perception level, to understand which new goals are achievable and/or which hurdles to take to achieve these new goals. Within the IT value perception context, an integrated IT strategy is based on the combination of business choices and IT choices.

6.2.4.1 Business choices

- *Environment*: e.g. choices on the role in the value system, analyses of competitive forces, legislator impact, customer wants and needs.
- *Positioning*: e.g. choices of products, markets and channels, product/pricing strategies.
- *Configuration*: e.g. value creation web, business capability description, business scenarios and choices, business structure, choices on core competencies.

6.2.4.2 IT choices

- *Environment*: e.g. results of the technology watch in terms of the analyses of available and new technologies, analyses of available service provisioning, gap analyses of strategic demand from the business and current IT portfolio.
- *Positioning*: e.g. choices of core technologies, choices of strategic partnerships, defining principles for IT portfolio management, IT architecture, IT process and IT competencies.
- *Configuration*: e.g. the analyses of the IT value perception level and required actions to be taken, IT capability description, IT portfolio description, IT architecture description, choices on core competencies, IT governance model (IT organization, IT management system, IT process model), sourcing strategy.

The choices on IT and the business go hand in hand and are reflected in one strategic masterplan:

- *Major business and IT events*: e.g. (planned/expected/antici- pated) mergers and acquisitions, restructuring of the business and/or IT.
- *Major milestones*: e.g. the due dates for strategic restructuring activity for the next three years and related goals to be achieved.
- *Terms and conditions*: e.g. the available financial resources.

A strategy description like the strategic masterplan needs to be updated with a (bi-)annual frequency and has a planning horizon of three to five years. This strategy description serves as a basis for all activity in the company. Putting strategy into action starts with the impact on the architectures.

6.3 The role of architectures in IT performance management

Architectures are derived from a series of comprehensive decisions on business and IT strategy. This paragraph will give a high level, non-technical view on the role of architectures in IT performance management. Let us start with a terminology framework on architectures.

6.3.1 Architecture terminology definition

In order to look at architecture from a managerial/performance management perspective, we introduce a simple two by two grid that we call 'the architecture grid' (Figure 6.2).

	Reality	Abstract models
Business	Organizational infrastructure and process	Business architecture
IT	IT infrastructure and process	Information & technology architecture

Figure 6.2
The architecture grid

On the horizontal axis we distinguish between reality and abstract models of this reality.

On the vertical axis we distinguish between business and IT. We preserve the term 'architecture' to be within the domain of the abstract models. This results in two quadrants in which we can plot 'architectural objects and terms' and two quadrants in which we can plot 'real life objects and terms'.

In the reality quadrants we deal with the real issues of everyday activity. The major content of this book deals with the performance management issues in this reality. The abstract models of reality are necessary to understand and implement standardization. Abstract models tend to last longer than the turmoil in reality. The internal comprehensiveness of these objects is easier to create and maintain, because of the abstraction level used.

Because it is possible to move away from the tricky details, some of us have the tendency to linger in this realm forever or at least much longer than is productive. We will indicate how to use these models and protect you against the pitfalls available.

6.3.1.1 Organizational infrastructure and processes

This is the quadrant where it all happens. The day-to-day dynamics of doing business in some form or structure, focused on 'making money', 'gaining market access' or whatever the vision or mission statement may state. The objects in this quadrant are mentioned by all of us on a daily basis in our conversations without asking ourselves: does the other person have the same thing in mind?

6.3.1.2 IT infrastructure and processes

This quadrant expresses all activity within the IT function. Typical activities are 'helpdesk support', 'managing mainframes', the typical IT jargon that normal people think they understand, but that sometimes turns out to have a very specific meaning that is clear only to insiders. As stated before 'the devil is in the details', so let's not try to define everything. In this book, this is called IT service provisioning. In Chapter 3 we cover IT service provisioning extensively.

On the intersection between the two reality quadrants we find the continuous process of balancing IT demand and IT supply and more specifically *the IT services portfolio* we addressed earlier.

6.3.1.3 Business architecture

This is the quadrant where the abstractions of 'doing business' reside. We find two types of models here, which are related by a matrix:

(a) The organization model.
(b) The process model.
(c) The process ownership matrix.

(a) The organization model

Organizational entity, business functions, roles and responsibilities, and resources, describing the 'command structure' from a hierarchical 'budgeting/planning and control' perspective.

In many companies there are three types of structured organizational entity. We distinguish:

- 'Managing entity', which participates in the 'control' structure, which is usually organized along the line of value creation in the value chain. Frequently used names are 'line of business', 'division', business unit, etc.
- 'Legal entity', which participates in the legal structure, which is usually organized along the geographical/legislation line. Frequently used names are 'company', 'joint venture', etc.
- 'Functional entity', which participates in the functional structure, which is usually organized along the competencies needed to execute. Examples are finance, sales and marketing, purchasing, HR and IT functions.

There are intrinsic frictions/overlaps between the IT demands of these three organizational structures. For architectural choices all three structures need to be taken into account. Which of the three should be dominant is situational. In general one can say that it depends on:

- The level of decentralization of power/authority where the legal entity structure is dominant.
- The implementation of KPI-driven bonuses, where the managing entity structure is dominant.
- The size and business impact of the 'shared services' organizations, where the functional structure is dominant.

(b) The process model

The process model consists of the following objects:

- The 'value creation web' describing the value propositions and business capabilities needed to deliver value.
- Business events, business processes, KPIs, business rules, etc. describing a flow of events and triggered activity with the purpose of delivering value.

Nowadays there are many 'business process models' available in industry that you can use as a quick start option for describing and implementing your business architecture.

(c) The process ownership matrix

This is a simple high level matrix, with processes as rows and organizational entities as columns. The cells contain indications such as: 'O = owns the process' or 'U = uses services from this process'. The impact of changes in this matrix usually reflects company reorganization/restructuring and may have a large impact on the IT service provisioning. This matrix is not always available because it is considered obvious; however, when making this obvious matrix one usually identifies the basic misunderstandings on roles and responsibilities.

6.3.1.4 Information and technology architecture

This is the quadrant where the abstractions of 'providing IT services' reside. The information and technology architecture can provide a more stable basis for decision making on IT service structures, service delivery and all related IT architectural topics.

We find three types of models here that are related by a matrix:

(a) The information model.
(b) The IT architecture model.
(c) The source allocation matrix.

(a) The information model

The Information model consists of the following objects:

- Information sets, logical data architecture, (business-) object model, data cluster, data entities, describing the data and relationships between data.

Many companies do not have explicit information/data models or consider the effort in creating them outdated. We think this is a serious misunderstanding of the value these models can bring in terms of managing the integrity and redundancy of the IT services provided.

(b) The IT architecture model

In Chapter 2 we defined our terminology model and identified the following three layers within the IT architecture:

- The application architecture.
- The middleware architecture.
- The infrastructure architecture.

(c) The source allocation matrix

The source allocation matrix is a high level matrix, with applications as rows and data entities or data clusters as columns. The cells contain indications such as: 'S = primary source' or 'R = replicated from the primary source'. There can be advanced versions with columns such as 'type of data (H = historical, M = master, T = transaction), cells containing information on volume and/or frequency. However, the crucial part is to identify which application maintains the primary source of the data. The impact of changes in this matrix usually results in re-engineering of the middleware architecture.

6.3.2 Using the architecture grid for understanding performance management

In an effort to explain to senior management of a company what the diversity of the IT landscape was and which measures were to be decided, we used the grid in the way that is indicated in Figure 6.3.

	Reality	Abstract models
	Organizational infrastructure and process	**Business architecture**
Business: *Revenue* *$1500 m/yr* *15 000 End users*	26 countries 98 locations 67 organizational units 68 legal entities 3 business units	1 business process model 4 Business process type (box selling, turnkey project, frame contract, etc.)
	IT infrastructure and process	**Information & technology architecture**
IT: *Expenses* *$100 m/yr* *600 FTE's* *Workload*	573 application systems 1000+ interfaces >10 DBMSs >5 OSs ?? network component types ?? data processing component types 2500+ desktop configurations	Information model sales Information model product data

Figure 6.3
An example of the high level architecture grid

This very high level inventory of the state of IT service provisioning in this company triggered the awareness that something needed to change regarding the business/IT alignment. So a target was defined to grow from a 'local for local' approach to a 'global standardization' approach (see Figure 6.4).

It became apparent that the need for standardization was there and a more architecture-based planning and control in IT service provisioning was introduced.

6.3.3 Focus areas for managing the content of the IT portfolio

The architecture is just a comprehensive terminology framework. The key question still remains: 'where to focus' in order to

Continuous restructuring based on:

Reality   *Abstract models*

	Organizational infrastructure and process	Business architecture
From: *Local for local* *Suboptimal support* *'Keep my customer satisfied'* *One problem, one solution at a time*	26 countries 98 locations 67 organizational units 68 legal entities 3 business units	1 business process model 4 Business process type (box selling, turnkey project, frame contract, etc.)
To: *Controlled suport based on a standardization concept* *IT capability management* *IT service management*	**IT infrastructure and process** 573 application systems 1000+ interfaces >10 DBMSs >5 OSs ?? network component types ?? data processing component types 2500+ desktop configurations	**Information & technology architecture** Information model sales Information model product data

Figure 6.4
Target setting based on
the architecture grid

⟺ *'local for local'*   ⟶ *'global standardization'*

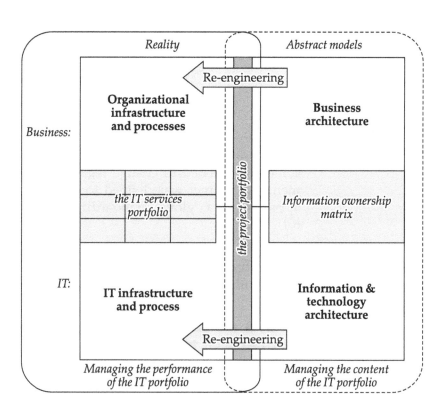

Figure 6.5
IT performance
management objects

manage the alignment between business and IT? We can use the architecture grid to identify these focus areas. Figure 6.5 distinguishes between focus areas for managing the content of the IT portfolio and focus areas for managing the performance of the IT portfolio. The latter will be discussed in the next section.

The content is based on the strategic choices that are being implemented in the next version of the architectures. The key management objects to focus on are as follows.

6.3.3.1 Information ownership matrix

The information ownership matrix is a high level grid with data entities or data clusters as rows and processes as columns. The cells contain indications such as: 'O = owns the data' or 'U = uses the data'. The purpose of this matrix is to identify which data is owned by which process. Since this is the most stable matrix with the architectures, the impact of changes in this matrix is the most far reaching in the IT architecture. This simple matrix plays a key role in architectural decision making. How changes in this matrix are being reflected in the IT architecture and how these architectural choices are implemented by means of the project portfolio highly impact the fit of the resulting IT services portfolio.

6.3.3.2 Project portfolio

In Chapter 3 we introduced the project portfolio as part of the IT portfolio and as the vehicle for new service introduction. In Chapter 5 we addressed decision making on the project portfolio. This project portfolio is a management object regarding not only the content of the IT portfolio, but also the performance.

6.3.4 Key objectives for managing the performance of the IT portfolio

The focus areas for performance of the IT portfolio (see Figure 6.5) directly relate to the matching of IT demand and IT supply. This matching comes together in the IT services portfolio and the IT project portfolio. In Chapter 3 we introduced both.

To manage this matching of IT demand and IT supply there are three key performance objectives:

- 'Fit between IT demand and IT supply'. This is the result of a, sometimes implicit, IT provisioning policy that is somewhere on a scale with a demand pull ('keep the customer satisfied') extreme on one end and a technology push ('one size fits all') extreme on the other. Both extremes are leading to a lack of effectiveness and an uncontrollable IT portfolio. The architectural approach to alignment will help managing this fit and finding the right IT provisioning policy.
- 'The speed of new IT service introduction', meaning the matching of the timeliness of required and provided new IT services. This matching is mainly the result of the technology used, the competencies available and the proper level of 'buy-in' on both the business and the IT side. The architectural approach will address the impact of technology and competency choices on this speed. The 'buy-in' aspect is of a non-architectural nature and for that reason left aside here.
- 'Flexibility of IT supply', meaning the agility of implementing change in the IT portfolio. Change is an everlasting thing, so architectural choices are subject to change as well. Finding the proper architectural scope helps providing flexibility to change.

We cannot separate these three objectives from each other, the mutual influences are many. So there is not a recipe for each of them, nor is there one recipe that can support all three.

6.4 Practical approaches to the alignment of business and IT

We will now address three architectural approaches that, although focusing on one performance objective, contribute to all three objectives mentioned above. These approaches were born in the day-to-day practice of implementing and managing IT, they are by no means exhaustive. We only mention them because of their proven value in creating alignment.

- Standardization of processes and IT services. This is a most common approach that is based on the concept of continuous improvement of processes. Standardization focuses on 'fit between IT demand and IT supply'.
- Implementing role – technology alignment. This is a concept that is based on the type of technology that is chosen to implement required IT functionality. This concept focuses on 'the speed of new IT service introduction'.

- Isolating IT architectural components. This is a concept that is based on enterprise architecture components and being able to 'plug and play' by means of a message bus. Isolating components focuses on 'flexibility of IT supply'.

6.4.1 Standardization of processes and IT services

In Chapter 4 we addressed the stages of IT optimization and a four-stage approach to standardization. The two top line gains and their successive order were:

- Business process standardization (HR/finance processes, order fulfilment processes, bid-to-cash processes).
- Information integration (common product, customer codes, information repository).

6.4.1.1 Business process standardization

One of the drivers for business process re-engineering (BPR) is cost optimization by means of standardization of processes and IT. This can be done from two perspectives:

- Promoting one particular successful implementation of a process to the standard and then duplicating this success elsewhere in the company. This is called a 'best practices' approach.
- 'What was successful elsewhere will also be successful for us.' This is usually the justification for implementing an ERP solution as the basis for BPR. We'd like to call this an 'ERP' approach.

Experiences with both approaches do not lead to a preference to either one of them. In general it depends on the scope of the processes, the size of the E (enterprise) in ERP and the persistence in senior management support whether standardization will be successful.

There is a potential threat that standardization will stand in the way of the required 'flexibility of IT supply'. The scope of the process standardization needs to be limited enough to stay flexible, yet large enough to be effective. Choices on the scope need to be in line with the strategic choices on the value system and the strategic positioning mentioned in section 6.2.

6.4.1.2 Information integration

The other top line gain mentioned is standardization of information. This approach in fact abstracts from the processes and puts the information central to decision making on IT architecture. Again the business strategic choices on the value system positioning and the value creation web are key to the IT architectural solution. No matter what exactly the technology is that is chosen for customer relationship management (CRM), product lifecycle management (PLM) and business intelligence (BI), the standardization of nomenclature and structures of customer and product data are key to their effectiveness.

The next section shows an example from practice on defining the scope of standardization of business processes and to a limited extent the associated information integration.

6.4.2 An example of implementing process and IT architecture standards

In the 1990s a globally operating telecom equipment manufacturer started process standardization using the ERP approach mentioned above. This went with varying degrees of success. An analysis was made of the relevant differences and similarities in the various process solutions that were implemented which led to the conclusion that not every 'standard process' was applicable everywhere. However, it turned out that there was a finite set of 'standard processes' with the associated IT services to support them, which could be 'configured' into a 'business type'. These business types were then used as 'blueprints' for organizational models.

Eventually from the learning experience a model emerged based on this business type concept that helped implement standardization.

6.4.2.1 The concept

The concept of a business type exists to assist in the analysis of the data and processes required by an organizational entity to conduct business in a specific area of the world. It enables the limiting of the information systems required to support the business entity based on the premise that similar data and processes can be supported by similar information systems.

Analysis of the dependencies led to the identification of the following business types:

- Sales operation.
- Sales operation and logistics.
- Manufacturing/assembly operation.
- Development lab.
- Full enterprise operation which includes all of the above + a series of support functions.

The 'natural' order for implementing new business in a specific geographic area turned out to be a three-phase approach.

Phase I 'Market entry'

- Sales operation.
- Sales operation + logistics.
- Sales operation + logistics + manufacturing/assembly.
- Sales operation + logistics + manufacturing/assembly + development lab.

Phase II 'Globalization/specialization'

- Full stream operation specialized in manufacturing and/or development and/or (regional/local) operational support centre.

Phase III 'Focus on core competencies/shared services'

- Local specialization on manufacturing and/or development.
- Regional shared services for operational support that are sourced.

6.4.2.2 The associated growth path for IT architecture

The third phase had not been reached in the timeframe of the example. Business evolution was through both mergers and acquisitions and changing command structures. In case of the third phase the managing of sourced shared services is the third influence on the IT architectural choices.

Market entry was realized by means of acquisition of existing business in a geographical area. Usually it started with a joint venture (JV). To facilitate a steady growth towards the usage of global IT architectures, the business type approach was accommodated with an IT architecture growth path in three phases. For the sake of creating a complete picture we added the fourth phase (see Figure 6.6).

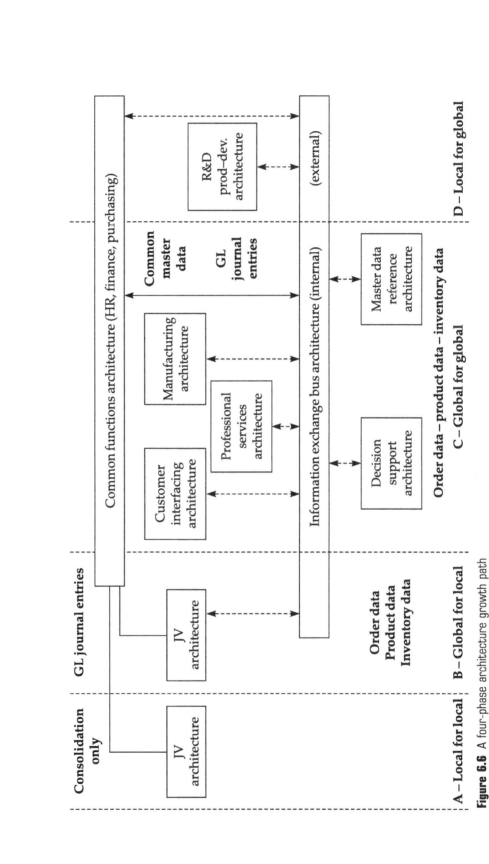

Figure 6.6 A four-phase architecture growth path

A – Local for local

The existing processes and IT architecture are kept in place; the only information exchange with the mother company is based on the yearly financial consolidation cycle. Usually in this phase the JV is partly owned by the mother company. Customer and product nomenclature is according to local standards and so is the information on the customer installed base.

B – Global for local

This is the situation where the JV is fully owned. The existing processes and IT architecture are gradually being replaced by the company-wide architecture standards, starting with the components in the functions architecture. For example, for the financial systems, the information exchange with the mother company is expanded to include general ledger journal entries on a monthly basis. As a next step product, order and inventory data is exchanged for the 'intra-company' business. Prerequisite is the adoption of the company standards for customer data, product data and the high level business events linked to a B2B information exchange protocol. In this phase the structure of the business can change to accommodate a future role globally.

C – Global for global

All processes and the IT architecture are gradually replaced to accommodate the role in the global operation of the existing JV. By definition the JV becomes a local subsidiary of the mother company.

D – Local for global

The back office support is reorganized in shared services organizations that are (partly) outsourced. By definition the shared service centres are outside the mother company. The information exchange bus has expanded into an external B2B e-business link.

6.4.2.3 Benefits

The approach of process and architecture standardization by means of business types brought the company several essential benefits:

- a start-up time of a new venture abroad within a period of 9 to 12 months;
- a two-year timeframe for a joint venture to become profitable (or not); and
- when profitable grow towards the mother company by means of the company standard processes and architecture; or
- when not profitable, downsize the operation to sales operation only.

The essential ingredients to be able to realize this concept are:

- Information integration based on global customer and product nomenclature and structures.
- Standardization of the information exchange by means of the 'information exchange bus architecture' closely in line with standardization of applications.

6.4.2.4 The performance management objectives involved

Looking at the three performance management objectives we can summarize:

- 'Fit between IT demand and IT supply' was created by mixing the learning experience of both the 'ERP' and 'best practices' approaches into business types with a finite set of defined standard processes and IT services to support them.
- 'The speed' was created by implementing new operations based on these business types and their standard processes and IT services.
- 'Flexibility of IT supply' was created by introducing the standardized information exchange.

6.4.3 Implementing role – technology alignment

The second approach to improving alignment is totally different and based on the type of technology that is applied when designing, developing and implementing IT services. We will take a look at technology from the perspective of the role types in which one end user can be engaged. In fact we focus on the application architecture layer only. The middleware and infrastructure architecture layers are not mentioned, because in this case their influence is minimal.

6.4.3.1 IT technology from an end user perspective

Looking at the type of activity of one individual, we distinguish three different role types with related IT services based on three technology types (see also Figure 6.7):

- As an individual, the 'personal toolset' is provided. This is the standard desktop/laptop functionality that every 'knowledge worker' gets as a basic toolset.
- As a member of one or more teams, 'workgroup tools' (including workflow functionality) are used. This is the common functionality that every member of a specific team needs to exchange information with other team members in some predefined way.
- As an actor/player in a business process, 'business applications' are used, the robust IT solutions that are used by many individuals. These applications have a defined functionality associated with the role type of the individual in the business process.

In many cases all three types of technology are referred to as 'applications' or 'solutions' and in fact this is correct; however, the impact of the choice of one of those three technology types to resolve a specific IT demand is totally different.

6.4.3.2 Balancing speed and integrity

The three technology types all have their pros and cons.

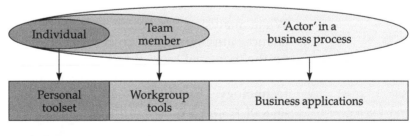

Figure 6.7
Technology from an end user perspective

Regarding the ability and speed of changing IT functionality

- Personal toolset: very flexible, lead times for implementing new functionality/IT services are in days or weeks (two to three weeks maximum).
- Workgroup tools: flexible, lead times for implementing new functionality/IT services are in weeks or months (two to three months maximum).
- Business applications: inflexible, lead times for implementing new functionality/IT services are in months or years.

Regarding the integrity, reliability, timeliness and accuracy of the data

- Personal toolset: very unstructured, hardly any integrity capabilities, duplication of information, lots of ways to influence reliability, easy to access but hard to find the proper information, very vulnerable, only sporadic back-up/recovery capabilities in use.
- Workgroup tools: limited structuring capabilities, some integrity capabilities, reasonably strong security capabilities, reasonably well-organized and accessible data, back-up/recovery capabilities in use.
- Business applications: strong structuring capabilities, strong integrity capabilities, strong security capabilities, well-organized and accessible data, back-up/recovery capabilities in use.

Applying the proper technology for a specific IT demand is a trade-off between speed of implementation and the price to pay in terms of integrity. In some cases one cannot afford to prefer speed to integrity, in some cases one can.

When analysing the overall application portfolio of a company, chances are high that a great number of applications are based on the 'personal toolset' technology type that for data integrity reasons should have been designed with 'business application' technology. Usually the reason given for that is the perceived lack of responsiveness of the IT department.

6.4.3.3 An example from our practice

In a project where we developed an IT master plan based on a new business and IT strategy we used this model to project the 'AS-IS' application portfolio and plot some potential applications. The result made senior management realize that the most mission critical IT had been implemented with technology from the personal toolset, such as spreadsheets, desktop database tools, and email connections with attachments. This came as a shock and the result was that the focus for priority setting drastically changed towards managing the risk involved.

6.4.3.4 The performance management objectives involved

Looking at the three performance management objectives we can summarize:

- 'Speed in new IT service introduction' can be improved by implementing flexible technologies (personal and workgroup tools) where possible, based on end user roles.
- 'Fit between IT demand and IT supply' can be facilitated through improved alignment between the technology and the role of the end user. Stable where needed, flexible where possible. The technologies provide for easy/fast adaptability which supports the required fit.
- 'Flexibility in IT supply' is created by the speed of the adaptability.

6.4.4 Isolating IT architectural components

Our third approach to improving alignment is based on the usage of information exchange technology and architecturally isolated components. When we say 'component' do not immediately think that we are entering the realm of object orientation or component-based development. The word component is used as a generic term here.

6.4.4.1 Example of an application architecture based on a bus concept

Figure 6.8 shows an example of a 'target application architecture' based on a 'bus' concept. The bus components consist of workflow management functionality and an internal message bus.

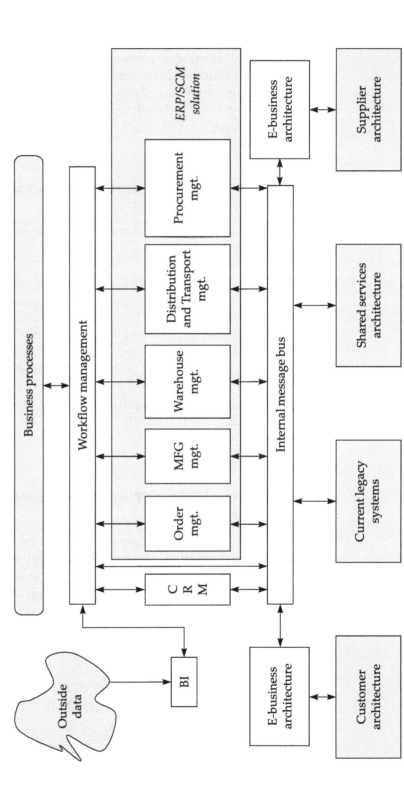

Figure 6.8 Information bus architecture

This approach is used for multiple purposes:

- *Phase-out current legacy systems*: create a growth path to move functionality from the existing legacy applications to new components in the application architecture. What actually happens is that when implementing the new component the required interfacing to the existing architecture is realized using 'message-oriented middleware' technology. Preferably with 'standard messages' based on an industry-specific definition of a message.
- *Implement a shared services architecture*: with shared services we mean functionality that is not business process specific, such as HR, finance, procurement, etc. The reason for isolating these applications is twofold:
  - it supports the strategic choices on the configuration of these services; and
  - it provides for potential savings for the company by creating economies of scale based on standardization.

A next step could be creating even bigger economies of scale by 'business process outsourcing (BPO)'. This bus approach can be seen as a preparation to a potential strategic sourcing decision.

- *Implement a standard user interface*: the workflow capabilities of the middleware implementation serves two purposes:
  - it creates an envelope around the applications (new and legacy) and as such it isolates the impact of application changes to the end user;
  - it manages the information exchange on a 'non-application-specific' basis and as such provides the standard workflow functionality.
- *Implement the 'mission critical' components*: business intelligence (BI), customer relationship management (CRM) and the e-business architecture are considered mission critical in this company. Since the market place is changing rapidly it is not precisely clear upfront whether the company can really benefit from this new technology. Also what exactly will be a competitive advantage cannot be anticipated. This resulted in the option of isolating these 'leading edge' applications from the other applications. The bus architecture plays a key role in the information exchange between the two.
- *Implement the new business process support functionality*: it has not been decided whether the business process support functionality will be replaced by an ERP/SCM solution or by means of a 'best of breed' approach. When some parts of the company already implemented some 'best of breed'

components, it was not yet clear whether these components were to be considered 'legacy'. The bus concept provides for extra time in deciding what the target component will eventually be.

The preferred order of implementing such an application architecture is:

- Start with the workflow capabilities and the internal message bus.
- Implement the mission critical components assuming that speed of new IT service introduction is of the utmost importance for these components.
- Replace the business process support functionality.

The choices of the appropriate message standards are key in this approach.

6.4.4.2 Technologies to implement a 'bus' concept

Nowadays this concept is related to the use of enterprise application integration (EAI) technology; however, it had already been implemented in the 1980s with the use of electronic data interchange (EDI)-based technology and protocols.

There are a number of technologies available with which to implement the 'bus' concept. One can make extensive studies on the technology to use; however, eventually there will always be a new and better/faster to implement technology available. This means that in the end we will always end up with a hybrid technological situation that needs to be managed. From a performance management perspective lifecycle management issues are also applicable to middleware implementations.

Choosing the proper technology is mainly based on the required timeliness of the information exchange.

6.4.4.3 The strategic choice of where to isolate architectures

By far the most important question to answer is where to isolate the components. To address this strategic architectural choice we will define an essential principle.

There are two different reasons for applying this type of bus concept:

- *Isolating* major architectural components. Isolating is what we do when information is passed on to an architectural area that is managed and owned by a separate entity.
- *Linking* major architectural components. Linking is what we do when information is passed on to an architectural area that is managed and owned by the same entity.

Information ownership can be determined in the following way:

- It is a process that owns a data entity or data cluster.
- And the process is owned by an organizational entity.
- There is only one application that is the primary source of a data entity or data cluster.
- This application takes part in only one application architecture.

This establishes the relationship between the managing and owning organizational entity and the (components in the) application architecture.

In the example from Figure 6.8, the shared services architecture and the legacy architecture are linked to the other architectures. The BI and e-business architectures are isolated.

The value system in which the company plays is by far the most stable basis for choosing isolation. The business strategic choices can cover multiple chains in the value system. In this case it is our firm belief that isolating architectures based on these chains creates the most flexible overall application architecture.

Information exchange *in isolated architectures* should *always* be based on 'external' industrial standard messages and message protocols. Adhering to this principle is of the utmost importance for the strategic flexibility/agility of the company. This is the key difference between IT being a showstopper or being an enabler for mergers, acquisitions and divestitures.

Information exchange *in linked architectures* should *preferably* be based on industry message standards; however, for reasons of competitive advantage at the early adoption of new technology, these will not always be available.

6.4.4.4 The performance management objectives involved

Looking at the three performance management objectives we can summarize:

- 'Flexibility in IT supply' is the key objective here and is based on the isolation principle in line with the strategic positioning choices in the value system.
- 'Fit between IT demand and IT supply' is facilitated by using industry-specific standard messages for information exchange.
- 'Speed of new IT service introduction' is based on using industry-specific standard messages for information exchange.

6.5 Managing the demand axis of the IT portfolio

Managing the IT demand axis (Figure 6.9) is the most challenging and most rewarding dimension of managing the IT portfolio. This is where senior management attention as well as a thorough understanding of the impact of strategic choices is vital for the results.

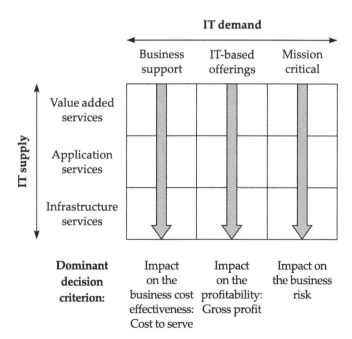

Figure 6.9
Decision criteria for IT demand

The main focus in this part of the IT portfolio is on the impact on value creation. There is never a pure/isolated cost or a pure/isolated value orientation, because lowering cost = increasing value.

All three IT demand types in the IT portfolio will be discussed separately:

- Mission critical.
- IT-based offerings.
- Business process support.

For every demand type the following subjects will be elaborated:

- An explanation of the type of demand/services we are referring to.
- The performance management objective in terms of type of value creation.
- The impact of strategic choices.
- The impact of architectural choices.
- The impact of service provisioning.

The strategic choice on sourcing will be addressed separately in Chapter 8, and only briefly mentioned here.

6.5.1 Managing mission critical IT

This is the most difficult, most challenging and the highest value add area of the IT portfolio. The difficulties of managing mission critical IT are manifold, for example:

- There is always a lot of senior management attention involved, which can be both helpful and bothering at times.
- There is a lot at stake and mistakes are killing (the company).
- Usually there are a lot of complex dependencies with other parts of the IT portfolio.

A distinction needs to be made between 'business critical' and 'mission critical'. Business criticality is not by definition mission critical. We consider business criticality a requirement that results in a certain service level that is required to be provided for that particular service. For example, email is in almost all cases business critical, yet we consider it a commodity service that belongs to the business support area of the IT portfolio. There are isolated cases where email can be mission critical, e.g. when vital, unstructured company information is exchanged to outside organizations. In that case the mission critical email service requires specific security levels that outrank all the other services.

Reasons why an IT service is mission critical can be either defensive or offensive:

- Defensive reasons express reacting to an initiative taken in the environment that can be killing for the company. Examples are changing legislation requires restructuring of (parts of) the business, drastically changing revenue streams ask for down-sizing parts of the business, uncontrolled growth in the past asks for drastic optimization.
- Offensive reasons express acting on an opportunity that arises in the environment. Examples are: new channels provide for competitive advantage and ask for the utmost speed in new IT service delivery, the integration as a result of a merger asks for drastic and fast business restructuring to cash in on synergies.

Mission critical IT can be in both business support and/or IT-based offering services; however, they are absolutely key to/vital for the success of the business as a whole. This means that some mission critical services can change over time into 'normal' services. What is mission critical today can be a normal service next year because of the changing environment of the business. Services that are mission critical in one industry can be of a normal type in another industry, or even within the same industry. For example, call centre services are mission critical for 'direct writers' but normal IT services for the other channels in the insurance industry. Defining what exactly is mission critical for the company is a business strategic issue that needs to be decided by the board and senior management. The criteria for this are by definition subjective estimates of threats and opportunities.

The management challenge regarding the IT portfolio lies in the required balance between:

- short-term, fast, risk avoiding response to the demanded services; and
- long-term, stable, efficient fit in the existing services portfolio that are not mission critical.

The biggest risk from an IT portfolio management perspective is that too many IT services are becoming 'mission critical' at the same time and also that the intervals of being mission critical are becoming shorter. This would be a sign of lack of stable strategy planning.

6.5.1.1 The performance management objective

When making investment decisions on mission critical IT services, the dominant decision criterion is the *business risk* involved. A lot depends on the magnitude of the risk involved. The added value can be in any of the four areas:

- Technological/infrastructure value is the least likely objective, but can be the goal for defensive mission critical services.
- Organizational/process value can be the objective for both offensive and defensive mission critical services.
- Extended reach value is an objective for offensive mission critical services.
- Competitive value is *the* most likely area for offensive mission critical services.

6.5.1.2 The impact of strategic choices

Mission criticality is not just highly impacted by strategic choices; it is completely driven by strategic choices.

Business choices

Typical areas for mission critical services based on 'focus' strategies of Treacy and Wiersema:

- Operational excellence: the replacement of IT business support services that are too costly by lean and mean low cost applications.
- Product leadership: implementation of knowledge management capabilities, knowledge transfer and design transfer capabilities.
- Customer intimacy: decentralized, workgroup-based customer knowledge capabilities.

Typical areas for mission critical services based on the strategies of Boynton, Victor and Pine:

- Industrial revolution strategy: all cost optimization related activity, such as business support in the area of process lead time reduction and the area of design transfer from invention to mass production.
- Dynamic stability strategy: the ability to isolate and link product and services components into customer-specific offerings.

IT choices

- Choices on *environment and positioning* will increase mission criticality when leading edge technologies are applied or novelty service provisioning. In both cases next to the business risk already involved, there is also technology risk.
- Choices on *configuration* will increase mission criticality when strategic partnerships are involved without a strong risk/ reward component in the partnership contract. And/or core technologies are chosen with little to no skills available in the marketplace. And/or architectural solutions are extensively using information from components in the existing IT architecture and stability of the new technology has not yet been proven.

6.5.1.3 The impact of architectural choices

In case of offensive mission critical IT services, the process and IT architecture standardization is not an option, because both the process and the IT service are new. There is little chance that the software to support this is available. If this is the case then one has to ask oneself whether one has backlog on the competition. In case of defensive mission critical IT, the process and IT architecture standardization is an option. However, when speed is required (which most of the time is the case in mission critical) this could be too long a path.

Using workgroup solutions is a strong option, because 'learning' and 'learning fast' are what is needed here. This implies that design and implementation of tailor-made application software should be postponed until the IT service has proven viable and the requirements have stabilized. Most of the time the workflow capabilities can speed up the implementation of lead time reduction programmes. Because this technology is 'wrapping' the existing architectures one should be carefully planning the 'sun setting' of redundant functionality in the legacy archi-tectures. Leaving it as is does not optimize cost.

Use of a bus architecture approach is based preferably on isolation of the IT service, at least until the service has proven viable. 'Don't touch the system and the technical nerds' can be considered as the most extreme form of isolation. Only when information from existing architecture components is needed, is linking an option.

6.5.1.4 The impact of service provisioning

Since isolation of mission critical IT is key in achieving the required speed, the service provisioning management model based on a 'tuning zone approach', which is described in Chapter 3, is mandatory to the implementation of mission critical IT services. Any type of new technology can be used and as such must be isolated, stabilized and optimized, given viability over time.

A potential problem can arise when these mission critical services are outsourced. There can be very good strategic reasons for outsourcing offensive mission critical IT services (speed and competencies being the obvious ones), but can the external service provider's organization be considered to be the 'tuning zone' and can the services be insourced, optimized and stabilized later on? If not, a new 'vendor lock-in' is created. It all depends on the strategic intentions and the contract with the vendor.

6.5.2 Managing IT-based offerings

Next in the line of value added IT are the IT services that are (part of) an offering to the end customer of the company. When we take a closer look at this group of IT services we can see three different types of offering falling in this area:

- E-business services, with various sell and buy versions:
  - business to consumer (B2C) services;
  - business to business (B2B) services like partnerships in supply chain management/e-procurement;
  - Electronic funds transfer (EFT).
- Embedded knowledge offerings, with various versions based on:
  - knowledge of customer installed base;
  - design transfer capability in the manufacturing industry;
  - call centre implementations with a strong CRM component;
  - knowledge embedded in software that is available hard coded in the end product.
- Process automation, with various industry specific versions.

All three types directly contribute to the companies' profit and loss statement. The biggest challenge from an IT portfolio management perspective is providing continuity of service.

6.5.2.1 The performance management objective

When making investment decisions on IT-based offerings, the dominant decision criterion is the *impact on the business profitability*. This is mainly in terms of additional revenue. Sometimes it can be in terms of cost reduction, when these offerings are compared to more traditional equivalents. A high cost level can be good, when the company has a strategy that is heavily based on IT and the application of the Internet. The gross profit is more important than the cost level. For this type of IT service the expense will be booked as cost of goods sold (COGS).

The added value can be in one of the four areas, depending on the type of offering:

- Technological/infrastructure value is the most likely objective for process automation.
- Organizational/process value can be the objective for both process automation and embedded knowledge offerings.
- Extended reach value is the most likely objective for e-business offerings.
- Competitive value can be the objective for both embedded knowledge offerings and e-business.

6.5.2.2 The impact of strategic choices

IT-based offerings are highly impacted by IT strategic choices and completely driven by business strategic choices.

Business choices

- Choices on *environment and positioning* are the basis for IT-based offerings. The environment must offer opportunities for implementing these IT services, both from a financial feasibility and from a technical feasibility point of view. There is a difference between the three types of offerings:
  - in many cases e-business will be seen as a new channel that can become part of the business strategy; however, it can also be a vehicle to lead time reduction in 'cross value chain' processes;

- – embedded knowledge offerings are a means to enable customer retention and as such is a competitive force;
- – process automation can provide IT-based features that will create competitive advantage.
- Choices on *configuration* determine to what extent IT-based offerings can be deployed. The level of integration/linkages between business strategy and IT strategy determines the amount of management attention that will be available for IT-based offerings.

Typical areas for IT-based offerings in the 'focus' strategies of Treacy and Wiersema:

- Operational excellence: all three types of offerings can help reduce process lead times. Process automation supports internal efficiency. Embedded knowledge offerings and e-procurement/SCM support cross value chain lead time reduction. B2C e-business will be used to reduce the cost to serve.
- Product leadership: only in an IT-based industry like financial services, will IT-based offerings be a strategic issue (and a very important one!). In all other industries companies with a profit and loss focus will only use IT-based offerings when driven by their environment.
- Customer intimacy: all e-business and embedded knowledge offerings are key to the success of the company in this focus strategy. B2B e-business and embedded knowledge offerings are vital when a company operates in the middle of a value system. B2C e-business and call centres are vital when a company operates at the end of a value system.

Typical areas for IT-based offerings in the strategies of Boynton, Victor and Pine:

- Industrial revolution strategy: as in 'operational excellence', all three types of offerings can help reduce process lead times. The embedded knowledge offerings will be mainly focused on 'design transfer capabilities' in an 'early adoption mode'.
- Dynamic stability strategy: as in 'customer intimacy' all e-business and embedded knowledge offerings are viable here. B2B e-business and embedded knowledge offerings are vital. The 'design transfer capabilities' need to be mature with an emphasis on 'standardized component identifications and descriptions'. There is a very mature cross industry partner-ship thinking needed to implement this strategy.

IT choices

- Choices on *environment and positioning* are important for the success of IT-based offerings. Taking the management challenge of continuity of service into account, the application of leading edge technologies or novelty service provisioning in many cases turns out to be the vital choice to make. Deliberate choices on which technology wave to surf and which wave to pass need to be based on their impact on the profitability of the IT-based offerings.
- Choices on *configuration* influence the effectiveness of IT-based offerings. Especially the key role played by IT governance issues. Providing B2C offerings in a separate line of business and as such implementing an 'IT-based channel' is closely linked to the customer intimacy and dynamic stability strategies mentioned above. Process automation and embedded knowledge offerings are usually fully integrated in the business unit that is providing the offering to the customer.

6.5.2.3 The impact of architectural choices

The architectural options differ for the three types of services that we identified:

- Architectural impact on e-business services:
  - process and IT standardization is a very viable architectural approach in the case of separating these e-business offerings in an organizational unit/channel;
  - team and workgroup application is only advised to be used when speed in start-up situations is needed. 'Personal toolset'-based applications are absolutely forbidden, given the business impact that is at stake;
  - middleware implementation is highly recommended for isolating e-business architectures.
- Architectural impact on embedded knowledge offerings:
  - process and IT standardization is key to the success of providing these services. In particular cross value chain process and data standardization are key to the success;
  - team and workgroup applications are highly recommended in the case of offering knowledge of customer installed base as a component and in the case of design transfer capability in the manufacturing industry. 'Personal toolset'-based applications can only be tolerated in a start-up learning phase. Replacement needs to be planned from the moment the technology is implemented;

- middleware implementation is highly recommended in the case of call centre/CRM/BI implementation given the need for linking to other architectures.
- Architectural impact on process automation:
  - process and IT standardization is highly recommended;
  - team and workgroup application as well as 'personal toolset'-based applications are out of the question, because of the required stability of the IT services and service provisioning;
  - middleware implementation is highly recommended to both isolate the process automation architectures and link the required administrative data flows.

6.5.2.4 The impact of service provisioning

IT-based offerings require a stable service provisioning. The service provisioning management model based on a 'tuning zone approach', which was described in Chapter 3, is necessary for the implementation. The isolation of new IT-based offerings that are in a market entry stage needs to be managed specifically. Any type of new technology can be used and as such must be isolated, stabilized and optimized, given viability over time.

The embedded knowledge offerings and the process automation are usually services that are provided internally because the knowledge component involved is core to the business.

As with mission critical services, a potential problem can arise when e-business offerings are outsourced. There can be very good strategic reasons for outsourcing B2C e-business offerings (speed and competencies being the obvious ones), but can the external service provider's organization be considered to be the 'tuning zone' and can the services be insourced, optimized and stabilized later on? Or is a new 'vendor lock-in' created? It all depends on the strategic intentions and the contract with the vendor.

6.5.3 Managing business process support

The IT services that support business processes is the third group of IT demand types. When we take a closer look at this group of IT services we can see two different types falling in the area:

- Support of primary processes, such as:
  - the 'order realization' processes: sales and marketing, logistics and distribution, manufacturing, procurement of product components;

    – the 'product realization' processes: R&D, product design, process design, product and process implementation.
- Support of secondary processes and business functions, such as:
  - centralized procurement, facilities management;
  - HR, finance, IT.

The common element in all of these is that IT service demand is defined from the perspective that a process needs to be supported, which results in IT capabilities and IT services that are subordinate to the value delivered by the process.

The primary processes can be divided into a product realization process and an order realization process. The concepts we need to understand are common business economics and go for all industries, but in Figure 6.10 a 'manufacturing'-based terminology is used.

It is important to understand that the product realization process (PRP) has other value drivers and associated KPIs than the order realization process (ORP). Yet the two are related and are linked at the point of 'design transfer', which in the picture is between product and process implementation and manufacturing. The IT services portfolio to support these processes requires cautious design on all intersections mentioned in the picture, but on the 'design transfer' intersection in particular. One can consider each intersection as a potential (external) market and as such every process as a potential player in a value chain. From that perspective managing the IT services portfolio becomes easier.

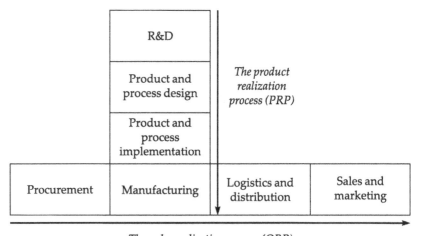

Figure 6.10
Business processes

To a certain extent this also goes for the secondary processes/ business functions. In the concept of business process out- sourcing (BPO) these activities are usually considered non-core to the company and as such targeted for outsourcing or at least centralized in 'shared services' operations. Considering these to be a separate business within the business helps simplifying the management of the IT portfolio.

6.5.3.1 The performance management objective

When making investment decisions on IT services that support business processes, the dominant decision criterion is the *impact on the cost level of the business*. Industry-specific levels of the 'cost to serve' provide the targets. A high cost level is not by definition bad, when the company has a strategy that is heavily based on IT. It is not the IT cost level that is important but the business cost level. For this type of IT service the expense will be booked as sales, general and administrative (SG&A).

The added value can be in one of the four areas, depending on the type of offering:

- Technological/infrastructure value can be an objective, for all types of business process support.
- Organizational/process value is *the* most likely objective, for all types of business process support.
- Extended reach value can be an objective in the ORP process support as well as in the PRP support.
- Competitive value is the most important objective in the support of the PRP.

6.5.3.2 The impact of strategic choices

Business process support is highly impacted by strategic choices.

Business choices

- Choices on *environment and positioning* are basic to the configuration of the product realization process and the order realization process.
- Choices on *configuration* determine the actual process struc- tures of both process types. The ability to source certain processes to partners in the value system highly influences the structure and content of the IT portfolio.

171

Typical areas for business process support in the 'focus' strategies of Treacy and Wiersema:

- Operational excellence: all three types of processes, ORP, PRP and shared services operations are getting key management attention in terms of cost efficiencies. IT services can play a key role in implementing this focus strategy.
- Product leadership: primary management focus is on the PRP processes. Success of the business is directly linked with the speed of new IT services implementation in the PRP processes. Understanding and dealing with product/service structures and component-based production are the main areas for IT services.
- Customer intimacy: primary management focus is on the ORP processes. Success of the business is directly linked with the fit of customer demand and the company offering. The required IT services to support this are based on customer knowledge related to product/service delivery flexibility. These are the main areas for IT services.

Typical areas for business process support in the strategies of Boynton, Victor and Pine:

- Industrial revolution strategy: as in 'operational excellence', all three types of processes require 'low cost' IT solutions to support 'low cost' processes.
- Dynamic stability strategy: both PRP and ORP processes need maximum flexibility in IT services provided.

IT choices

- Choices on *environment and positioning* influence the effectiveness of IT services that support the processes.
- Choices on *configuration* only marginally influence the effectiveness of the IT services that support these processes.

6.5.3.3 The impact of architectural choices

Looking at the three types of business processes that we identified, the architectural options are very much alike:

- Process and IT standardization is a very viable architectural approach provided that the processes are stable. Use of 'off-the-shelf' software can speed up the process, but doesn't provide for a competitive advantage.

- Team and workgroup application is a very good alternative when speed in start-up situations is needed. 'Personal toolset'-based applications are absolutely forbidden, given the business impact that is at stake.
- Middleware implementation is highly recommended for isolating PRP, ORP and shared services IT architectures. A thorough design based on the information ownership matrix will create the flexibility needed in the business.

6.5.3.3 The impact of service provisioning

Stable service provisioning as well as speed in implementation are required here. This intrinsic conflict is addressed in Chapter 3. The service levels required are subject to negotiation between the demand and supply organizations involved. For these types of services along the IT demand axis of the IT performance management grid, the service levels are the least critical.

6.6 Managing the supply axis of the IT portfolio

Managing the IT supply axis (Figure 6.11) is somewhat closer to the IT management practices. This is where senior management attention usually lacks and the required IT competencies, IT assets and IT governance are left to the CIO. However, the management along this axis is just as vital to the overall results as the IT demand axis.

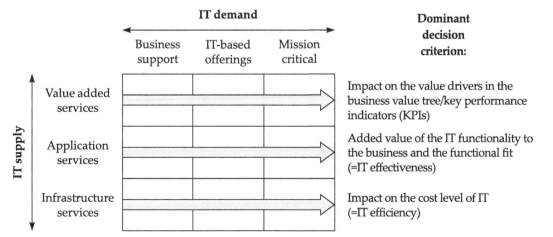

Figure 6.11 Decision criteria for IT supply

The main focus in this part of the IT portfolio is on cost management.

Before we deal with every row on the IT supply axis, we want to take a closer look at the basic ingredients that we have available.

6.6.1 Managing IT CAP-abilities

Delivering value can only be done by managing the IT capabilities. In Chapter 2 we gave the following definition of IT capability. We consider an IT capability to be 'an integrated and internally coherent set of competencies + assets + processes (=supporting processes and tooling)' (CAP-ability).

This provides us with the following performance management objectives:

- Competencies, effectiveness of the available competencies now and in the near future, which is driven by strategic choices in both the business and technology realm.
- Assets, exploitation of assets now and in the near future, which is driven by strategic and architectural choices in the technology realm.
- Processes, efficiency of the interaction between competencies and assets focused on the intended process result.

The result of the interaction of these three is the IT services delivered at a certain level of quality.

When taking a closer look at *competencies* we can see that:

- Competencies are people business, which means that nurturing the development and in particular the professional development is essential.
- Competencies comprise 'know-how' (=skills) + 'know-what' (=knowledge) + 'know-why' (=relevant experience), which means the fit of this mixture on the required competencies together with the individual's attitude will account for the results.
- Competencies always have a business relevance, an IT relevance or a mix of both and as such are subject to erosion of a level that is linked to the level of erosion of the related business and IT relevancy.

When looking at *assets*, we can see that:

- Assets are technology business, which means that technology watch and timely refresh are vital.

- Assets provide functionality, which means that the fit of the provided and required functionality together with the level of standardization achieved will account for the results.
- Assets erode over time driven by business and technology change/evolution, which requires monitoring.

When looking at *processes*, we can see that:

- Processes bring competencies and assets together and provide defined repeatable results called services or products, which means that process monitoring and continuous improvement are important.

The above-mentioned CAP-abilities will be our major management objective along the IT supply axis of the IT portfolio.

We will now deal with all three supply types in the IT portfolio separately:

- Value added services.
- Application services.
- IT infrastructure services.

For every supply type we will deal with the following subjects:

- An explanation of the type of services we are referring to.
- The performance management objective in terms of CAP-ability impact.
- The impact of strategic choices.
- The impact of architectural choices.

The strategic choice on sourcing will be addressed separately in Chapter 8.

6.6.2 Managing value added services

Value added services are the most business sensitive supply type of services. These services deliver value to the business in the broadest sense: translating demand into supply, operational business/IT alignment, managing service provisioning, etc.

Value added services consist of three groups:

- Consultancy and architecture services to provide for the company- and IT-specific expertise to *match IT demand and IT supply on a content basis*. Type of activities:
  - business enhancement, opportunity modelling, business change justification, process change consulting, information analysis, defining and implementing IT services policies,

product/process support ('key users'), technology watch, defining and implementing technology policies, architectural design and development, functional evolution, requirements definition, parameter configuration, etc.

- Service management, service level management and vendor management services to provide for the competencies to *match IT demand and IT supply on a performance basis*. Type of activities:
  - service performance monitoring and management, monitoring compliance with policies, internal marketing and sales/account management, service integration, charging/billing, product support (1st level), vendor contract management, etc.
- Programme and project management services to provide for the competencies to implement new IT services. Type of activities:
  - project management, business change management.

6.6.2.1 The performance management objective

This is 'people business', which means that managing the required professional capabilities is the obvious performance objective of this area in the IT portfolio.

The main investment decision criterion is the *impact on the value driver trees of the business*. However, not all companies have explicit value driver trees that can be used. This sometimes results in a very distributed approach to delivering these services ('key users'), where it becomes blurry whether we are discussing IT services or activities that belong in the business. We always include the value added services in the management objective of the IT portfolio, regardless of organizational implementation.

Looking at the CAP-ability model:

- Managing competencies is focused on the ability to acquire and retain the competencies for all three types of service mentioned. There are basically three sources for competency development in this area:
  - from the business community, to the IT community, resulting in either service managers or project/programme managers;
  - from the application services area to the value added services area, resulting in consultants and architects;

  – from external service providers either in terms of 'training
  on the job' of their own staff when hiring external expertise
  or in terms of professional development services.
- Managing assets is not relevant.
- Managing processes is focused on standardization of the
  methods and terminology/jargon. Here the number of external consultants, architects and project managers and the
  associated 'schools of thought' they bring to the process can
  become very ineffective. For the service management services,
  KPIs can be defined more easily because processes are more
  structured and of a repetitive nature.

6.6.2.2 The impact of strategic choices

Business strategic choices only influence the type of business
specific knowledge/competencies that are required to deliver
the consultancy services.

IT strategic choices deeply impact the required competencies
with regard to consultancy, architecture, service management
and service level management. The biggest impact is created by
the sourcing strategy, which is addressed in Chapter 8.

All value added service types mentioned define and implement
the IT strategy. So all mentioned IT choices to be made are based
on advice to senior management by the people delivering the
value added services.

6.6.2.3 The impact of architectural choices

The architectural principles that were addressed in the first part
of this chapter need to be fully understood and implemented by
the people delivering value added services. In addition:

- The consultants need to understand and control the changes
  in the information ownership matrix and be able to address
  the issues related to those changes.
- The architects need to have a thorough knowledge of the IT
  architectural components that were chosen in the IT
  strategy.
- The service management people need to have a thorough
  knowledge of the service structures and the relationships
  between the service components and the IT architectural
  components.

6.6.3 Managing application services

Next in line in the IT supply axis of the IT performance management grid are the application services. These services consist of the development and maintenance of applications. The subjects of these services are:

- The 'application architecture', which is the most business-sensitive part of the IT architecture consisting of:
  - application software with defined capabilities/functionality and operational support services;
  - generic software on the high end (browser, office tools, TP monitor, security SW, etc.) with defined capabilities and operational support services.
- The business-related functionality of the middleware architecture, which bridges the gap between business sensitivity/business change and technology sensitivity/technology refreshment consisting of:
  - generic software on the middleware layer (DBMS, object brokers, message-based service SW, etc.) with defined capabilities and operational support services.

These services can be divided into three types:

- Application management and maintenance of service components to provide for the availability of the functionality of the application architecture to the user. Type of activities:
  - corrective maintenance, small changes/minor impact new functionality, second line user support with access to third line support at the software provider's organization, version upgrades, packages and licences management, change management, installation, version upgrade, load balancing/application performance management.
- Application development services to provide for the design, development and testing of new functionality in the application architecture. Type of activities:
  - functional and technical design, software enhancements, application programming, parameter setting and testing.
- Project management services to provide for the competencies to implement new functionality in the application architecture. Type of activities:
  - project management, business change management.

6.6.3.1 The performance management objective

These services are a mix of 'people-based' activity with the required competencies and architectural components with their capabilities. For performance management, we regard the integral service perception. For the overall application services the main investment decision criterion is the *'functional fit'* of the services delivered, in general the *IT effectiveness*. This is 'people business', which means that managing the professional capabilities required is the primary performance objective of this area in the IT portfolio.

Looking at the CAP-ability model:

- Managing competencies is focused on the ability to acquire and retain the competencies. There are basically three sources for competency development in this area:
  - from the application development activity to the application implementation activity resulting in consultants and architects;
  - from the project management to the service management activity;
  - from external service providers either in terms of 'training on the job' of the own staff when hiring external expertise or in terms of professional development services.
- Managing assets is managing the technology that is used in the application and middleware architectures. The management objective is standardization and optimization of the used technology as well as timely refresh:
  - a number of generally accepted principles/management focus areas can be given here;
  - buy is preferable to build, reuse is supported actively, minimize the number of different 'programming languages', monitor the pace of change in the adopted application technology;
  - support the implementation of external/industry specific standards.

In Chapter 4 and section 6.4 we addressed standardization. In particular what was written about architectures and isolating and linking architectures is of the utmost relevance in managing application services assets.

- Managing processes is focused on standardization of the methods and terminology/jargon. Here the number of external analysts, programmers, project managers and the associated 'schools of thought' they bring to the process can become very ineffective. Only when architectures are isolated properly can this 'school of thought' phenomenon be controlled. For both application development and application maintenance service lots of standard processes and KPIs are defined.

6.6.3.2 The impact of strategic choices

The business strategic choices only influence the type of functionality/applications that are serviced. The IT strategic choices deeply impact the required competencies with regard to application development and maintenance. Technology refresh cycles and the required time to (re-)build the competencies are key. Timely availability of application development and maintenance competencies can be a competitive advantage.

6.6.3.3 The impact of architectural choices

The architectural principles that were addressed in the first part of this chapter need to be fully understood and implemented by the people delivering application services. These persons need to have a thorough knowledge of the IT architectural components that were chosen in the IT strategy.

6.6.4 Managing IT infrastructure services

Last in line of the IT supply axis of the IT performance management grid are the IT infrastructure services. These services relate to keeping IT up and running in the broadest sense. We can consider most of these services to be non-business sensitive.

They can be divided in three groups:

- Desktop services to provide for the availability of the functionality of the desktop to the user.
- Datacentre services to provide for the availability of the processing power to the user.
- Network-related services to provide for the availability of connectivity to the user.

In Chapter 3 we gave more details on the type of activity that is associated with these services. We consider these services to be commodities, given the maturity of the market for these services.

6.6.4.1 The performance management objective

These services are a mix of 'people-based' activity with the required competencies and architectural components with their capabilities. The main investment decision criterion is the impact on the cost level of IT. In general we are speaking of *IT efficiency* with a dominant asset-related cost orientation. It is the match between required and available technical capabilities that provides the quality of the IT service.

Looking at the CAP-ability model:

- Managing competencies is of a lesser importance, given that we are dealing with commodity services. This is the realm for sourcing, see also Chapter 8.
- Managing assets is managing the technology that is used for IT infrastructure architecture. The management objective is standardization and optimization of the used technology as well as timely refresh. In Chapter 4 we addressed standardization and optimization of these services extensively. In Chapter 8 we will address the issue of assets and the control on the technology refresh when these services are being sourced.
- Managing infrastructure services processes is focused on efficiency. There are many process management experiences available, e.g. in the ITIL process descriptions (ITIL, 2002).

6.6.4.2 The impact of strategic choices

The business strategic choices do not influence these services, because they are 'non-business sensitive'. The IT strategic choices impact the required competencies, more specifically the sourcing strategy which we will address in Chapter 8.

6.6.4.3 The impact of architectural choices

The architectural principles that were addressed in the first part of this chapter will have an impact on the infrastructure. This impact needs to be fully understood and implemented by the people delivering infrastructure services. These persons need to have a thorough knowledge of the IT architectural components that were chosen in the IT strategy.

6.7 Managing IT performance

What are the processes to introduce and execute IT performance management? We use a four-step approach to manage the IT performance cycle (see Figure 6.12) involving:

- Strategy planning and implementation (steps 1 and 2).
- Tactical planning and control (step 3).
- Operational planning and control (step 4).

The strategic, tactical and operational planning and control cycles go at a different pace; however, the content is deeply related.

6.7.1 Strategic planning and control

The usual strategic planning and control cycle covers a three-year forward-looking timeframe which is updated once every

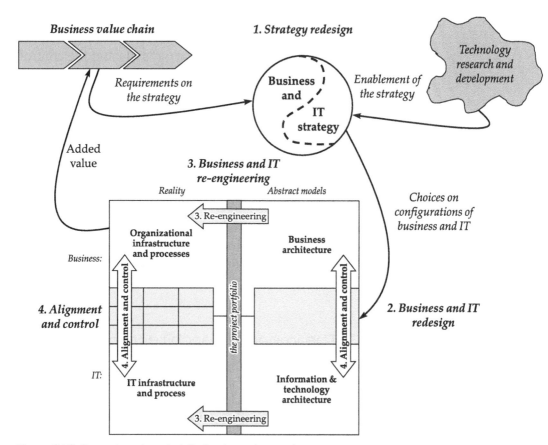

Figure 6.12 Strategic and tactical IT planning and control

year. There is a lot of business unit-related activity that consolidates in the strategic masterplan (introduced in section 6.2). This strategic masterplan becomes the basis for verification/control of every management decision with a strategic impact for the next years. Within this masterplan the *configuration of IT* is described, resulting in the IT performance management grid. This grid is the instrument for directing and controlling the flow of money that is involved in IT.

Step 1 Strategy (re-)design

(Re-)design of the strategy is triggered by:

(a) changing requirements/demand from the environment in which the business operates;
(b) new technology enabling new strategies.

A clear distinction between business strategy and IT strategy is not needed. The two go hand in hand and are two flipsides of the same coin. Whether we consider this to be redesign or design is irrelevant. In this step we need to be open to any kind of architectural option or approach.

Step 2 Business and IT redesign

Based on the new strategies, business and IT redesign leads to (the next version of) both the business and information and technology architectures. Again the two go hand in hand.

6.7.2 Tactical planning and control

Tactical IT planning and control is the co-ordination of and reporting on decision making on IT. The IT performance management grid is the instrument for this level of planning and control. We have addressed the decision making on the project portfolio to a large extent in Chapter 5. It is this tactical planning and control activity that provides for management information to the senior management layers in the business.

Step 3 Business and IT re-engineering

A series/programme of re-engineering projects implements the new strategy and associated architectures in both business and IT. This includes the managing of all IT projects for whatever purpose, as long as they are related to the IT performance management grid that was defined in the masterplan.

6.7.3 Operational planning and control

Operational IT planning and control is much more a day-to-day process that provides the basic information for decision making on IT.

Step 4 Alignment and control

The IT scorecard is the instrument that aggregates all lower level detailed management reporting. The organizational level at which IT scorecards are defined and implemented depends on the IT governance structure that is part of the *configuration* of the IT strategy as described in the strategic masterplan. A series of service agreements and service level agreements is the basis for controlling the IT service provisioning.

6.7.4 Important roles in IT portfolio management

In the three planning and control levels the decisions are made and supported by a number of key players. We already addressed the key roles in IT service provisioning in Chapter 3 and we will also mention several roles in Chapter 8. Here we limit ourselves to the key roles regarding strategy, architecture and IT portfolio management. In Chapter 9 we will put all these roles in an organizational perspective.

6.7.4.1 Strategist

This role is focused on the highest level of IT demand from the options of IT enablement of the business strategy. The strategist continuously monitors and analyses the business and IT environment for business opportunities. A specific area of interest is the opportunity for IT to enable the business. The most important ingredient of IT performance that is influenced/managed by the strategist is IT competency. IT competency and competency-related decisions determine the success of the new strategies.

Specific tasks:

- Understanding and analysing the competitive situation.
- Understanding business practices and approaches.
- Understanding business politics, organization and culture.

- Performing scenario and opportunity modelling.
- Analysing and redesigning business processes on a high level.
- Overseeing IT governance, structures and cultures.
- Developing, implementing and managing IT competency policies.

6.7.4.2 Strategic architect

This role is focused on the translation of strategy into architecture. The strategic architect continuously monitors technology and technology development to decide on applicability in the business. The strategic architect is defining architectural boundaries and setting technology-related standards and monitors the usage of such standards.

Specific tasks:

- Performing continuous technology watch.
- Understanding and implementing emerging technologies.
- Designing architectures and architecture isolation and linking.
- Setting interface policies and standards.
- Designing standards for all architecture layers.
- Understanding existing systems and technologies.
- Monitoring compliance with technical and architectural policies and standards.

6.7.4.3 IT portfolio manager

This role is focused on the realization of the strategy and architecture. The IT portfolio manager continuously monitors the matching of demand and supply. The available budget and the allocation of budget to IT service provisioning and the project portfolio is the key responsibility of the portfolio manager. He is the owner of the IT paragraphs in the strategic masterplan.

Specific tasks:

- Planning, prioritizing and reporting on business and IT change.
- Supporting the business case and the case for priority activities.
- Analysing performance and taking measures to improve.
- Managing change in business and IT.
- Managing specific re-engineering programmes.

6.8 Summary

In this chapter we addressed the complexity of managing an IT portfolio aligned with the ever changing business portfolio. The strategy and strategic alignment issues of business and IT were only briefly touched on by giving an overview of the major lines of thinking on strategy.

Strategy implementation starts with architecture (re-)design and implementation. A high level framework for strategic architecture planning and development has been introduced. This framework is used to help manage the content of an IT portfolio.

After that, a closer look was taken at three specific architectural approaches that were successfully used to improve alignment between business and IT. After that we returned to the IT performance management grid.

The content, management objectives, strategy impact, architecture impact and service provisioning impact on every row and column of the performance management grid have been discussed. By doing this we created a high level introduction to the use of the IT performance grid in managing both content and performance of IT.

This chapter ended addressing the IT performance management processes and the key roles that are involved in IT portfolio management.

7 The market place for IT services

7.1 Introduction

So far in this book we have covered both the cost and the value of IT, and both the demand for IT capabilities and the supply of IT services. Now it is time to take a closer look at the way demand and supply come together in a market place.

What does the market place look like, how many market places are available? What does it take for a customer to be a good 'IT services consumer'?

What are the economic principles for an IT service provider to be able to stay in business and sell good IT services for reasonable prices. Can we compare the internal tariffs with external market prices? What are reasonable market prices anyway?

It is good to note at this stage that although two of the authors of this book work for an IT services provider, the contents of this chapter reflect personal opinions only.

7.2 Classification of market places

The first distinction must be between the internal and external market place. In the internal market place a limited number of service providers exist. Probably there is a central IT department; additionally there can be IT departments in business units providing IT services in the offering and mission critical areas of the IT portfolio. Usually, the internal service providers do not compete with each other, at least not openly.

The external market place often consists of multiple IT service providers who compete with each other. Business units may or may not have free choice between internal and external IT service provisioning. If there is no free choice and the IT services have to be delivered by the internal IT department, this is called forced supply.

The most common type of external market place for IT services is the free market. This market is characterized by its multi-vendor and multi-client nature. Market prices will be based on the balance between demand and supply. Where skills are rare, prices will go up; if there is overcapacity on the supply side, prices will drop. The economy, alternately declining and booming, will constantly change the market rules, forcing the vendors to adjust prices and adapt to new circumstances.

We have seen that the IT services market place is highly dependent on the economic situation, under high pressure in the booming days of the Internet hype and seriously in trouble after the decline of the telecommunication industry in the new millennium.

Another market place type which is contrary to the free market is the monopoly. In this market, there is only one vendor and multiple clients. The monopolist has a market share that will be above 90 per cent and thus is able to raise its prices at its will, because the clients do not have any alternatives.

From the client perspective, this is not to be preferred. However, some IT services can be very specific and highly specialized, which will lead to very few vendors in that market niche. An example might be an application for the radar traffic control of harbours and airports. Additionally, new innovative services will be very expensive at the start of the product lifecycle, where no competitors are able yet to copy the new concept. In some cases, for example when related to technological innovations, these new services may even be patented for some time, blocking competitors to enter the market.

In most countries, however, the majority of IT services are sold and bought in a free market model, creating the opportunity for companies to compare and select the external service providers with whom business shall be done.

7.3 The internal market place of IT services

In Chapter 3, we covered the subject of IT services in depth. We saw that IT services need to be defined, and service levels used to differentiate between quality and price. The total of IT services will be described by the IT department in a service catalogue, which is the basis for the internal market place of IT services, where service delivery managers of the IT department meet with the business unit representatives (information manager and service manager), in order to agree on the delivery of IT services to the business unit in the next period.

The outcome of these discussions is a service level agreement (SLA). An SLA defines the responsibilities of both the business unit and the IT department and describes the quality of service within agreed limits. The advantage of the SLA model is that the relationship between business and IT becomes formalized.

Many organizations have implemented a system of forced supply: this means that (a subset of) IT services can only be delivered by the internal service provider (ISP): for these services, competition from external service providers (ESP) is not allowed.

The advantage of treating an ISP as if it were an ESP is limited:

- It does help in implementing customer focus in the ISP.
- It does help in a cost management focus in the ISP.
- It does help in educating the service requestor and growing in maturity of demand.
- It does not help in speeding up the delivery process, all of sudden there will be many misunderstandings and disputes about what was requested vs what was delivered, vs what was charged, which almost by definition is interpreted as 'imma-ture IT supply'. It asks for additional management attention to resolve these issues.
- It does help in learning to deal with mature vendor/supplier relations on the IT demand side as a prelude to sourcing.
- As a pitfall it can introduce a charging circus with lots of people involved and little value add when charging is based on 'market conformity' + 'transparent pricing structures'. The two do not go together. Transparent pricing means: 'show me your pricing per component so I can select which components I think are too expensive'. Market conformity meaning: 'the end-to-end service is charged at a price/ performance level that can compete with the external market'.

7.4 IT services in the context of the IT value chain

In order to classify the large number of IT services, we will use the IT value chain that was introduced in Chapter 3.

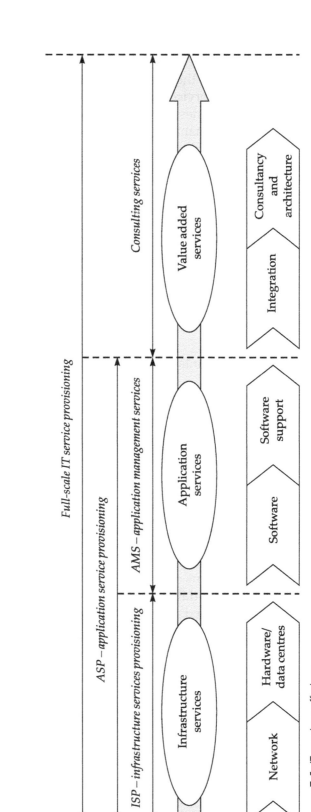

Figure 7.1 IT services offerings

In the day-to-day practice a wide range of IT services provisioning has developed. Nearly every service provider uses his own terminology, service structures, scope, service level elements, etc. The most common terminology used to group the IT services offerings is indicated in Figure 7.1.

Full-scale IT service provisioning relates to integral service provisioning by a separate organization, usually an independent player in the value chain. The process of implementing full-scale IT service provisioning is called outsourcing. In Chapter 8 we will discuss sourcing strategy and outsourcing in more detail.

ISP – infrastructure service provisioning relates to the basic IT services: providing availability of IT infrastructures and their capabilities. Typical services are: hosting servers, managing back-up/disaster recovery, managing networks, managing servers, large-scale print services, etc. By nature this type of IT service is 'non-business sensitive' which helps implementing economies of scale to a large extend, leading to competitive price/performance ratios.

AMS – application management services relates to providing development and maintenance of (business) applications. Typical services are: legacy maintenance for, e.g., Cobol, PL/1, etc., SAP competence centres, C++ competence centres, etc. The applications involved can be both generic and business specific/business sensitive.

ASP – application service provisioning relates to providing application functionality 'end to end'. Usually this is based on the sharing of application functionality on a 'per user' basis.

Typical services are: SAP finance capabilities, pay-check calculation, billing services, printing and delivery, e-business services, etc.

Consulting services is a very broad range of services delivering value added to the business by adding value to the other activities in the IT value chain. The number of IT professionals who refer to themselves as consultants is very large, and the activities they perform can be very different. To structure this, we need to distinguish the work that is being performed by consultants into two main dimensions (Figure 7.2):

- The clarity of the problem that is subject for consulting.
- The clarity of the (IT) solution that is subject for consulting.

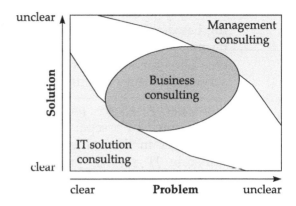

Figure 7.2
Consulting offerings

When neither the problem nor the solution is not very clear, we are in the field of business strategic management consulting. The types of questions that are challenged here are:

● What will our company look like in five years?
● Which markets do we need to address? Which products?
● Should we invest in new emerging technologies?
● Etc.

When the problem as well as the IT solution are clear, the type of consulting is called IT solution consulting. These consultants, for example, perform the implementation of ERP or CRM software packages, or offer expertise on performance management for a specific hardware platform.

The category in between often is called 'business consulting', where, for example, questions around the optimal use of IT for a given business strategy are answered. We regard this book as a guide for business consultants and their clients.

Beyond the scope of this book are services that address not only the IT value chain, but have an impact on the business processes themselves. The term business process outsourcing is more and more used for this type of service. A lot of supporting processes are provided by specialized companies for a long time, for example catering, security and distribution. But administrative processes can also be outsourced, such as salary administration and invoicing.

Another evolving type of service is called business transformation outsourcing or BTO. This type of service addresses the organizational change management issues that accompany a large organizational transformation. BTO is beyond the scope of this book as well.

7.5 The maturity of IT service provisioning

7.5.1 The lifecycle concept

In business economics, the concept of a product lifecycle has been the subject of research since the 1960s (Kotler, 1980). The analogy with human life results in a five-phase approach of the 'life' of a product (Figure 7.3). The phases of this lifecycle are:

- Introduction: a new product enters the market place.
- Growth: the new product is a success.
- Maturity: a solid position in the market with a stable market share.
- Saturation: erosion of sales and/or market share.
- Decline: sales and profit are dropping quickly; the end of the product's life.

Companies all over the world develop product management practices in order to replace legacy products in due time for new products. An important element in the research and development of new products is technology. More often than not, the introduction of a new product includes the introduction of a new technology. See, for example, the music and entertainment industry: compact disc replaces record, DVD replaces video, etc. This is why the lifecycle concept can be applied to a technology as well.

The technology lifecycle has a number of phases:

- Bleeding edge: the technology is brand new, only experimental users.

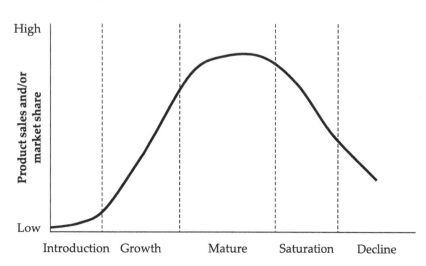

Figure 7.3
Product lifecycle

- Leading edge: the technology is well received by trendsetters, the 'early adopters'.
- Mature: the technology is middle of the road, well accepted.
- Legacy: the technology has become old-fashioned, because a new kind of technology enters the maturity stage.

This technology lifecycle differs considerably from the perceived technology lifecycle. The bleeding edge and leading edge phase of the technology lifecycle can include technology hype. This hype is a result of self-enforced media attention, overestimation and uninformed optimism in the market. Usually, the hype is over very soon, leaving a lot of disappointed people and a relatively small number of success stories. It is only after the hype that a technology will start to mature. The large number of disappointing trial and errors during the hype has led to a steep learning curve, which is fastening the technology lifecycle more and more. The broad adoption of new technologies is faster nowadays than 20 or 30 years ago. For example, compare the 50 years that were needed to spread TV around the world (TV was invented in the 1920s) with ten years of worldwide mobile phone adoption.

7.5.2 Combining the technology and service lifecycle

Beneath the technology lifecycle, a service lifecycle can be defined (Figure 7.4). When a new technology emerges as bleeding edge, the development for accompanying services will start, often on an ad hoc basis. Most pioneers in this first stage

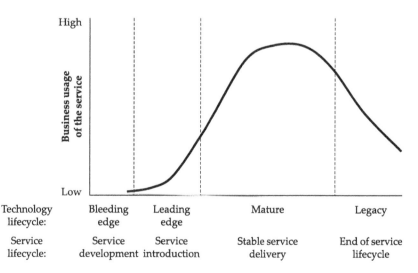

Figure 7.4

Technology and service lifecycle

Technology lifecycle:	Bleeding edge	Leading edge	Mature	Legacy
Service lifecycle:	Service development	Service introduction	Stable service delivery	End of service lifecycle

will deliver a self-supporting service. For example, consider the car repair service at the beginning of the twentieth century. Car drivers had to fix their punctures and other minor discomforts themselves. When the new technology spreads, a market place for car repair services emerges.

Technology has a lifecycle from bleeding edge to legacy, and IT services have this lifecycle as well. The IT industry is characterized by a number of technological revolutions, unprecedented in any industry. There are two laws that describe the explosive rate of change in the IT industry:

● Moore's law: predicts that the processing power of microchips will double every 18 months. This law can be used to estimate when new technology based on microchips reaches an acceptable customer quality level.
● Metcalf's law: states that while the cost of a network expands linearly, the value of a network increases exponentially. This law can be used to estimate when the critical volume can be reached of the adoption of network-based technologies.

We have become used to PC hardware that runs through the lifecycle stages from bleeding edge to legacy in no more than four years. Consequently, the IT profession has suffered from an enduring technology push over the last decades, and it is expected to continue. Therefore, an ISP must be an adaptive department, always expecting the next wave of technology. In order to do this, the IT service provider needs a service lifecycle in parallel with the technology lifecycle.

The IT services market is dependent on the IT technology waves. The more mature an IT service becomes, the more likely is the birth of a competitive market place for that particular IT service.

7.5.3 The growth path of IT services

In Chapter 3 we introduced the hourglass model of IT services. Another effect of the maturity of an IT service is the evolution from specific business capabilities to assets and products. Grains of sand representing business knowledge fall down through the hourglass to become a commodity. An example in Figure 7.5 will illustrate this.

In the 1970s and 1980s most companies had a tailor-made financial information system, usually built in COBOL with a

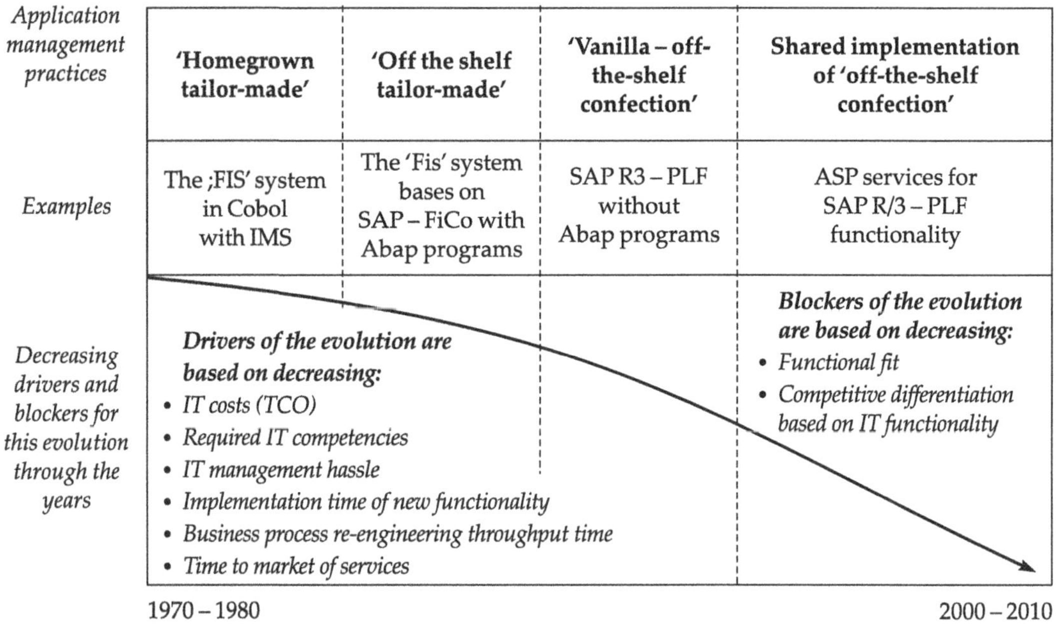

Application management practices	'Homegrown tailor-made'	'Off the shelf tailor-made'	'Vanilla – off-the-shelf confection'	Shared implementation of 'off-the-shelf confection'
Examples	The ;FIS' system in Cobol with IMS	The 'Fis' system bases on SAP – FiCo with Abap programs	SAP R3 – PLF without Abap programs	ASP services for SAP R/3 – PLF functionality
Decreasing drivers and blockers for this evolution through the years	*Drivers of the evolution are based on decreasing:* • *IT costs (TCO)* • *Required IT competencies* • *IT management hassle* • *Implementation time of new functionality* • *Business process re-engineering throughput time* • *Time to market of services*			*Blockers of the evolution are based on decreasing:* • *Functional fit* • *Competitive differentiation based on IT functionality*

1970 – 1980   2000 – 2010

Figure 7.5 Evolution of IT services

database management system such as IMS or IDMS. These systems had a good functional fit for the financial department, but there were some disadvantages:

- The full lifecycle costs of these applications were relatively high, because functional changes needed to be programmed manually.
- The IT skills that were required were scarce and expensive; a lot of organizations needed to hire expensive external programmers and database managers.
- The changes of these applications needed a lot of extra IT management processes, such as configuration management, project management, testing and change management.
- The implementation time of new functionality was high; for instance, the introduction of a new product type caused an additional product code to be included hard-coded and manually in a dozen old COBOL programs.

These disadvantages of tailor-made software led to the rise of application packages like SAP. However, the first wave of package implementations still had a lot of tailor-made programs in order to create a maximal functional fit for the organization. When these implementations did not succeed in the expected cost reduction, a new wave of implementations arose; this time, the application packages were no longer changed in order to fit with the organization, but the processes and the organization were changed in order to work with the application packages. This time, the tailor-made part of the implementation was minimal, reducing both implementation time and full lifecycle cost.

The IT service 'software application for financial administration' had become a stable service. The next step for this IT service is the development of application service providers that deliver financial management functionality as a component-based service.

This IT service evolution was accommodated by a number of key drivers:

- The need for decreasing cost levels.
- The decreasing availability of competencies for the legacy technology used.
- The need for decreasing management hassle.
- The need for decreasing intervals in implementation of new functionality.
- The need for decreasing business process re-engineering lead times.
- The need for shorter time to market intervals of new services.

The result/price to pay for the business are potential blockers:

- Decreasing functional fit.
- Decreasing competitive differentiation based on IT functionality.

This kind of evolution of an application management service can be observed for different kinds of functionalities in the Netherlands; the salary slip was among the first administrative process functionalities that became external software packages. In this case even the next step, business process outsourcing, has been widely accepted.

Of course, this kind of service will make the differences between companies for these processes disappear. Therefore, only the processes that support the primary business processes will be suited for this kind of outsourcing. When the financial department is a core competency for an organization (for example, in a leasing company), the chances are low that an off-the-shelf package will suffice for the functional requirements.

7.6 Pricing and charging of IT services

The matching of demand and supply in a market is based on price. The subject of pricing is a large field of economic theory, where pricing mechanisms of different markets (free market, monopoly, oligopoly, etc.) have been studied. We will only scratch the surface of these theories and discuss some practices around internal market pricing (charging) and pricing for an external market.

7.6.1 Pricing with regard to the market

In a free market, prices will be established by the balance of demand and supply for a product. The demand for a product can be described as a function between price and volume. In figure 7.6 this is represented by demand 1: when prices are low, the demand volume will be high and vice versa.

The supply of the product (supply 1 in Figure 7.6) will be high if prices are high and low when prices are low. At the cross-section of the lines, demand and supply are balanced, resulting in market price 1 for a given market volume. When demand for a product diminishes, the customers will buy less when the prices remain the same (demand 2). Because vendors want to keep their market share, prices will drop (market price 2); the market volume will drop as well.

When vendors run out of stock and supply becomes low, there will be less supply at the same price (supply 2) and prices will rise because customers are willing to pay a higher price for

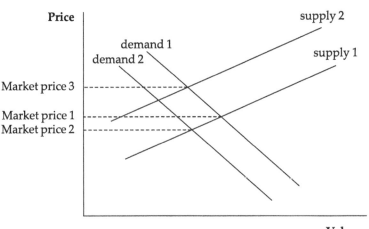

Figure 7.6
Economic model of demand, supply and price

scarce goods (market price 3). Again, the market volume will drop.

In a monopolist market, there is one supplier who has total control over the supply side of the market. This enables the monopolist to limit its supply and get higher prices for its goods and services. This is the main reason why free market and free competition have become the preferred economic market place model for consumers and governments around the world.

In a lot of companies, however, the supply of IT services is in the hands of one supplier, the internal IT services department. In this case, the question of market prices becomes relevant. How do the prices of the ISP compare with the external market? Would the ISP be able to compete in a free market? For these discussions, it is important to introduce a third element into the market place that we did not include in the simple free market model above: the quality of the delivered services or goods may differ between suppliers. In Chapter 3 we saw that the quality of IT services can be expressed in terms of service levels. However, to compare services of the ISP with ESP's, one has to be able to compare the quality of delivered service as well. When we expect the IT department to deliver at market standard, we not only have to look at the prices, but at the performance in terms of quality of service as well.

Consider Figure 7.7, where price and performance are visualized. Market standard is a range of price/performance ratios. Performance can be relative low, but if the price is low as well, the service can be a market standard.

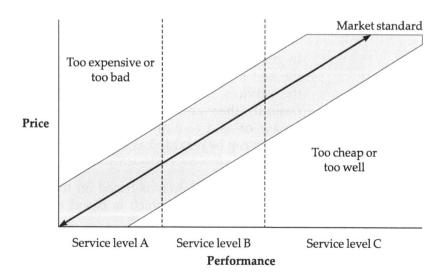

Figure 7.7
Market standard

We can compare the IT services market with the automobile market: there are market-standard, small, cheap cars and there are market-standard, large, expensive cars. The expensive cars have more features, such as air conditioning, on board computer and navigation systems. In IT services these features can be compared with service levels: for example, availability. In the example of the figure:

- Service level A   availability 5×8 hours
- Service level B   availability 6×10 hours
- Service level C   availability 7×24 hours

It is only natural that service level C will be more expensive, but all service levels can be at market-standard prices. A modular services catalogue will help the business units to understand the components of a given IT service. If each component is priced separately, the tariff for the service as a whole will be transparent.

From this simple example, it becomes clear that the prices of an internal IT department cannot be compared with market-standard prices, without a proper comparison of the service levels involved.

7.6.2 Pricing with regard to the IT service characteristics

In Chapter 3 we showed an example of the classification of services. Now we take a closer look at these services and the way they are delivered. The service characteristics provide a basis for the way the service usage is tracked and charged. This is illustrated in Figure 7.8.

In general, the contract in which a supplier of IT services (both ISP and ESP) and a client agree to do business will depend on the services that will be provided and their characteristics. Basically, there are two ways to deliver services: by means of a project or as a continuous process. In Chapter 3 we saw that projects can be regarded as the introduction of new (versions of) services.

The pricing of projects is based on the number of hours spent and the hour tariff, which is based on skill level and market conditions.

For projects and professional services (man hours) the contracts may be classified along three dimensions.

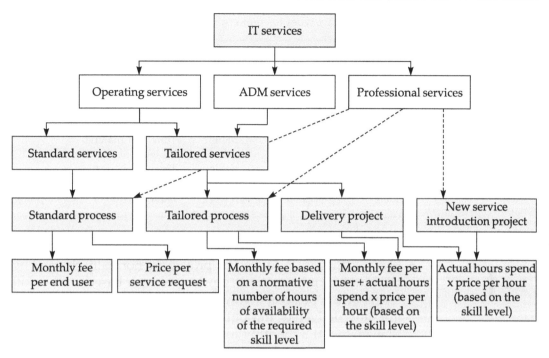

Figure 7.8 Charging of IT services

1 The deliverables of the contract can be fixed or variable; when the deliverables are fixed there is accountability of results, when the deliverables are variable there is accountability for effort only.
2 The agreed time span to deliver the services can be fixed or variable.
3 The money that will be paid by the client can be fixed or variable.

These dimensions lead to eight different contract types. Real life contracts often will blend multiple types, for example by using caps and floors for variable components. The eight contract types are shown in Table 7.1.

The contract structures for managed services will be explained in Chapter 8.

The two general ways to deliver services by means of a project or a continuous process require different ways of charging:

● Services delivered as an internal standard process may be charged on a monthly fee per user, or, if the service is triggered by the end user, there may be a price per service request. It even may be a combination of both.

Table 7.1 Contract types for projects.

Deliverables	Date	Price	Contract
Fixed	Fixed	Fixed	Fixed price, fixed date
Fixed	Fixed	Variable	Fixed date
Fixed	Variable	Fixed	Fixed price
Fixed	Variable	Variable	Time and material
Variable	Fixed	Fixed	Budget box, time box
Variable	Fixed	Variable	Time box
Variable	Variable	Fixed	Budget box
Variable	Variable	Variable	Blank cheque or bodyshopping

- Services that are delivered by project are normally charged by the number of hours times a price per hour based on the skill levels of the persons involved. For professional services that are not delivered through projects (for example, interim management) a monthly fee may be charged.

The charging of the services will require a detailed administration. For example, the administration of hours spent is an important application, because most of the services will be charged by the number of hours spent.

For software, the charging based on the number of users will be done by licences. As a client organization, it is important to register the licences of the used software. For expensive software, the licences should be linked to individual users. Some software packages enable the usage of concurrent users. In this way, the number of licences bought can be much smaller than the actual number of users. A registration of user licences can also enable the reuse of software licences that were used by people who leave the organization. If the number of users for the software is high, a corporate licence might be cost effective; most software vendors use some kind of high volume discount model.

Another important example of an administration that is very useful in the charging of IT services is the configuration management database (CMDB). In this database all data regarding IT resources and services and their users is kept. For instance, for each desktop the meta-data with respect to the desktop, accessories, the user, the installed software (with configuration levels) is kept.

In many organizations the data in the CMDB is not accurate; the reason for this is the fact that it is not always clear who is responsible for the content management of the CMDB: the demand side or the supply side of the IT services. The point is, both parties need to deliver input to this CMDB, it is a shared responsibility. But a shared responsibility can be a farce if no one is accountable for the quality of the data in the CMDB. Therefore, both at the demand and at the supply side, a person accountable must be appointed.

7.6.3 Pricing with regard to the IT service lifecycle

The pricing level of services related to the service lifecycle is illustrated in Figure 7.9.

The market characteristics in these phases will be as follows:

- Service development: low volumes, high margins.
- Service introduction: low volumes, high margins.
- Stable service delivery: high volumes, low margins.
- End of service lifecycle: low volumes, high margins.

The skill and competency characteristics in these phases will be as follows:

- Service development: no skills available.
- Service introduction: skilled people are rare and expensive, high demand for education.

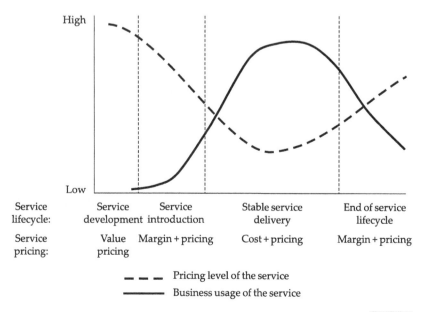

Figure 7.9
Pricing of IT services

- Stable service delivery: many skilled people available, prices will drop.
- End of service lifecycle: skills become rare and expensive again.

What lessons can we learn from the analysis of these lifecycles?

First, it should be noted that the development of IT services is lagging behind the technology. There will be no external service offerings from ESPs. Using bleeding edge technology can only be useful for technological companies that see an opportunity in the emerging technology to gain a competitive advantage in their markets. This type of experimenting will be done typically by the research and development department, the IT department will be supporting at best.

The ESP can support the development by providing professional services (man hours). If an ESP shares the risk of developing the usage of new technologies, the pricing can be based on a risk reward basis (value pricing). Because there will not be any services available, the application of bleeding edge technology can not be outsourced by the way of a formalized service contract. The only way to do this is to use venture capital to buy small, starting, promising companies and let them experiment.

Second, IT service providers need to create their business plans based on the services lifecycle. At the start of a new service, skills will be scarce and margins will be high. It is important to deliver new services fast. On the other hand, at the end of the maturity stage for a technology there will be a growing demand for outsourcing of a specific service. Organizations want to move on using new technology and often a transformation plan has been made to sunset the legacy services (both infrastructure and applications). We call this the 'window of opportunity' for out-tasking services.

7.7 IT vendor management

7.7.1 The importance of a sourcing strategy

Organizations need to think about which IT services will be delivered by internal IT staff and which IT services will be bought from a third party. The answer to this question is often referred to as the sourcing strategy of an organization. We will briefly introduce this topic here and elaborate on it in the next chapter.

If an organization does not have a clear sourcing strategy, chances are high that over time a myriad of third party IT vendors will have a relationship with the organization, but what kind of relationship is not always crystal clear. The sourcing strategy holds guidelines:

1 For which kind of services the external market is used.
2 At which kind of vendors these services will be bought.

Two different aspects play an important role in the sourcing strategy:

1 Are these IT services core competences for my organization?
2 Do we have the necessary skills available to deliver these IT services?

7.7.2 Preferred suppliers and how to select them

As said before, the lack of a clear sourcing strategy can cause an organization to work with a lot of different vendors. There are some disadvantages to this kind of approach:

- Many vendors will need to co-operate in order to deliver a high quality end-to-end service; the more vendors there are, the harder it gets.
- Each vendor will have its own relationship or account manager, who wants to talk with the decision makers of your organization; the more vendors, the more time it will take.
- The chance of lower rates because of the economies of scale for the vendor is small.
- Vendors are likely to blame each other in case of technological problems; a lot of discussions on responsibilities will be inevitable.
- Each vendor will have its own methodologies and will not want to share these with other vendors.

Some ways to get around these problems:

- Create a central staff function within your IT organization, named vendor management; these staff are responsible for the relationships with IT service providers.

- For each large project, appoint one vendor as a solution integrator, and hold this vendor responsible for the end-to-end quality of the project or service that is at stake.
- Select a limited number of preferred suppliers, and build a partnership with these vendors.

The selection of a limited number of preferred suppliers should be based on a number of criteria such as:

- Price.
- Quality of service.
- Proven track record within the organization.
- References outside the organization.
- Trust.
- Ability to deliver innovative solutions.
- Etc.

Be sure always to appoint a minimum of three preferred suppliers to prevent monopolistic behaviour from your ESPs.

7.8 Summary

In this chapter we covered the subject of the IT services market place, although this is not to be seen as a comprehensive and complete research guide of an industry. We have only scratched the surface to look at some points that are relevant in the field of IT performance management.

We looked at different types of market places and different types of contracts. We discussed internal and external market places. An internal market place may use the principle of forced supply. The advantage is that the alignment between business and IT can become very strong, but if the business units perceive the IT department as underperforming, forced supply can be a catalyst for escalation of conflicts.

We showed many ways in which an IT service can be charged, and explained the interaction between the technology lifecycle and the IT services life cycle. The pricing of IT services will for the most part depend on the phase of the service lifecycle.

Finally we looked at the way an organization should look at the IT services market place and its actors. The selection of IT services vendors and the management of the relationships with these external service providers become more and more important. Therefore, the introduction of strategic sourcing of IT services is at the heart of IT performance management. This is the subject of the next chapter.

Sourcing IT and managing a mixed IT portfolio

8.1 Introduction

Many IT services offerings are available in the external market place, and there are many more to come. Yet, the IT services industry is still young if not 'at the break of dawn'. Lots of new offerings are emerging from the IT industry to help you improve your business value.

How do we know 'when to jump on which bandwagon'? This is a question of IT strategy implementation; with a very widespread impact. 'Strategic sourcing' is the term that is usually used for these types of choices.

We define sourcing as: 'the activity of obtaining IT services, competencies or assets from an external service provider'. The word external is essential here. Internal service providers provide IT services but even though they can be in a separate organization we do not consider the internal IT service provisioning to be sourced.

Related to this are:

- 'Outsourcing': 'the activity of moving IT services (including the resources to provide these IT services) and/or competencies and/or assets from an internal service provider to an external service provider'.
- 'Out-tasking': 'the activity of moving IT services (excluding the resources to provide these IT services) from an internal service provider to an external service provider'. In other words out-tasking is also a sourcing activity.

This means that there is a world of difference between sourcing and outsourcing. Implementing a sourcing strategy usually includes an outsourcing activity, but managing sourcing is something completely different from managing outsourcing. Over the last 10 to 15 years a lot of companies have (out-)sourced IT or parts of it. Sometimes this was successful, sometimes it was not. A great deal has been published on this subject, we would like to take sourcing of IT services as a given and assume this is a proven good practice. The result of a number of years of sourcing, however, is a mixed bag of IT service provisioning contracts that needs to be managed.

In this chapter we will address the aspects of integrally managing an IT portfolio that consists of IT services that are (partially) delivered by a mix of internal/external service providers.

We will start with defining a sourcing strategy. Next we will focus on what is needed to stay in control of the overall value add of the IT service delivery. We will discuss the sourcing deal and the question of how to set up a sourcing deal. Then we will address the management roles needed to manage the resulting IT portfolio with a mixed bag of internal service providers (ISP) and external service providers (ESP) service delivery organizations.

8.2 Building an IT sourcing strategy

Primary questions that need to be answered when building a sourcing strategy are:

- Why sourcing? How do we decide on sourcing? When do we source IT? The answers to these questions highly influence the added value of the sourced IT services.
- What to source and what not to source? What is the appropriate level of sourcing?

8.2.1 The 'why' question in the IT sourcing strategy

The drivers for strategic sourcing come from two concurrent directions:

8.2.1.1. Outside-in: from competitive pressure to strategic sourcing

The business market place asks for excellence, but it is impossible to excel in everything. Businesses must make tough decisions regarding the core value and specialization that will drive the entire business strategy. These decisions will then affect the entire sourcing strategy in the organization including the IT sourcing strategy. Success requires that everything that is part of the core business must achieve excellence and become a true competitive weapon and differentiator. This requires very mature management standards, regulations and professions for managing complex sourcing arrangements.

8.2.1.2 Inside-out: from internal IT and outsourcing to strategic sourcing

When companies admit that their internal IT capabilities can no longer cope with their changing business needs, sourcing is considered. Changing technologies and competitive pressure are leading to increasing use of ESPs. At the same time, change management and process innovation start to go well beyond the company boundaries in terms of interoperability.

These two directions are pushing a more strategic use of internal and external sources of knowledge, work and IT services. Because of the complexity of the changes, the amount of sourcing options available and a lack of adequate management practices, many sourcing decisions are just the most obvious or simple and, therefore, not necessarily the right ones. However, sourcing is strategic, and every company needs to build its own approach and management practices for it. Companies must learn how to leverage sourcing, while creating the required abilities to manage it. Building a sourcing strategy and developing the required sourcing competencies are the steps to take in this direction.

8.2.2 Are we up to an IT sourcing strategy?

The next step is a process of conducting the sourcing strategy. This process starts with a pragmatic assessment of how strong the change pressure is and how ready the organization is to change. This assessment involves cultural, financial, contractual and statutory factors, and will vary widely between companies. If the organization requires a significant change, a strategic gap analysis should be prepared.

The four core questions of the strategic gap analysis are:

- Are we doing the right things?
- Are we doing those things well?

- Are we able to achieve the short- to medium-term business objectives?
- Are we able to react quickly enough to unexpected business changes?

As part of the first two questions, the most important internal elements that need to be analysed are:

- Current IT service provision (i.e. in terms of financials, efficiency, effectiveness, and market availability of equivalent or better IT services or resources) and business implications.
- Current sourcing management capability (i.e. projects, IT services and processes).
- Ability of the company to change (i.e. entrepreneurship, management, staff, culture and unions).
- Relationship between business and IT organizations.

All of this is an integral part of strategy and strategy implementation. Building a good sourcing strategy is directly linked to all the subjects mentioned in Chapter 6. In summary: we need to analyse the ability to adequately match the IT demand in terms of required IT capabilities with the IT supply in terms of provided IT services.

8.2.3 Required IT competencies are key to IT sourcing

When trying to match demand and supply the required IT capabilities are leading. Looking at the key ingredients of required IT CAP-abilities one can make the following observation regarding the ease at which they can be adapted to the required change:

1 The P of processes can be continually improved, with or without outside help.
2 The A of assets can be continually adjusted based on technology watch.
3 The C of competencies is derived from these technology choices and improved processes.

Competencies are crucial to the success of providing IT services. It is the pace at which IT competencies can be adjusted to the changing business that is crucial to the ability to match IT supply to IT demand. In practice the development of the required competencies for new technologies lags behind the pace at which they are needed.

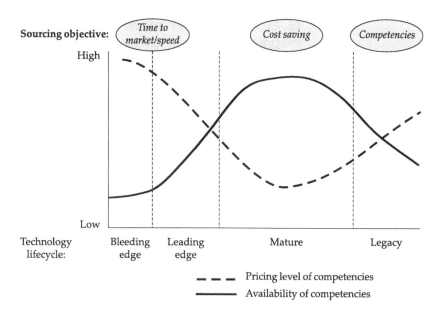

Figure 8.1
Technology, competencies and sourcing objectives

When new technologies become available, the required competencies are scarce and the price to pay for them is high. It takes years to develop new competencies at a certain level and with a certain volume. Once a technology has become mature, the availability of competencies has reached the level of market demand and the price has dropped to normal. At the end of the technology lifecycle, the technology is not interesting anymore to people and the level of the available competencies drops again, raising market prices (see Figure 8.1).

This results in three major sourcing objectives which are derived from the availability of competencies:

1 Time to market/speed of new IT service introduction is the major sourcing objective when competencies are scarce and prices are high because we are implementing bleeding edge or leading edge technology.

2 Cost saving is the major sourcing objective when ESPs can achieve more economies of scale, because the available competencies for mature technology are high, prices are normal/low.

3 Competencies are the major sourcing objective when we need to support legacy technology, because again economies of scale lead to a better carrier perspective of the people involved with the ESPs, which in turn leads to ESPs being able to offer a better deal for the IT services.

8.2.4 The 'what and what not' question regarding sourcing of IT

After all the good strategy work on the 'why' question that has been undertaken (usually with the help of many outside consultants) we come to the question: 'what to source and what not to source?'

8.2.4.1 Sourcing strategy directions

Taking the IT performance management grid as a starting point, there are two directions in which we can look for deciding what to source (Figure 8.2):

- 'Sourcing based on IT supply'.
- 'Sourcing based on IT demand'.

The two directions are strategically very different. So when building a sourcing strategy one should take a number of criteria into account when deciding the services direction, or the demand direction, or a mix of both.

In Chapter 5 we introduced the concept of dominant decision criteria in the IT performance management grid for decision making. We can apply the same model for finding the decision criteria on the sourcing direction. Every row and every column has one dominant criterion. This results in two dominant criteria per cell which need to be judged on their mutual influence.

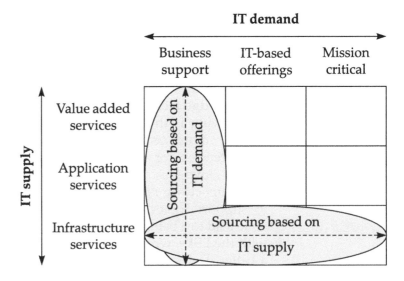

Figure 8.2
Sourcing directions in the IT performance management grid

8.2.4.2 Sourcing based on IT supply

Choices in the three rows are basically a matter of achievable economies of scale. The pluses to sourcing based on IT supply are:

- Efficiencies that can be reached are the highest, because the scales are the largest.
- Management of IT services provisioning can be centralized to support overall effectiveness and efficiency.
- Managing technology refresh is relatively easier than in the vertical direction.

The minuses are:

- High level of implemented standardization needed.
- Managing the introduction of new IT services involves a wide range of processes and is harder to achieve.

Value added services

This is the key area in which the IT core competencies of every organization reside, it is the area where business-specific expertise resides to be able to do this translation of IT demand into IT supply and where IT service provisioning is managed. From that perspective this area by definition is the last area to be considered for outsourcing. Sourcing is limited to hiring competencies.

Application services

Sourcing of the entire application services provisioning will only be beneficial when IT effectiveness can be improved by sourcing vs doing it oneself. The choices made in the application architecture regarding technologies and related competencies play an important role and influence the sourcing options. Application technology lifecycle influences the competencies resulting in the three major sourcing objectives mentioned in section 8.2.3.

Infrastructure services

This is the area where IT infrastructure standardization and economies of scale bear most fruit for the business. Optimization along this axis is very beneficial. For this reason this is the area where outsourcing practices have their roots.

213

8.2.4.3 Sourcing based on IT demand

Choices in the three columns are basically a matter of scope and level of decentralized decision making in the business. The pluses to sourcing based on IT demand are:

- Scope of the sourcing is easier to manage.
- Implementation of standardized approaches and solutions is easier because the scope is limited.
- Management of IT services provisioning can be more easily decentralized.

The minuses to this approach are:

- Optimal IT effectiveness on a company level for infrastructure services will never be reached.
- Managing the introduction of new technologies and improving overall effectiveness of IT will be suboptimal.

Business support

Sourcing the integral and complete IT service provisioning for business support can be an option when the architectural choices in the past were made on standardization by business unit or along the line of processes within a business unit. The compelling reason for sourcing these IT services is usually based on the 'non-core' nature of the IT solutions involved.

IT based offerings

Sourcing the IT service provisioning for these IT services is usually based on:

- Providing 'a quick start' in a new market/channel.
- Keeping the stable business support processes untouched.
- Unavailability of required IT capabilities and competencies.

Mission critical IT

Sourcing considerations are the following:

- Is the partner willing to share the risk?
- Can we easily do away with the results when it fails?
- Are we really into a new 'killer application/IT service' that provides competitive advantage?

8.2.4.4 The mix of the sourcing strategy directions

The management challenge is that the directions each have appealing pros. Choices are not easy and are influenced by expected change over time, planning horizons of the business and the business partners. Eventually we will always end up with an IT portfolio that contains a mix. A strategic direction will look roughly like Figure 8.3.

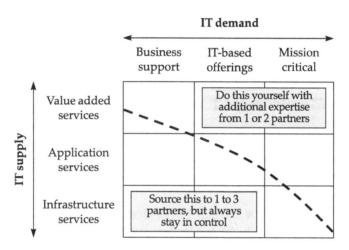

Figure 8.3
High level sourcing strategy in the IT performance management grid

8.2.5 The appropriate level of sourcing

In today's practice we can distinguish four levels of IT sourcing, with increasing complexity:

- Hiring capacity. The goal for this level of sourcing is to fill in a gap in our own capacity. In this case we are completely accountable for the work to be done and the quality level at which the IT service is delivered.
- Hiring know-how/expertise. The goal for this level of sourcing is to acquire know-how/expertise from an external source and learn from it to be able to do without within a reasonable timeframe. In this case we are completely account-able for the work to be done and the quality level at which the IT service is delivered.
- Out-tasking. The goal for this level of sourcing is to simplify management hassle with regard to IT and stay in control of the resources. The assets will stay within our own books, only the work to be done is externalized. In this case we are accountable for strategic and tactical control of the IT services

rendered. The operational management and the quality level at which the IT service is delivered is the responsibility of the external partner.

- Outsourcing. The goal for this level of sourcing is to ultimately simplify management hassle with regard to IT. All resources (assets and humans) are externalized. In this case we are only accountable for strategic control of the IT services rendered. The tactical and operational management and the quality level at which the IT service is delivered is the responsibility of the external partner.

You will never have just one of these levels. Deliberate choices of the level are part of continuously managing the IT portfolio.

8.3 Crafting IT sourcing deals

Now that we have addressed the strategic issues around sourcing, we want to look at the deals. In the most simplified situation there is a sourcing contract between the company and the ESP stating:

- Which IT services will be delivered, e.g. datacentre services.
- At what service level, e.g. 7 by 24 hours at 99.8 per cent availability.
- At what price, e.g. at xxx.xxx € per month.
- For what period of time, e.g. five years from the day that the contract was signed.

Unfortunately this is an oversimplification of reality. In most cases it is not that simple to craft a clear and measurable deal. First of all there is the issue that the end user always has the perception that his requirements are unique, so he wants a say in the contract negotiation. Then there usually is a centralized body called 'corporate IT' that reasons that we should use sourcing to enforce standardization, so they should be in the lead when crafting the contract.

Both arguments are justifiable but lead to opposed input to the deal. In order to address these and similar issues we need some key principles:

- Effectiveness of IT sourcing: align the IT sourcing responsibilities with the profit and loss responsibilities. When profit and loss responsibility is decentralized, e.g. in a business unit, they should get the appropriate level of input and control on the contract.

- Efficiency: leverage economies of scale and bargaining power (standards, joint IT services, common vendors, etc.). Leveraging economies of scale is based on the contract volume. The more standardization of IT services can be negotiated internally, the more efficiency results will be reached in the contract. Bargaining power comes from the volume of the required IT services as well as the brand image of the company. Centralization and standardization lead to efficiency effects in this respect.
- Critical competencies: enable the building of critical sourcing competencies within the company. The critical competencies are vendor and contract management at a centralized organizational level, service management at both centralized and decentralized organizational levels and service level management at a decentralized organizational level.
- Simplicity: keep the number of vendors low. There is a lot of space between 'one size fits all' and '38 strategic partnerships'. One vendor with a long-term contract is a vendor lock-in with very little management hassle at an uncontrollable expense rate. At the 38 strategic partnerships end the functional fit will be ideal and the control and management hassle will be unaffordable.
- Transparency: create the conditions for communication across the company. This starts with recognizing that both decentral and central forces make sense.

8.3.1 Structuring the contract

Implementing the principles for IT sourcing deals is supported by the use of a three-level contract structure (see Figure 8.4).

Frame agreement is a non-financially binding contract that contains procedure arrangements and overarching terms and conditions. Examples: the payment conditions and process, details on intellectual property rights, escalation process, the role of the configuration management database (CMDB), etc.

Service agreement is a non-financial binding contract that contains the IT services descriptions which can be agreed in the service level agreements (SLAs). It provides choices for SLAs based on a combination of business requirement and ESP offerings. The available choices are based on a finite set of IT services with the associated service level boundaries and price level boundaries. As such it is the 'IT services catalogue' for the SLAs that are underpinning. This is the middle layer in the contract structure. Here is where the level of standardization

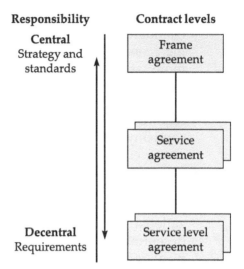

Figure 8.4
The structure of a
sourcing deal

and the level of differentiation in unique requirements come
together. The structuring and the level of detail of the service
agreement have a very high impact on the management effort
involved. The more options that are defined in the service
agreement the more service management and service level
management attention is needed.

An SLA is a financially binding contract between the ESP and an
organizational and legal entity that is the contract owner as
mentioned in the frame agreement. It contains the detailed
agreement on IT services, service levels, pricing, organizational
scope of the IT service delivery, duration, etc. All these terms
and conditions are a detailed level of the terms and conditions
mentioned in the service agreement and the frame agreement.

8.3.2 Implementing control levers

It is important to create the means to control the IT service
delivery from an IT demand perspective. When crafting the
frame agreement and the service agreement a limited number of
options are available to create such a lever for control. When
dealing with a frame agreement we are usually discussing a
major contract with a strategic partner that can provide multiple
types of IT services. The structure of service agreements per
frame agreement can vary. There can be separate service
agreements:

- Per IT service type, e.g. 'professional services' will be in a
  different service agreement than 'hosting services'.

- Per type of IT demand, e.g. business support services separated from business unit-specific IT-based offering services.
- Per organizational unit on the demand side.

The type of separation highly influences the level of control that we have on the IT demand side. All of the above-mentioned principles play their own role here and the balancing of these principles will result in the choices on what will be in which service agreement.

A general issue is asset ownership. It depends on the maturity of IT demand whether the sourcing of 'end-to-end' IT services without the transparency of IT service structures is an acceptable level of control. Architectural structures and effectiveness play a key role here. The issue of asset ownership is usually addressed when:

- Technology refresh still needs to take place.
- Optimization of the IT infrastructure can still become beneficial.

In these cases the service agreements need to contain target settings for the ESP that are controllable. One of the ways to do this is to keep the assets in your own books.

A very important lever for IT service delivery control is based on ownership of the configuration data. The configuration management database (CMDB) as is defined in the ITIL standards for IT service delivery processes (ITIL, 2002) is the database where all information on IT service structures, architecture structures, users, user authorities, etc. is being tracked. This database is the prime source for the charging of IT service delivery. The frame agreement should contain agreements on:

- Ownership of the configuration data on the demand side and the supply side.
- Level of accuracy of the CMDB and related penalties.
- Access to the content of the CMDB by the service requestor.
- The use of the CMDB regarding the billing of IT services by the ESP.

8.4 Managing the integral IT services portfolio

All of the above by definition results in a mixed bag of contracts that need to be managed. The performance management challenge is to manage these contracts in line with the internal service provisioning. This is the most complex management challenge. The business demands flexibility. This issue is addressed with the help of architectural and IT service structural concepts, but how flexible do we need to be and how flexible can we be?

8.4.1 The impact of required business flexibility

In Chapter 6 we already addressed the importance of business and IT alignment from a content point of view. The business strategy of an organization constantly changes, acting on new opportunities and reacting to threats from the organization's environment. The resulting business flexibility requires a high flexibility of the IT services portfolio as well. With regard to making decisions on the IT services portfolio there are some specific areas that need to be taken into account:

8.4.1.1 Volume growth at the existing markets and across the country borders

- Which countries?
- Is there local legislation that influences choices on IT architectures?
- Who are potential merger and acquisition candidates?
- What is the status of their IT services portfolio?
- What is their strategy and how do they deal with architectural issues?
- What are their internal IT competencies and what is their policy with regard to competency development?
- Who are their current sourcing partners?
- Which legacy technology do they apply?

8.4.1.2 Increasing profitability by means of new product/market combinations

- What is the impact of the IT services/IT service components in the product?
- How vulnerable/mature is the technology used?
- What are the available competencies internally?
- What is the business risk involved in applying the IT technology?
- Does the IT component fit into the existing IT infrastructures?

This is by no means a complete list of questions to be asked. We only want to give you a flavour of the kind of questions that need to be answered continuously in the process of strategic planning and control of IT. They are at the basis of decisions regarding the IT architecture and the IT services portfolio.

8.4.2 The challenge of managing 'end-to-end' services

Managing the mix of IT services across several providers asks for an architectural basis on which IT services are built and maintained. We can identify a strong relationship between:

● Contract length.
● Architectural isolation of the IT service components.
● Structural design of IT services, IT service components and service level requirements.

From an end user perspective the IT service must be delivered 'end to end', no matter who the service provider of which component is. This requires a well-devised process for managing services.

Bundling of IT services in a contract is a prerequisite for being able to manage change.

In the example in Figure 8.5 we have multiple bundles of supply-driven sourced activities.

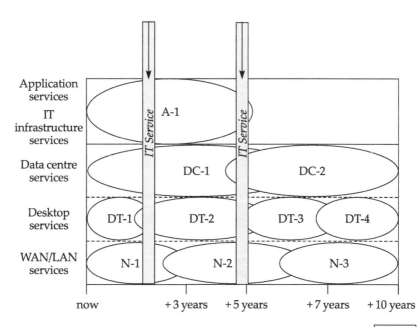

Figure 8.5
The complexity of managing multiple ESP contracts

In the situation presented in Figure 8.5, at the starting point a particular IT service is built from the following component bundles:

N-1: WAN/LAN services + DT-1 or DT-2: desktop services depending on the status of roll-out of DT-2 + DC-1: datacentre services + A-1: application services

Three years later that same IT service can be built from the following components:

N-2: WAN/LAN services + DT-2 or DT-3: desktop services depending on the status of roll-out of DT-3 + DC-1 or DC-2: datacentre services depending on the status of the DC consolidation/ optimization status + A-1 or A2: application services depending on the status of the new functionality roll-out of that application

As you can imagine this requires fundamental architectural and IT service component planning and implementation. It is the role of the 'service architect' to manage all dependencies between IT service components, architecture components and the way they are reflected in bundles in specific service agreements.

Conclusion: don't go for 38 strategic partnerships because that seems to be the cheapest solution!

8.4.3 The key roles and responsibilities in IT sourcing management

We will now summarize the roles and responsibilities of the key players regarding sourcing.

8.4.3.1 Vendor manager

This role is focused on analysing potential partners and building and maintaining the relationship with (strategic) partners that provide IT services and manage and realize business/IT re-engineering projects. It is the highest authority for contracting IT and for escalation of problems and as such it is the highest authority for monitoring and managing all ESPs.

Specific tasks:

- Develop, communicate and control sourcing strategy and vendor strategy.
- Monitor IT supply market.
- Perform vendor portfolio analysis.

- Manage high level vendor relations.
- Measure, evaluate and communicate long-term and cross-contract vendor performance.
- Develop/refine procurement process.
- Develop supporting tools (templates, methodologies, systems).

8.4.3.2 Contract manager

This role is focused on preparing, negotiating, closing and managing contracts with ESPs. The main focus is on the terms and conditions of the contracts and contract renewals as well as the execution of the procurement process.

Specific tasks:

- Define contract specifications.
- Negotiate and write contracts.

8.4.3.3 Services architect

This role is focused on understanding IT demand in terms of required capabilities and translating it into an 'end-to-end' IT service, consisting of service components that can be integrally delivered and managed by the ESP. Most of the results of the services architect's work are the core of the service agreement and service level agreement.

Specific tasks:

- Define business specifications.
- Co-ordinate cross-demand management unit needs.
- Decide on nature of required services (specific vs generic).
- Integrate business unit specific conditions in frame and service agreements.
- Track and communicate to decentral demand management units similar existing IT services.
- Communicate on existing frame and service agreements.
- Provide support upon request.

8.4.3.4 Service manager

This role is focused on the day-to-day matching of delivered services with the required capabilities. The service agreement and the service level agreement are the basis for managing the ESP. The service manager negotiates the match of IT demand

and IT supply with the service delivery manager. The service manager is responsible for the effectiveness of the services delivered. Note that the service manager is positioned here at the IT demand side. In some reference models (e.g. ITIL, 2002), this role is positioned on the IT supply side.

Specific tasks:

- Manage and monitor service delivery.
- Define service specifications.
- Support vendor selection.
- Renegotiate service agreements and service level agreements.

8.4.3.5 Service level manager

This role is focused on the day-to-day matching of delivered services with the required capabilities. The service level agreement is the basis for managing the ESP. The service level manager is the direct counterpart of the service delivery manager on the supply side. Note that the service level manager is positioned here at the IT demand side. In some reference models (e.g. ITIL, 2002), this role is positioned on the IT supply side.

Specific tasks:

- Order.
- Manage and monitor.
- Evaluate.

8.5 Some lessons learned in outsourcing of IT

A great deal has been published on 'outsourcing IT', so for the purpose of this book we limit ourselves to a number of lessons learned that are based on personal experiences and that are confirmed to be common.

8.5.1 The basics

8.5.1.1 Always source with a business objective in mind

Don't start to consider outsourcing before you have a defined sourcing strategy. Sourcing is never a goal, it is a means to achieve a higher order goal, e.g.:

- Speed: time to market of new IT services to support business processes, time to market of business offerings with a substantial IT component.
- Revenue/cost: 'best in class' cost levels through the implementation of standardization, affordability now and in the future, added value to the business, added value to the end customer of the business.
- Competency: adaptability/ability to learn of the IT community.
- Innovation: introduction of new technologies.

8.5.1.2 In many cases the original objectives for outsourcing were not achieved

Common causes:

- Unclear agreements at the start.
- Expectations were not made explicit enough.
- Changing demand for IT services that wasn't taken into account upfront.
- Insufficient experience on the demand side with a business-like approach to IT service delivery.
- Lack of 'control' of the execution in the ESP.

8.5.1.3 Never in splendid isolation

You never engage in outsourcing without adequate involvement of all stakeholders:

- Make sure executives are engaged in the process and stay engaged throughout.
- Build executive review and approval to proceed into the project plan to keep momentum and focus among the selection team.
- The responsible business management (board of directors, CEO, CFO, business management, IT management).
- The responsible competency management (HR, workers council).
- The advisory boards (on strategy, legal affairs, finance, risk management).

8.5.2 Some rules of thumb

Some hints and tips to manage the risk of a vendor lock-in in sourcing:

- Clean up the mess before you outsource, outsourcing is not a purchasing activity but a sales activity, so present your offering nice and shining when you put it in the showroom.
- Stay in control of continuous optimization of the assets.
- Stay in control of the technology refresh.
- Decide on the length of an outsourcing contract depending on the business environment and reasonably expectable change in the business environment (3–5 year contracts vs 10 year contracts).
- The longer the contract the more 'risk/reward' options are needed.
- All good sourcing contracts need a 'shared risk component'.
- Organize and staff 'vendor management' with knowledge of IT service structures to prevent redundancy in contract negotiation across the business.
- Organize and staff 'end-to-end service management' which has control on the IT service delivery from the demand perspective with the required know-how of IT service structures; make sure that the measurement system is in place before you outsource.
- Always decide on 'chunks'/'bundles' of IT services/IT service components based on an architectural direction, where business/IT alignment and the required ability to change is a prerequisite.
- Hire outside help to assist with the evaluation and selection process, and listen to the advice.
- Define the IT services and evaluation criteria before the RFP is sent out.
- Make sure that each phase of the evaluation and selection process is reviewed against the sourcing strategy to ensure that the strategic objectives for sourcing don't get lost in the detail.
- If you want to consider alternatives, make sure the RFP is developed to allow and encourage ESPs to propose the scope of IT services that make sense for them.
- Require ESPs to agree to work together via a memorandum of understanding that defines accountability for service levels, escalation procedures and management commitment to work together.
- Sourcing is not a one time event, it is continuously on the IT management agenda.

8.6 Summary

In this chapter we addressed the performance management issues regarding external service provisioning. We started with the why question and the related definition of a sourcing strategy.

After that we addressed the crafting of a sourcing deal with a three-level contract consisting of frame agreement, service agreement and service level agreement. Then we returned to the difficulties encountered in managing multiple external service providers. We identified key roles regarding sourcing.

The chapter finished with lessons learned on sourcing.

9 Organizing the demand and supply of IT

9.1 Introduction

In Chapters 2 to 8 we addressed IT performance management mostly from an abstract level. Real life management is performed by people and happens where people are working together. Some of the abstractions we gave may be appealing, some may not. This always depends on the situation.

Before finishing this book with a 'back to business' section, two chapters (9 and 10) provide the necessary illustration of the performance management principles in this book. These illustrations will give the reader a sense of recognition, which will help to put the IT performance management principles into practice, starting tomorrow.

Chapter 9 shows a number of different ways the demand and supply of IT can be organized. Chapter 10 is an elaboration of the four IT value perception level cases that were introduced briefly in Chapter 1.

Organizing IT demand and IT supply and organizing IT performance management cannot be done with a recipe, because it is people business. In this chapter, four different demand/supply models with their advantages and disadvantages are described. In real life, there will be many varieties of the described models.

The models are based on an organization with a number of business units, with profit and loss responsibility for a set of product/market combinations. In all four models we assume that there is a 'corporate CIO' organization as well, which performs several company-wide tasks regarding IT.

The models are:

- Model A: Decentralized IT service provisioning in business units.
- Model B: Centralized IT service provisioning in corporate information services
- Model C: The IT service centre
- Model D: Business and IT fusion

It is important to note that the models presented in this chapter are examples of typical demand/supply interrelationships. These are not meant to be a complete, definitive list of all possible governance models. In real life, the demand/supply model will probably be a mixture of two or more of the presented models. This mixture may be the result of hectic discussions and political clashes between the IT function and the business units. The chief information officer, the CIO, has the responsibility to define and manage the demand/supply model of the organization. His staff may be thin or fat, depending on the level of centralization of the IT function.

Each demand/supply model description will show some characteristics and indicate where the performance management-related roles are positioned. First, we will summarize the key roles in IT performance management.

9.2 The key roles in IT performance management

The key roles need not always be management roles. The key players that influence IT performance and are involved in the matching of IT demand and IT supply can be grouped in three areas:

- Strategic roles.
- IT demand management roles.
- IT supply management roles.

9.2.1 Strategic roles

9.2.1.1 Strategist

This role is focused on the highest level of IT demand from the options of IT enablement of the business strategy. The strategist continuously monitors and analyses the business and its environment for business opportunities. The opportunities for

IT to enable the business are a specific area of interest. The most important ingredient of IT performance that is influenced/ managed by the strategist is IT competency. IT competency and competency-related decisions are key to the success of the new strategies.

9.2.1.2 Strategic architect

This role is focused on the translation of strategy into architecture. The strategic architect continuously monitors technology and technology development to decide on applicability in the business. The strategic architect is defining architectural boundaries and setting technology-related standards and monitors the usage of such standards.

9.2.1.3 IT portfolio manager

This role is focused on the realization of the strategy and architecture. The IT portfolio manager continuously monitors the matching of demand and supply. The available budget and the allocation of budget to IT service provisioning and the project portfolio is the key responsibility of the portfolio manager. He is the owner of the IT paragraphs in the strategic masterplan.

9.2.1.3 Vendor manager

This role is focused on analysing potential partners and building and maintaining the relationship with (strategic) partners that provide IT services and/or manage and realize business/IT re-engineering projects. It is the highest authority for contracting IT and for escalation of problems and as such it is the highest authority for monitoring and managing all external service providers.

9.2.2 IT demand management roles

9.2.2.1 Information manager

This role is focused on the matching of IT demand with IT supply for specific organizational areas, such as a business unit. All the IT performance management issues that relate to the demand side of the IT performance management grid are addressed by the information manager. This includes both the content of the IT portfolio and the performance of the IT portfolio.

9.2.2.2 Contract manager

This role is focused on preparing, negotiating, closing and managing contracts with external service providers. The main focus is on the terms and conditions of the contracts and contract renewals as well as the execution of the procurement process.

9.2.2.3 Services architect

This role is focused on understanding IT demand in terms of required capabilities and translating it into an end-to-end IT service, consisting of service components that can be integrally delivered and managed by the service provider. Most of the results of his work are the core of the service agreement and service level agreement.

9.2.2.3 Service (level) manager

This role is focused on the day-to-day matching of delivered services with the required capabilities. The service agreement and the service level agreement are the basis for managing the internal or external service provider. The service manager negotiates the match of IT demand and IT supply with the service delivery manager. The service manager is responsible for the effectiveness of the services delivered.

9.2.3 IT supply management roles

9.2.3.1 Service delivery manager

This role is focused on the matching of IT demand with IT supply for specific organizational areas, for example a business unit from a supply perspective. The service delivery manager negotiates the match of IT demand and IT supply with the business IT representative: the service manager. The service delivery manager is responsible for the end-to-end service delivery, for the value added service and its components as well as the effectiveness of the services delivered. His key performance management target is customer satisfaction. The service delivery manager provides for the buckets of funding to the operations manager.

9.2.3.2 Operations manager

This role is focused on effectiveness and efficiency of the supported products he delivers. The operations managers manage the availability of stable IT services with their application services and infrastructure services components, more specifically the supported product.

9.2.3.3 Project manager service delivery

This role is focused on the effectiveness of the new services his project delivers. The project manager for service delivery has the end-to-end responsibility for delivering a new IT service or service group from a tuning zone. The project manager for service delivery also manages the optimization, stabilization and transition of the new IT service to the stable IT service delivery environment. In this case there are no detailed service level agreements, only high level service agreements between the project manager and the information manager.

9.2.3.4 Project/programme manager

This role is focused on timely delivery of new IT services. The programme or project manager manages a service development and implementation project. He has the responsibility to deliver the defined project deliverables in a timely manner and to transfer control of the project results to the project manager for service delivery.

9.3 Model A: decentralized in business units

9.3.1 Characteristics

In this model (Figure 9.1), the supply of IT services is fully contained within each business unit. The total responsibility of IT development, maintenance and operations lies with the management team of the business unit. There will be no chief information officer (CIO) or only a very small corporate body advising the board on high level strategic issues.

This model has a lot of advantages for the business units. Short communication cycles will lead to fast decision making on IT. IT staff will be dedicated to the business of the business unit, improving understanding of business issues and requirements. In the development of new products, this model will enable the business unit to involve IT at an early stage.

There are also some disadvantages. These concern the business as a whole. Decentralization may lead to inefficient IT investments. The risk is that each business unit will reinvent the wheel

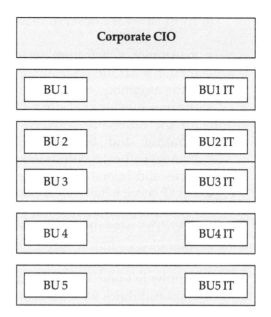

Figure 9.1
Demand/supply model:
decentralized

in its own way, which leads to a diversified landscape of IT solutions. Various hardware platforms, software packages and tailor-made software are often the result of a decentralized model. This is no problem if the business units have nothing in common, and are located far away from each other. However, most companies share a common IT infrastructure with a network, email, intranet, etc. Working together on the subject of IT infrastructure and more specifically on the non-business-sensitive IT will lead to economies of scale for the business as a whole.

9.3.2 IT performance management roles

In this model, the supply of IT services is fully contained within each business unit. This implicates that the scope of the IT portfolio is limited to the business unit. There is an IT performance management grid per business unit and there is an IT service provisioning approach per business unit.

It depends on two situations whether the key management roles in IT service provisioning are implemented:

- The maturity level of both IT demand and IT supply of a specific business unit.
- The size of the IT supply operation within the business unit.

233

In most cases we observe the following:

- 'Customer satisfaction' is the number one focus area, no matter what the costs are.
- Little attention is paid to synergies and economies of scale in the non-business sensitive IT. This leads to a lack of attention for the difference between the roles of the service delivery manager and the operations manager, resulting in one manager that incorporates the conflict between customer focus and operational efficiency.
- All IT service delivery is managed from a 'continuous new IT service delivery project approach', without the transitioning step. The overall landscape of IT solutions contains various technology-related islands and islanders.
- There is no explicit process for matching IT demand and IT supply, leading to a integration of the service management responsibilities with the service delivery management responsibilities. This results in a lack of measurability of the provided price/performance ratio.
- The programme and project management role is highly regarded. The perception of senior management is that today's service delivery will be dramatically improved by the IT project portfolio.
- When external service providers are being used the contracting and service (level) management roles are located in the business unit-specific IT department. The same goes for the strategic performance management roles.

9.4 Model B: centralized in corporate information services

9.4.1 Characteristics

This model (Figure 9.2) is largely the opposite of model A. The corporate information services is the organizational unit where the supply of IT services is managed. This unit is neatly organized in applications, operations and projects. For the end users of the business unit there is a helpdesk for all their operational questions. The alignment between demand and supply on a strategic level is centralized on the business level. The IT committee, chaired by the chief financial officer with the business unit managers and the IT manager as members, decides on the IT investments and budgets.

Most of the advantages of this model were mentioned as disadvantages of model A. This model enables the organization

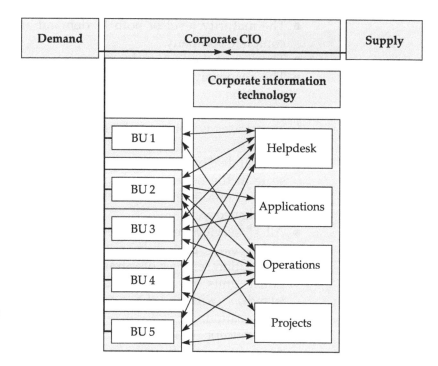

Figure 9.2
Demand/supply model:
your wish is my
command

to maximize its economies of scale for investments in IT infrastructure.

The main disadvantage of this model is the lack of operational alignment between the IT department and the business units. The IT people are not committed to a specific business unit, and the business units do not have an IT staff of their own. Translating business unit-specific requirements in general IT solutions may lead to misunderstandings and a general feeling at the business units that IT is not delivering a good quality service.

9.4.2 IT performance management roles

In this model the corporate information services is the organizational unit where the supply of IT services is managed. This model usually works with a 'one stop shop dictate' from senior management. By definition there is one IT portfolio, one IT performance management grid and one IT service provisioning structure for the entire company.

It depends on three situations whether the management roles for IT service provisioning are implemented:

- The maturity level of both IT demand and IT supply of the complete company.
- The size of the IT supply operation.
- The responsiveness to business change by the IT supply operation.

In most cases we observe the following:

- A great deal of attention is paid to synergies and economies of scale in the non-business-sensitive IT. Cost cutting is target number one. The service delivery manager role has not been established yet.
- All IT services are delivered by dedicated operations managers, each providing either a value added service or application services of infrastructure services to all organizational units in the business. This results in 'functional islands' within the corporate information service organization.
- The concept of a 'tuning zone' for new IT service delivery does not exist. All new services are directly implemented in the existing service delivery organizations, resulting in negative impact on service levels.
- There is not an explicit process for matching IT demand and IT supply, leading to a wide range of contacts between the business and the IT organization. Every operation manager talks to 'his customer'. Every business manager has to communicate with at least four or five operation managers.
- The programme and project management role again is highly regarded. The corporate information services organization is involved in the new IT services introduction projects in the final stages of the design and implementation, resulting in serious discussions on service delivery levels that were promised by the programme or project manager.
- There is no specific demand management organization in the business units available. The information management is limited to participating in steering committees and aggregating required IT budgets. This is more a management reporting and representing role.
- Managing external service providers is completely centralized in the corporate information services organization.
- The corporate CIO organization does have the IT strategy and architecture roles; however, they are mainly focused on standards for the non-business-sensitive IT. Vendor and competency management are not organized.

9.5 Model C: the service centre

9.5.1 Characteristics

In this model (Figure 9.3), the IT department reorganized itself into a services organization. In fact, many IT departments made this change in the 1990s. The business units become more aware of the possibilities of IT and the business value that can be gained from it. This results in the rise of business unit information managers, often with an IT background, who are able to define a business unit-specific demand for IT services. For the central IT department, the only way to respond to this is to recognize the business units as clients, and become a service-oriented organization. The account managers in the IT department become the single point of formal contact with the business unit. Their task is to define and negotiate contracts with his clients: the service level agreements (SLA). In the SLA, the services are specified, along with the quality levels of that service and their prices. The IT services organization could even be (partly) outsourced.

In this model, the strategic alignment of demand and supply remains central. This means, for example, that decisions on enterprise architecture and the contents of the service catalogue will be taken at the central level.

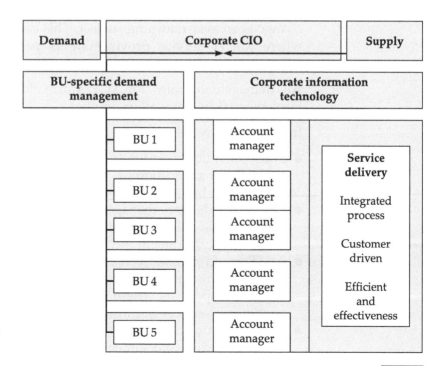

Figure 9.3
Demand/supply model:
the service centre

The advantage of this model is that it combines the advantages of the two previous models: it is harvesting the advantages of the economies of scale using a common infrastructure, and at the same time it is delivering tailor-made services to the business units.

However, there is a disadvantage to this model. The main disadvantage is that it is a closed system; the business units have to obtain their IT services from one source. This is not always in the best interest of the business units. In addition the model can generate a lot of administrative overhead because of the internal SLA and charging that is involved.

9.5.2 IT performance management roles

In this model, the IT department reorganized itself into a services organization. The model that we presented for IT service provisioning in Chapter 3 completely fits with this demand/supply model. The IT service centre can work with a 'one stop shop dictate' from senior management. In this case there is one IT portfolio, one IT performance management grid and one IT service provisioning structure for the entire company. Depending on the maturity of the IT demand and IT supply, this model can be subject to continuous debate between business and IT. In particular the responsiveness to business change is an ever returning subject. This can lead to a situation where the IT service provisioning is partly sourced to an external service provider.

All management roles for IT performance management are implemented in one way or another.

In most cases we observe the following:

- Much attention is paid to operational excellence through synergies and economies of scale in the non-business-sensitive IT, but also for customer satisfaction.
- The service delivery manager role has been established and in some cases is called 'account manager'; he is the single point of contact and problem escalation for the customer.
- All IT services are delivered by the service delivery team and supported by various operations managers, each providing service components. These can be a value added service or application services of infrastructure services.
- The concept of a 'tuning zone' for new IT service delivery sometimes exists and sometimes doesn't. All new services are

perceived by the IT service delivery organization as disturbing the day-to-day stable service delivery resulting in negative impact on service levels.

- There is an explicit process for matching IT demand and IT supply based on a services catalogue. The service delivery manager negotiates with his counterpart in the business, who is called the service manager or service level manager.
- In the case of bigger internal service providers the demand/supply agreement is split in a two-level agreement:
  - service agreement, which contains a range of IT services and associated service levels and pricing. This service agreement is subject to negotiation between the service manager on the demand side and the account manager on the supply side. It is an overarching agreement for a longer period of time;
  - service level agreement (SLA), which contains the details on service delivery for one particular customer organization. This SLA is subject to negotiation and the basis for the control on the delivery. The SLA is agreed within the terms and conditions of the service agreement and managed by the service level manager on the demand side and the service demand manager on the supply side.
- The programme and project management role again is highly regarded. The internal service provider is involved in the new IT services introduction projects from the beginning, yet there are still discussions on service delivery levels that were promised by the programme or project manager.
- The information management role as well as the service (level) management are established.
- It entirely depends on the adherence to market standards of the internal service provider whether it is possible to shop outside. If that is the case the contract management role occurs both in the business unit for the business-sensitive IT and in the internal service provider organization for the non-business-sensitive IT.
- The corporate CIO organization contains all strategic roles including vendor management to optimize buying power for the company as a whole.

9.6 Model D: business and IT fusion

9.6.1 Characteristics

This model (Figure 9.4) brings a lot of the alignment between business and IT back to the business units. In each business unit,

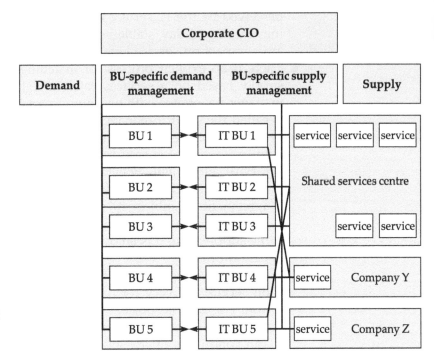

Figure 9.4
Demand/supply model: shared services with selective sourcing

a small number of highly skilled professionals translate the business model of the unit into IT solutions. For these solutions they orchestrate the IT supply from both internal and external sources. The organization has a shared services centre, where generic IT services are delivered at market prices. Some services that are very specific for a limited number of business units are bought from external parties.

The advantages of this model are a strong alignment between business and IT and a good balance between internal and external sourced IT services.

A disadvantage of the model is its complexity, which will require high skills in the management of the business unit IT departments.

9.6.2 IT performance management roles

In this model the 'one stop shop dictate' issue has been resolved into a 'selective sourcing strategy'. The organization has a shared services centre, where common IT services are delivered at cost+ prices. Some services that are very specific for a limited number of business units are bought from external parties.

There can be one IT portfolio and one IT performance management grid approach for the entire company. In this case the 'corporate IT function headed by the CIO' has a strong strategy and architecture influence and an active role in the strategic planning and control of IT. This is a good model for utilizing scarce competencies such as strategists, architects and vendor managers. It also is a good model when the synergies between business units are based on IT.

The other approach is more decentralized. Every business unit has:

- An IT portfolio.
- An IT performance management grid.
- A 'BU-specific demand management' organization.
- A 'BU-specific supply management' organization.

Key to the success of this model is the 'selective sourcing strategy' and the way this IT planning and control of service delivery is implemented.

In most cases we observe the following:

- 'Customer satisfaction' is the number one focus area, although at an affordable price level.
- Less attention is paid to operational excellence through synergies and economies of scale in the non-business-sensitive IT, negotiation with service providers is based on an 'all-in, end-to-end, price per seat' approach. Specifically for the commodity type of IT services that are non-business sensitive, such as desktops, datacentres, etc.
- The delivery of value added service is split:
  - matching demand and supply, business consultancy, project and programme management is delivered by the 'BU-specific demand management organization';
- architecture design and management, solution design and integration, end-to-end service level management is delivered by the 'BU-specific supply management organization'.
- The service delivery manager role has been established in the shared services organization, he is the single point of contact and problem escalation for the service manager or service level manager in the BU-specific supply management organization.
- Whether the service providers have implemented the key IT supply management roles is subject to negotiation in the sourcing contract.

- There is an explicit process for matching IT demand and IT supply based on a services catalogue. However, this has moved from the demand management organization to the 'BU-specific supply management organization'.
- Most of the time the contract has a three-level build-up:
  - frame agreement, which contains the overarching terms and conditions that are negotiated at a company level by the corporate IT vendor and contract management function;
  - service agreement, which contains a range of IT services and associated service levels and pricing, within the terms and conditions of the frame agreement. This service agreement is subject to negotiation between the service manager on the demand side and the account manager on the supply side. It is an overarching agreement for a longer period of time;
  - service level agreement (SLA), which contains the details on service delivery for one particular customer organization. This SLA is subject to negotiation and the basis for the control on the delivery. The SLA is agreed within the terms and conditions of the service agreement and managed by the service level manager on the demand side and the service delivery manager on the supply side.

<table>
<tr><td>**10**</td><td></td></tr>
</table>

Illustrating the IT value perception model

10.1 Introduction

The IT value of a company depends on the strategic focus of the company and the level of perception of the IT services that are delivered to that company. Therefore, the IT value perception model has been introduced (Figure 10.1).

In this chapter the four levels of the IT value perception model will be elaborated using four virtual IT organizations. These departments do not exist in real life; they are used for illustrative purposes only. The descriptions are partly based on our working life experiences, both as employees from within, and as external consultants with clients. The other part, though, is based on our imagination.

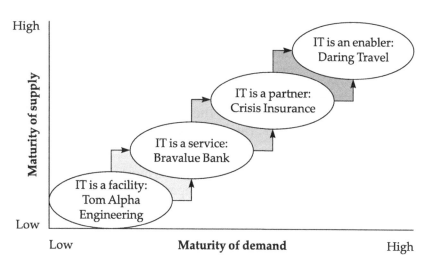

Figure 10.1
Illustrating the IT value perception model

It is important to note that the four cases in this chapter are not linked to the demand/supply models in the previous chapter. The cases will have a mixture of these models implemented, as any organization will have.

10.2 Level one: IT is a facility

Tom Alpha Engineering (TAE) was founded in 1981 by an electrical engineer named Tom Alpha. He was an employee of an electronic multinational. He had a lot of ideas to improve the production lines of his company, but did not succeed in getting the top managers' attention. Therefore, he left the company and started his own. Now, at the age of 52, Tom is the owner of a successful company with more than 500 employees.

TAE produces small electrical home appliances. These markets are characterized by many vendors and low margins. Their success is based on operational effectiveness, lean-and-mean low-cost production lines. Their product and development department remains relatively small. Tom Alpha says: 'we are not inventors. We copy the market leaders and improve their products to produce at low cost for the mass market.'

The business strategy of TAE is the sole responsibility of Tom and he is doing a fine job with clear directions for everybody. His original choice on positioning in the value system has proven to be right, considering the prosperous growth of the company. His strategy can be labelled: 'mass production – innovation', with a focus on 'operational excellence'. Tom is considering implementing ideas on 'continuous improvement'. There is no explicit IT strategy other than 'keep the business satisfied'.

Administration is a burden for Tom Alpha. It is an overhead to him, a necessary evil. With the margins staying as low as they are, too much overhead is killing the business.

The IT department of TAE is part of the business unit Facilities, along with the departments security, buildings, communications, catering and quality management.

IT consists of 12 people. The IT manager has been with the company for 15 years; most of that time as an assistant controller of the finance department. He is a star in cost management.

The expenses of the IT department are covered by the facilities budget of TAE. Once a year, the IT manager has to provide his budget for next year to the head of the facilities department.

This budget is based on the expected expense of this year + 15 per cent. The last few years, Tom has been cutting this budget with 10 per cent.

There is no cost management system. Simple bookkeeping is performed for the IT costs made by the IT department. IT spending for the production IT and by personnel outside the IT department is not part of the IT bookkeeping.

The costs of facilities are charged over the various lines of business, based on the number of employees for each business unit.

For the administrative IT services the alignment is good, because the IT manager has strong informal 'one-on-one' relationships with all department heads and managers. Communication is direct, unstructured, informal and speedy. Consequently, the administrative IT applications are not based on any architecture, they are developed over time based on requests from the users and the preferences (and skills) of the IT people.

The autonomous assembly line teams have the competencies and assets to design, implement and manage production control IT. They are not supported by the IT department.

Here, the alignment is optimal, because the IT competencies are completely integrated in the self-steering teams of the business.

There is no such thing as a services catalogue. The joint business and IT perception is that there is no need to become explicit about the obvious. As the IT services are not formalized, they are not priced either. Since services are not structured in any way, issues on the quality and improvements/enhancements of existing IT solutions are discussed between the business unit managers and the IT manager.

In this company, there is only one kind of value that the IT department can deliver, which is to cut costs. Therefore, the IT department is controlled by minimizing the cost. There is no structured process for IT investment appraisal. Applications are bought when necessary on an ad hoc basis. It is speedy, situational, with not much in-depth research. The IT specialist does a 'case-by-case' selection of technological solutions with the lowest cost of ownership as the most important criterion. Tom Alpha needs to approve investments over a certain amount.

A recent investment proposal was made by the sales manager. The outbound sales are able to dial into the TAE network to obtain their email. The sales manager wanted to enable them additionally with the capability to enter their sales into the sales administration directly. However, he was not able to quantify the business value of this change, and thus was not able to convince Tom Alpha of the need for this IT investment.

TAE does not have a sourcing strategy other than 'hire capacity when needed'. For the helpdesk, two employees have been hired from an external service provider. Their task is to handle the calls, and route them to the appropriate IT employee. Additionally, they sometimes perform easy desktop support activities. The IT manager is having the business contacts with the service provider.

The human resource and payroll application has been out-sourced. This contract was initiated and signed by Tom Alpha himself. The head of the human resources department is satisfied with the service provided, so the contract is automatically extended every year.

There is no real mission critical IT. The IT-based offerings are limited to production control, the actual value add is not made explicit because it is not visible as a separate IT activity. The administrative IT is not managed from a business perspective, but from an IT cost control perspective.

The infrastructure services for production control are completely separated from the administrative IT, resulting in a number of desktops and desktop applications that are unknown to the IT department. This has led to complications and loss of synergy, when a desktop standardization effort was planned and rolled out.

The datacentre activity is limited to a series of stand-alone (one application on one server) server parks. There is little to no documentation available. The main activity is desktop support related.

The application services are limited to:

- Report generator-based tailoring of output.
- Building and maintaining interfaces between the major applications for finance and billing.
- Maintaining complex spreadsheet applications for production planning.
- Maintaining a self-made procurement application that is linked to the finance system.

There is little to no documentation, everybody in the IT department is highly appreciated for his or her specific expertise of an application and the support they give to the user. Development and testing is done on a separate server. The consultancy and architecture services are included in the application services. Project management has not yet been implemented in the IT department.

The exchange of information between applications is based on 'one-on-one' interfaces with all kinds of technological solutions. There is no structured real time information exchange with the outside world. Product designs from third parties are transferred by exchanging CD-ROMs.

The management objective is completely focused on cost cutting opportunities. Potential synergies in server deployment are considered by the IT manager. Competency management is limited to yearly salary raises. There are no formal processes with key performance indicators implemented.

10.3 Level two: IT is a service

Bravalue is a financial institution with both a short history and a long tradition. Bravalue is the result of a merger between Braath Insurance and the VFM Bank. VFM stands for value for money.

The merger that resulted in Bravalue took place in 1999 and has proven to be a success. The original idea was to open new markets with 'cross-selling' and achieving economies of scale in the back office activity. The new IT-based offerings for stock portfolio management and stock portfolio-based mortgages contribute to the success of the merger greatly. In fact the merger was the implementation of a new strategy that is based on the 'mass customization' concept with an 'operational excellence' focus. Two 'mass production' organizations were successfully merged within a one-year timeframe. The result is a financial services organization with a broad services portfolio consisting of payments, savings and stock services, life insurance and mortgages. The main channel for this portfolio is the 300 offices of the original retail bank. The Internet is only recently and very cautiously identified as a channel opportunity.

A critical success factor for the merger was the fact that both companies were able to look at the new post-merger world with an open mind. They combined the best of two worlds, adopting best practices where possible and taking a green-field approach at some exceptional areas.

247

IT was such an exception. During the merger, external consultants assessed both IT departments and concluded that the companies' IT departments suffered from large, end-of-life legacy applications, and choosing between the two would only make things worse. The decision was made to create a new department, Bravalue Information Services (BIS). Within BIS, a separate team operates and maintains the old-legacy environment.

Strategic planning is executed by corporate planning. This board level staff organization doesn't communicate with IT in any structured way. The BIS organization is informed of the results but does not participate in the planning process. The Bravalue Bank has a policy of forced supply by the BIS organization. The BIS organization can define its own strategy goals, but the control on the funding of IT activity is within the business units. The larger portion of the IT budget is allocated for the newly defined IT-based offerings, instead of the optimization of the service provisioning and the legacy sunsetting.

Bravalue Information Services consists of 300 people, 30 per cent of whom are external hires. The alignment between business and IT is bad. The business is annoyed with the fact that the IT community cannot cope with the pace of the business restructuring. Expectations of the merger were high and rightfully so; however, IT turns out to be a ball on a chain.

The service level management department of BIS has developed a service catalogue from scratch, based on an inventory of the activities that were performed within the department. The project team has written down these services in an IT supply guide. They have asked several business units to review their service description. A lot of business units did not react at all; the business unit that reviewed the catalogue noted that the descriptions were very technical and hard to understand. The manager of the service level management department is aiming at a larger commitment for next year's version of the service catalogue, because he understands that the service catalogue needs to be an instrument between the business units and the IT department.

The charging is based on the service level agreements that have been signed by the various business unit managers. However, this process is subject to a lot of criticism by the business units. The main criticisms are:

- The descriptions in the services catalogue are too technical and cannot be understood.

- The service level reports are too technical as well; they state that the IT department has performed conform SLA, but the perception of the business units is they did not.
- The prices for the IT services are not transparent; in this way they cannot be compared with external service providers.
- The charging of several IT services is based on the configuration management database (CMDB); however, the business unit claim that the data in the CMDB does not reflect reality.

A lot of questions from the business unit have to be answered each year concerning the height and components of the tariffs. For example, the CPU second has become 10 per cent more expensive than last year, and IT was not able to explain why, faced with newspaper articles of ever cheaper hardware prices.

The budget process in Bravalue takes about three months. In this timeframe each business unit has to deliver a business plan for the next year, including number of desktops and laptops and specific projects. The business units derive these budgets from last year's results.

The IT services department needs to cover its expenses by the charging of IT services; therefore, the prices are based on last year's actual costs, but include a margin for technological renewal projects. At the end of the year, the positive or negative result of the IT services department is recovered.

The new IT environment and IT services were developed in a very short timeframe. They based the environment on a plug-and-play architecture; middleware is used to link the legacy environments with these new environments. The legacy team (as everybody calls it) is phasing out the legacy applications and hardware.

The four-year plan to sunset all legacy systems is two years behind schedule but making good progress. The progress is slowed down because of the introduction of new IT-based offerings. This had to be done quick and dirty, resulting in architectural solutions that are not durable. The 'bus' architecture concept has been developed only recently. The middleware solutions that help with the speedy implementation of the new IT-based offerings was implemented from a technology perspective. This resulted in a successful CRM package implementation, linked with the legacy systems in a dedicated way.

Thus, the IT services portfolio contains a mixture of legacy-based services and recently started 'killer apps'. Most of the legacy-based services have a simple straightforward structure with 'supported product' at the top level. For these services the 'knowledge-based service components' traditionally were and still are in the demand management organization of the business units. The IT-based offering services/the perceived 'killer apps' contain a large portion of 'knowledge-based service components', which is provided by the BIS organization.

The IT manager (experienced in IT optimization) and the IT planning and control department have a strong focus on the planning and spending of the legacy team. This planning was created as a result of the study performed during the merger. They are strictly managed to their project plan and supporting business case. When this team needs new equipment there is a lot of hassle.

For the new environment there are budgets based on investment plans and business cases. These investments are made easily, when supported by the business. Cost management is not really performed and the information available from the merger study is no longer used. Cost charging is based on service rates, and planning and control determines the rates based on last year's rates and the overall budget. There is no direct relation with the costs made to deliver the service.

BIS has a mission to deliver IT services for all business units of Bravalue. Therefore, they regard themselves as a service centre. Investments are made to introduce new services. The need for those services is expressed by the clients of the IT department, i.e. the business.

BIS has implemented a process for the justification of IT investments. This process is facilitated by the IT planning and control department. For this purpose, the IT controller has developed a template from the business case model that was made by an external consultant, two years ago, for the consolidation of the data centres during the mergers. The project managers rarely use this template, because it is too complicated, not self-explanatory and contains too many complex formulas. Consequently, each project manager uses his own template, and business cases are not standardized.

Project managers develop the business cases without much help from the business unit sponsor; therefore, there is limited attention for the business value that may be obtained from the IT investments. If business value is addressed, it will imply reducing operating costs.

The communication with the outside world is still based on the traditional electronic funds transfer (EFT) applications. Plans to use the Internet as a channel are still in the pilot phase and completely stand-alone from the rest of the architecture.

The CRM implementation was considered mission critical for the first nine months of the initiative. As soon as the delivery turned out to be speedy and successful, the attention level of senior management dropped and the services became part of the IT-based offerings. The traditional IT-based offerings for electronic funds transfer are outside the responsibility of the BIS organization. They are linked to the core banking applications by dedicated interfaces of a batch nature. The value add of these services is completely integrated with the result of the 'payments' business unit.

In the merger the IT department began to structure its management and processes, because they faced budget cuts. The speedy CRM implementation was mainly successful because a limited number of dedicated IT specialists made it happen. There was no time available to document the implementation: application support and maintenance depends on two individuals. The implementation of ITIL-based processes went smoothly and is almost finished, except for the strategic processes. Most of the problems with the business are based on the time needed to learn the value added services – account management and service level management. Because of the business restructuring that went on at a very high speed, the configuration management database (CMDB) became unreliable. This is the root cause for the majority of the alignment problems. A planned desktop standardization refresh programme is intended to resolve these problems. Recently a capability maturity model (CMM) audit was done for the application services of the core business applications. Results were dramatic and new plans have been initiated for improvement.

The sourcing strategy of Bravalue Bank is limited to 'hiring capacity' and 'hiring know-how'. Around 30 per cent of the IT staff are external employees. The IT procurement department is responsible for the resource management of external resources. They are hired based on skills, expertise and lowest prices.

10.4 Level three: IT is a partner

The Crisis Insurance Company has been a direct writer insurance company right from its start in the 1980s. Crisis does not use agents to sell insurance policies, but handles all their customer contacts by phone. 'Crisis? Call Crisis!' was at the heart of their award-winning marketing campaign for many years. With the rise of the Internet, Crisis was among the first insurance companies to offer their customers direct online access to policy information and claim status.

The company has always been one of the early adopters of new technologies, for example in call centre technology and customer relationship management (CRM). This CRM implementation provides for the basic information to achieve the strategy, which is based on the 'mass customization' concept with an 'operational excellence' focus.

It is not a coincidence that their current CEO started his career at the IT department and was IT manager for three years before his appointment to the board.

The IT department consists of 200 people, 20 per cent of whom are external hires. The IT department has a staff for IT planning and control, vendor management and architects. There is a large competence centre for call centre technology.

At Crisis Insurance, the IT strategy is derived directly from the business strategy. The alignment between business and IT is pretty strong. There is a strong relationship between the IT manager and the CEO, who was his former boss as IT manager. Therefore, executive sponsorship is not a problem for the IT department in this company. The perception of IT in the business is good. Communication is based on formal and informal structures such as steering committees, service level agreements and knowledge exchange circles throughout the entire company.

The quarterly 'Watch IT!' sessions facilitate the mutual brainstorming of business and IT employees in order to create new opportunities to improve products, services and business processes with the use of IT. The IT employees use these sessions to explain technological innovations, which may lead to new ideas for Crisis. The major part of the IT portfolio is in the IT-based offerings area.

The introduction of new products and services is a critical success factor for Crisis. After introduction, the call centres must be able to respond to customers' questions from day one. That is why the lines of business and IT work together closely in multidisciplinary teams in the introduction of new products and services. The people involved leave their 'normal' workplace to work as a team in dedicated project war rooms.

Over the years, business and IT of Crisis Insurance have developed a smooth and mature project process, where the business and the IT owner of the proposed IT investment create a joint business case. In this business case costs and value of both business and IT are part of the financial model. The model is mutually agreed by business and IT before proposing it to the board. It is regarded as a product innovation plan instead of an IT investment, because it is developed as a business enhancement proposal to bring new products and services to the market. IT is 'just' one of the technical components to make this happen.

The architectures are based on a solid business capabilities framework that was established several years ago. The resulting IT capabilities were designed and implemented in an application architecture that is based on 'off-the-shelf' software that was highly and intensely customized by the staff of the IT department. The basis for the customizations was always the degree of integration of functionality that was possible and the assurance of data integrity.

The high level of integration has led to a 'tailor-made' ERP system. The implementation of a bus architecture is neither available nor planned. This will be a potential stumbling block when a merger with other companies is considered. That would result in either of the two companies having to adopt the solutions of one of them. Crisis IT staff are convinced that their solution is superior given the success of the company. The IT department considers offering their extensive knowledge on IT insurance solutions on the external market.

Together with user groups, the IT department has created a structured service catalogue. This catalogue is written in a style that the business units understand; crisp and clear, without technological details. The descriptions are based on the delivered added value to the business and not on the technological components. Phrases like 'the availability of the servers will be 99.4 per cent' have been replaced by 'the applications will be out of business to a maximum of 10 minutes per year'.

Many services have multiple service levels with differentiation in prices for different service levels. This offers the business units a choice between 'simple, but cheap' and 'world class, expensive'. Service level agreements have been agreed with all business units.

The IT services portfolio contains a large portion of IT-based offerings, which have many 'knowledge-based components'. In particular the call center and CRM implementations contain large knowledge-based service components. The infrastructure services have been outsourced to a third party.

The service provisioning roles are jointly managed by the business and IT. The supported product level is where the responsibility of the IT department stops and the responsibility of the business starts. Most of the value added service components are realized in the business units.

Crisis has developed an extensive ABC cost management system. The IT planning and control department is responsible for this cost management system.

Last year the Insurance Association did a benchmark on IT costs in the insurance business. Crisis used the information from their ABC cost management system in this benchmark. Upfront they expected to be one of the organizations with the highest IT costs, which is in line with their strategy as a technology frontrunner. The results were as expected, although the benchmark showed that other organizations were also increasing their investments in new technology. Asked for comment, the CEO said: 'Yes, we spend more on IT than average in the industry, and we're proud of it. It is our competitive advantage.' Nevertheless, Crisis is planning to further analyse these high costs in the coming year.

Each year, the business units deliver a new business plan to corporate portfolio management. The project calendar of each business unit has been consolidated at a company level. The IT projects are a subset of this overall calendar. The budgets are derived from the business plans of every business unit and the choices on the IT portfolio.

The charging of IT services is based on the product costs, with an additional margin, dependent on the phase of the technology lifecycle. Prices of services are calculated using the cost management principles of activity-based costing.

Crisis Insurance has outsourced all infrastructure services to an external service provider. The service management of the outsourced IT infrastructure services is organized in a separate department within the IT department which delivers a value added service for the whole company. This service management function is staffed from IT planning and control, vendor management and architect functions in the IT department.

Next to the outsourced infrastructure services, 20 per cent of the IT department staff are external hires. The procurement office is responsible for the hiring of external personnel. They have also described a procedure for the selection of third party software and services.

10.4 Level four: IT is an enabler

Daring Travel started as a hobby in 1997. Daring Publishers is a well-established publisher of non-fiction. Since the 1950s they have been publishing all kinds of books on a great variety of subjects, such as automobiles, animals and pets, health, home improvement and gardening. One of their best-selling series is the home-abroad travel books, delivering high quality information for backpackers on holidays, far away from home.

When the Internet became popular, one of the editors of the travel books started a website on backpack travelling, which became very popular. It turned out that the buyers and readers of the travel books were a cohesive community, sharing a lot of mutual interest. On the website, more and more questions were posed on the subject of travelling. This caused Daring Publishers to start an experimental company, Daring Travel. The mission of Daring Travel is to be a travel agency on the web. And it is a success, growing 30 per cent year over year in both sales and profit. IT is regarded a crucial resource for the company to reach its strategic goals. Without IT, there would be no Daring Travel.

Asked what was the secret of their success, Doris Daring, CEO of Daring Travel and daughter of the deceased founder of the publishing company, said: 'Well, it's the quality of the books that created a community around our brand. But without the IT department of Daring Publishers we would have been nowhere.'

The IT department of Daring Travel originated from the project team that developed the Daring Publisher's bookshop online. They don't really act as a department on their own, because they work together closely with Doris Daring and the other content editors.

255

Every two weeks, Doris Daring heads a 'How Dare You?' session. These sessions challenge all employees of Daring Travel to come up with new ideas. The mix of IT freaks and experienced backpackers in these sessions seems to be the critical success factor. Ideas are gathered and in strategic follow-up sessions the prioritization of the product ideas is translated in a prioritized project portfolio. In these sessions, the IT investments are assessed on their expected business value using the Daring Travel balanced scorecard. This scorecard combines business economic indicators with web analytics.

For example, they found out that the customers, who were interested in books on horses, also had a significant interest in travel destinations in Ireland. When they showed this to Doris, she immediately started to make a number of phone calls. One month later, Daring Travel offered a new, very successful travel arrangement on its website: horseback riding in Ireland. In this way, Daring Travel is able to add new products and services bases to their portfolio very quickly. Sometimes, Daring Travel doesn't follow the hype, it creates the hype.

Stagnation of growth in the existing portfolio has led to further building of new communities. As such the reuse of existing technologies was an implementation of the 'dynamic stability' strategy. The dominant focus is on 'customer intimacy'.

The basis for the success of Doris lies in the architecture of the mother company. The fact that there was a CRM application successfully implemented provided for the starting point of the whole new company. This knowledge base on customer wants and needs was exploited through the use of a middleware implementation and simple groupware-based solutions for providing content management capabilities to the new company. Combined with a business intelligence tool performing 'enterprise customer analytics' this architecture turned out to be the key success factor for the new company. The architectural structure and the use of isolation principles with the architecture of the mother company simplify mergers or divestitures when needed.

Decision making on IT is based on integral planning of business and IT. The portfolio management group plays a key role here in supporting the planning, reporting and control activity. Internal charging is not done. Since IT is regarded as a part of the product and services of Doris Travel, the IT costs are part of the overall product costs.

Daring Travel performs cost management using an integral ABC cost management system, where IT is one of the resources. The prices of the products and services are also based on this cost management system.

The IT organization is very small. The very high skilled team of IT whiz-kids is reporting directly to Doris Daring. The IT budget is derived from the business plan of each business unit.

The IT department of Doris Travel does not have a services catalogue. The IT services are completely interwoven with the day-to-day activity of the business. Roughly 90 per cent of the IT portfolio consists of IT-based offerings.

New service introduction cycle times are short because of the way the IT business communities work together. Last year, the website crashed two times within a month. After that, Doris decided to sign a web hosting contract with a service provider. Nowadays, all infrastructure services are outsourced through a web hosting contract, which is managed by the IT manager.

The business support services are only very few, and not structured. They consist of a standard administration package, running on an NT server, which is operated by one of the IT staff members on a part-time 'need to do' basis.

The business knowledge-based competencies are value added services that are provided by the internal team. Every IT-based offering has a key individual managing the content of the web page. The concept of new IT services introduction and the tuning zone is only slightly available through the way new web pages are installed by the external service provider. The service management role, managing the external service provider, is only small and executed by Doris herself.

Back to business

11.1 Introduction

In Chapter 2 until Chapter 9, we described the principles and theory of performance management. We supported our theory by using examples from our work experience. In Chapter 10 four virtual IT organizations were introduced to better understand the levels of the IT value perception model. These virtual IT organizations were used to describe the specifics and attributes of the four value perception levels. These elements were created to help you better understand performance management and relate it to your working environment.

In this chapter we will show how to use the principles and basics of performance management in your own IT department. It is written to be a practical guide, not a cook book; it will give you the hints and tips to start using and implementing performance management in your situation. Please always be aware that your situation is unique and that the theory and practical examples we give you do not always apply to your situation.

This chapter starts with a recapture of the IT value perception model which was introduced in the first chapter and further elaborated in the book. For this recapture we will focus on the management attention and business goals of each level and the role performance management can and should play on each level. References are given to detailed descriptions of the different aspects of the value perception model. To start using the model, each organization should determine its value perception level. A self-assessment checklist is created to determine this level. This checklist is described in the third section of this chapter. In the following section some assistance is given on how to introduce and use the performance management principles on each level. We have created so-called first aid kits, describing the ten activities per level to introduce and use performance management.

Chapter 1 described the order or growth path that exists in the model, although it should be recalled that each level can be an end stage for a specific organization. In section 11.5 the IT departments of Tom Alpha Engineering, Bravalue and Crisis Insurance Company experience enormous changes in their organization and business. This leads to a need for migration to the following level. This practical chapter will end with a description of how to migrate to the following level.

11.2 IT value perception model

Understanding the differences and similarities between the four IT value perception levels is key in understanding where to focus in your situation. Again, we cannot give you a clean-cut recipe; however, we will now give you a summary of management focus areas and characteristics per IT value perception level.

11.2.1 High level characteristics

We start with a first high level glance at the characteristics of the four levels.

Level one: IT is a facility

- Focus on reducing the overall cost of manual operations, e.g. administrative.
- Approach is based on automation of standard functionality.
- Business justification is to control expense (not necessarily increase value).

Level two: IT is a service

- Automation moves into the managerial levels (e.g. sales forecasting).
- Focus turns to quality.
- Business justification based upon cost control.

Level three: IT is a partner

- Moves toward creating a strategic advantage.
- Focus turns outside the IT organization.
- Goal is increased market share.
- Business justification is in capturing mind share.

Level four: IT is an enabler

- Moves toward industry domination.
- Focus is creating sustainable new revenue streams.
- Purpose is to create competitive barriers.

11.2.2 Performance management focus/goals

This section contains the top ten performance management goals and their relative importance per IT value perception level. The goals are sorted in alphabetical order.

Added value of IT

As in speed of new service introduction it is only when the enabling role of IT is being recognized by senior management on the demand side that value-based thinking is finding a solid ground to grow on. At levels three and four this is a prerequisite for good results and as such the key management focus area for IT performance management.

Competency development

The importance of competency development is recognized for the first time at level two. In this level it is usually addressed from the IT supply side. The perception level reaches level three, only when both the IT demand and IT supply side recognize the importance and start actively developing specific IT competencies. At level four it is still recognized as important; however, the processes and results are already in place.

Cost management/cost saving

In levels one and two this is the dominant area of performance management focus; initiated by the IT demand side the focus is cost saving. At levels three and four cost saving becomes less important, the IT supply side will be measured on their cost management, although the IT demand side will see this as a less important focus area.

Customer focus

As level two progresses the meaning of the word customer is starting to come to IT management's attention. At levels two and three the focus will be on the internal customer/end user which consumes the IT service provided. Somewhere in level three and definitely in level four the focus will shift to the external customer.

Fit of business and IT alignment

It is mainly the perception on the IT demand side that influences the level that you are in. Most often there is a push from the IT supply side towards business and IT alignment in level one and definitely in level two. Only when the awareness of this fit within the business becomes apparent in their actions towards IT supply, one can state to have reached level three.

Operational excellence

This management target is highly related to the above-mentioned cost management/cost saving target. At level two the competition with external service providers is becoming apparent which forces the management to focus on operational excellence and quality of service. At levels three and four operational excellence is a given, meaning still very important, but other areas need more attention.

Quality of service

At level one this is only a topic from the supply perspective; the demand side doesn't expect anything. At level two the pressure from potential external service provisioning awakens the demand for quality and makes it become a management-focus issue for the supply side. At levels three and four quality of service is a key discriminator for both the internal service provider and the external service provider.

Speed of new service introduction

The awareness of the enabling role of IT is the main driver for increasing management focus on the speed of new service introduction. It takes at least to levels three and four before this becomes apparent in the (senior) management focus.

Transparency

At level two, transparency is usually focused on tariff structures for internal charging. At level three the transparency focus is based more on understanding service structures and service components in order to facilitate reuse of service components. It is mainly the perception at the demand side that is the key differentiator for transparency.

Vendor relationship management

The balance between the internal service provisioning and the external service provider part of the IT portfolio is the key discriminator for the importance of vendor relationship management. At all levels there can be an external service provider; however, when value-based thinking on the demand side is at level three, there will be 'strategic' partnerships providing the essential IT services in the portfolio.

Table 11.1 contains a summary of the top ten performance management goals and their relative importance per IT value perception level. The goals are sorted in alphabetical order.

Table 11.1 Performance management goals per performance level

Performance management goals	Level 1: IT is a facility	Level 2: IT is a service	Level 3: IT is a partner	Level 4: IT is an enabler
Added value of IT	low	medium	very high	very high
Competency development	low	medium	high	medium
Cost management/Cost saving	very high	high	medium	medium
Customer focus	low	high	high	very high
Fit of business – IT alignment	low	medium	high	very high
Operational excellence	high	very high	high	low
Quality of service	medium	high	very high	high
Speed of new service introduction	low	medium	high	very high
Transparency	low	medium	high	low
Vendor relationship management	low	high	very high	high

11.2.3 Detailed characteristics

In Table 11.2 we give you more detailed characteristics per IT value perception level and a reference to where in this book you can read about that subject.

11.3 Self-assessment checklist

Now it is up to you. We will give a checklist to understand where your organization stands on the IT value perception level. Always keep in mind that we are talking about the match of the perception of IT value on the demand side and the supply side, so the checklists should be answered by both communities.

1. What is the primary area in which the board expects a value contribution from IT?

1 Process efficiency
2 Organizational effectiveness
3 Enterprise reach
4 Strategic

2. What is IT's primary business driver?

1 Expense control
2 Business unit measurements
3 Market share (horizontal and vertical linkages)
4 Industry domination

3. At what level is IT management influential within the management of the business?

1 IT users
2 Business unit
3 Executive team
4 Board

4. What is IT's perceived role within senior management?

1 Provider of technical capability
2 Basis for organizational efficiency
3 Strategic alignment with the business
4 Enablement of corporate vision

Table 11.2 Detailed characteristics of the IT Value Perception model

Characteristics	Reference to chapter/section	Level 1: IT is a facility	Level 2: IT is a service	Level 3: IT is a partner	Level 4: IT is an enabler
Architecture-based decision making	6.3, 6.4, 6.5 and 6.6	• Case-by-case technical solutions • One-to-one interfaces	• Mixed bag of best of breed and ERP solutions • First successes of middleware visible	• Relatively more IT-based offerings in the IT portfolio based on best of breed	• IT-based offerings are dominant in the IT portfolio based on best of breed • Mostly sourced infrastructure services • Linked by means of a bus architecture
Business/IT alignment	2.6, 6.2, 6.4 and Chapter nine	IT used to support business operations, no IT strategy	IT strategy used to define IT services for current business operations	Business strategy determines IT strategy, good alignment	Fusion of business and IT
Charging of services	7.7	Through facilities, based on number of employees	Based on service level agreements	Based on activity-based costing	Not applicable
Cost management	4.2, 4.3 and 4.4	Expense control	Control of cost	Cost management	Integral cost management systems
Implementation of IT service procurement and management processes	8.3 and 8.4	No specific processes for IT services procurement; this is part of facilities procurement	IT services procurement on a one at a time basis. No specific processes for ESP management	Sourcing strategy established with a limited number of strategic partnerships for the non-business-sensitive IT	Sourcing strategy established and mature IT demand management and IT service management in the business
IT investment practices	5.5, 5.6 and 5.7	No formal investment appraisal	Stand-alone non-standard business cases focusing on decreasing operational costs	Integrated portfolio management and pipeline management with standardized business cases	Integrated portfolio management and pipeline management with standardized business cases

Table 11.2 Continued

Characteristics	Reference to chapter/section	Level 1: IT is a facility	Level 2: IT is a service	Level 3: IT is a partner	Level 4: IT is an enabler
IT optimization stage	4.5 and 6.4	None or stage 1: infrastructure standardization	Stage 1 and stage 2: IT consolidation	Stage 3: business process standardization and stage 4: information integration	Stage 4: information integration
IT perception	1.3 and the remainder of the book	Cost centre	Service centre	Profit centre	Investment centre
Managing IT demand side of the IT portfolio	6.5	Mainly business support IT, a few IT-based offerings	Some implementations are labelled mission critical, tending to become IT-based offerings six months after introduction	A balanced IT portfolio with all three areas represented. Mission critical can be both business support and IT-based offerings	Mainly IT-based offerings with a substantial mission critical volume that in time becomes IT based offerings. Managing IT supply side of the IT portfolio
Managing IT supply side of the IT portfolio	6.6	Suboptimal infrastructure, application 'heroes'	ITIL processes implemented; starting with CMM but a lot has to be done	Infrastructure services have been outsourced. Main focus on application services competencies in the IT-based offerings	Strategic sourcing of selected IT and business processes with strong service management capabilities in the business
Organizational structure of service provisioning	3.5 and Chapter 9	Facility management	Application development, operations and user services; small IT support office	Model C: The service centre	Model D: Business and IT fusion

Table 11.2 Continued

Characteristics	Reference to chapter/section	Level 1: IT is a facility	Level 2: IT is a service	Level 3: IT is a partner	Level 4: IT is an enabler
Performance management practices	5.3, 5.4 and 6.7	Ad hoc measurements	First version of IT scorecard	Business balanced scorecard and IT scorecard alignment	Business balanced scorecard and IT scorecard integrated
Planning and control of IT	6.7	Budget-driven with cost cutting goals	Formalized budget process based on business plans of business units	Formalized budget process based on business plans of business units	Business and IT budget are one and the same
Pricing of services	7.6 and 7.7	No prices	Non-transparent prices derived from last years actual costs	Product costs with margin	Integrated in the customer product pricing strategy
Roles and responsibilities for service provisioning	3.5, 8.4 and 9.2	IT manager with cost focus discusses with LOB managers	Service level management	Service management and service level management	Service management for external service providers
Research and development on IT	6.2, 6.3 and 6.7	Anyone who is interested roams the Internet	Consultants and architects exchange interesting books	IT strategist and strategic architect role established	Strategic architect is key advisor to the board
Services catalogue	3.3	No service catalogue	Supply-driven service catalogue with extensive number of entries	Demand drives services catalogue with a limited number of entries from multiple external service providers	No service catalogue, mainly one or two external service providers providing (dedicated) services
Service structures	3.2	No formal structure	Defined services	Defined services with differentiated service levels	Complex services with substantial knowledge-based components
Services of external parties	Chapter 8	Ad hoc external hiring	Resource management for external hires	Infrastructure services have been outsourced	Strategic sourcing of selected IT and business processes

5. At what level is IT perceived to make a valuable contribution?

1 Technology
2 Service level
3 Strategy
4 Competitive

6. On what basis does alignment between business strategies and IT occur?

1 Piecemeal hardware/software
2 Application system with process
3 Business unit function
4 Holistic/synergy

7. What approach do executives take to the management of IT?

1 Cost/expense centre
2 Service centre
3 Profit contributor
4 Value centre

Answering these seven multiple choice questions will give you a glance at your IT value perception level. This checklist is a starting point; the next step is looking at the detailed characteristics (Table 11.2). Using these characteristics you can verify whether this first assessment suits you and where the deviations are. This helps you in determining the focus for your organization. When your organization seems to be in between levels, we also refer you to sections 11.5 and 11.6.

11.4 The next ten steps per perception level

The first aid kits for each perception level are described using the detailed characteristics of each level.

Level 1: IT as a facility

1 Find out whether you want to stay a facility, or want to become a service.
2 If you want to become a service, then define your growth path using sections 11.5 and 11.6.
3 Check out the IT optimization stages in Chapter 4, and initiate projects that have not been considered yet.

4 Start projects only when business case (Chapter 5) shows IT cost reduction.
5 Standardize, standardize, standardize.
6 Minimize your budgets for research and development, new technology pilots and proofs of concept.
7 List your projects to obtain a project calendar.
8 Structure your communication with the business by starting steering committees.
9 Find external help in defining your service structures and associated charging.
10 Introduce standard services for desktop functionality with a competing tariff.

Level 2: IT as a service

1 (Re-)define your IT service catalogue based on Chapter 3.
2 Create an IT cost model to get a transparent view on IT services costs.
3 Discuss measurements for IT processes and IT customer satisfaction.
4 Develop IT scorecard using these measurements.
5 Map your service catalogue to the performance management grid and perform a gap analysis of your services portfolio.
6 Introduce new services and sunset old services.
7 Define a sourcing strategy.
8 Select a limited set of preferred suppliers.
9 Include business unit-specific service provisioning in the competency development activities.
10 Involve business unit management in communication on IT.

Level 3: IT as a partner

1 Introduce multiple value levels in your service catalogue.
2 Review and improve IT scorecard continuously.
3 Define IT governance processes to ensure the joint strategy definition of business and IT.
4 Optimize service portfolio management, project prioritization and introduce standard business cases.
5 Introduce activity-based costing or perform cost management based on a cost model.
6 Review and optimize sourcing strategy to include IT-based offerings.
7 Introduce budget responsibilities based on the demand axis of the IT performance management grid.

8 Introduce the strategist and strategic architect role.
9 Provide support in the business planning cycle and start making an IT masterplan with a three year timeframe.
10 Involve information managers in the business unit in the strategic planning activity.

Level 4: IT as an enabler

1 Find out whether you want to stay an enabler, or want to become a service; if you want to become a service, then define your growth path using Level 1 → Level 2 in Sections 11.5 and 11.6.
2 Maximize your budgets for research and development, new technology pilots and proofs of concept.
3 Outsource mature technology infrastructure and infrastructure services where possible.
4 Implement component-based architectures and isolation principles as much as possible.
5 List your projects to obtain a project calendar.
6 Make IT an integral part of the organization's cost management system (ABC).
7 Manage your IT portfolio from the demand side with an emphasis on the profitability of the IT-based offerings.
8 Restructure your IT-based offerings to be able to reuse the knowledge-based components.
9 Develop IT core competencies in the business knowledge area and sustain these competencies for the lifecycle of the IT service.
10 Concentrate successful IT-based offerings in a separate managing entity to be able to implement lifecycle management principles.

11.5 The growth path through the IT value perception model

Changing circumstances in the business organization, the IT organization and the economy in general can lead to a need for a migration to the next level. Using the virtual organizations of Chapter 10 we will describe such migrations.

11.5.1 Tom Alpha Engineering, from facility to service

In recent years the margins in the small electrical home appliances business have stayed very low. This led to some major take-overs. Tom Alpha, now at the age of 52, starts to think about his future. He would like to work until the age of 57 and then start enjoying his pension with his wife and possible grandchildren. None of his children will be a successor to his company.

To protect his organization from a take-over and to guarantee his future, he decides to find a partner for Tom Alpha Engineering. ALTA home appliances, an engineering company focusing on new types of home appliances for reasonable prices, is soon interested. ALTA is led by Jim Casey, age 32, a very young but high skilled person.

Together they set up plans for their new organization. Jim proposes to improve the use of suppliers. By out-tasking more activities to these suppliers the production costs of AlPhaTa (APT) can be decreased. Together with their other plans for the new organization there is a need for a better linkage between the production and the administration, and better IT support for the business processes.

They decide that they need a separate IT organization with a strong focus on service and quality. A new manager is recruited, with long experience in IT as a service delivery manager and a quality manager.

11.5.2 Bravalue

During the merger Bravalue has been led by the two former CEOs. Although they were a perfect team the board of directors decides that a new CEO is needed to lead Bravalue into the future. This also facilitates creating a new common culture, because personnel still seems to operate in their old familiar culture of Braath Insurance or VFM Bank.

After his announcement the CEO contacts the CIO (they worked together ten years ago for another financial institution). The CIO is finally able to propose all kinds of plans for the future of IT in the organization. The CEO is especially interested in creating new products based on Internet technology. They decide that the CEO will focus on promoting the possibilities of IT for the business, while in the meantime the CIO will make plans for transforming the IT organization into a partner organization.

The CIO recognizes that if his IT organization should be focusing on delivering added value to the business, they need to reorganize and outsource some activities to free up personnel. In his plans he proposes to outsource their infrastructure services, set up competency centres around essential business-oriented competencies, and to improve their service management area.

11.5.3 Crisis Insurance Company

After recent benchmarks the CEO of Crisis discusses the possibilities of new technology with his management team. Although Crisis is already using IT as a competitive advantage, they want to make a new step.

At their current Internet site and forum they receive a number of questions from their customers about how to improve home security. Until now they have always given information about reliable local partners. One of the managers proposes to create a new security company that uses Internet technology. Customers can then see their own home via the Internet and check their houses when they are away.

The other managers like the idea, and even propose to develop additional services. Customers could use the Internet connection to their home to manage their home temperature, their sunshades, etc. All managers like the idea of creating a new company and propose to create some changes especially in the IT organization to support this new company. IT should be an integral part of the new company; some IT whiz-kids should be working dedicated to the new company to make technology a real competitive enabler.

11.6 Practical guide on migration

The growth path in the IT value perception model is based on two axes: maturity of the demand side and maturity of the supply side. A growth path can be initiated by either side, but needs to be supported by both sides. This is also the first step in the growth path, because a better understanding of each other's objectives and focus is essential.

We give per level some main focus areas or first aid kits for the migration. In section 11.2.3 the details of each level are described; these can be used for further detailing of the migration plans.

Level 1 → level 2

General:

- IT strategy supported by both IT demand and IT supply.
- Steering committees with business and IT members.

Demand side:

- Better understanding of business needs.
- Less focus on costs, focus on quality of service.

Supply side:

- Creation of a service catalogue.
- Introduction of service level management, starting with simple levels and measurements.
- Cost control by separated department for planning, control and support.
- Separated departments for operations, maintenance and development.

Level 2 → level 3

General:

- Create a business strategy, and create an IT strategy aligned to it.

Demand side:

- Involve IT people in the creation of new business plans.
- Senior management is involved in the development activities of IT.

Supply side:

- Outsource infrastructure services.
- Create competency centres, and introduce the IT strategist and IT architect role to the organization.
- Develop service catalogue into differentiated service levels and include services of external service providers.
- Pricing of services, including margin to facilitate new developments.

Level 3 → level 4

General:

- A integral strategy for the organization, including IT.
- Create an integral business plan and budget, including IT.

Demand side:

- Better understand IT and the possibilities of new technology.

Supply side

- Be a part of the business organization.

Appendix A: Glossary of terms

Application a programme designed to perform a particular task for the user, the software that provides specific functionality to the end user.

Architecture (IT architecture) the underlying framework of technology, its structure, its limitations, its choices from the perspective of the technological capabilities and the way they are implemented and used in the enterprise. It is an abstract representation in terms of models and frameworks of the technology that is available or will become available to provide specific functionality.

Alignment the continuous effort of matching business requirements with provided services/solutions.

Assets (IT assets) the technology that provides a defined functionality, which is owned or used by a company and which provides value.

Benchmark comparing metrics/performance indicators with internal or external sources to conclude on performance.

Business case the result of a process of comparing the various costs associated with an investment with the profits and benefits that it returns.

Capability (IT capability) an integrated and internally coherent set of competencies, assets and processes.

Capacity (IT capacity) the outcome of a required IT capability or provided IT services in terms of the volume and/or load.

Centralization an activity to make information technology come under the control of one central authority.

Concentration an activity of gathering people or information technology.

Configuration management database (CMDB) A registration of the structure of IT service components.

Consolidation an activity to make information technology more solid, secure, or strong and/or to unite or combine information technology into one.

Competency (IT competency) competencies comprise a balanced and coherent mixture of know-how (=skills), know-what (=knowledge), know-why (=relevant experience) and individual attitude. The level of competency accounts for the level of quality of the results in IT.

Cost the amount of money needed to obtain and/or maintain something.

Customer focus the attitude of a person or organization towards providing high quality service to the customer.

Demand (IT demand) the desire of customers or end users for IT capabilities which they buy or use.

Effectiveness having the desired effect; producing the intended result.

Efficiency producing a satisfactory result without wasting time or resources.

Enabler the perception level at which IT service provisioning is considered key to the success of the company.

External service provider (ESP) an organization that is outside the realm of the company and provides IT services to the company.

Expense the spending of resources, especially money resulting in a cash flow.

Expertise see Competency.

Facility the perception level at which IT service provisioning is considered a necessary evil.

Financing to provide money for a project, purchase, etc.; to fund something,

Fit of business and IT the level at which IT demand and IT supply match with each other. See also Alignment.

Flexibility the ability of the IT service provisioning to adapt the services and quality of the services to changing needs.

Forced supply a dictate from senior management that (particular) IT services will only be supplied by a named internal or external service provider.

Funding see Financing.

Infrastructure (IT infrastructure) a cohesive set of technologies that provides the basic capabilities needed to run applications.

Internal service provider (ISP) an organization that provides IT services to the company and is part of that company.

Investment an activity that leads to buying or building information technology and that is worth undertaking, because it may be profitable or useful in the future.

Killer application an application that provides overwhelming and decisive competitive advantage.

Market place the system of buying and selling goods and/or services under competitive conditions.

Maturity the stage of having reached a level of development; sophistication.

Measurements the basic ingredients for metrics/performance indicators that express the size, length, or amount of something.

Metric metrics are the quantifiable objects that management needs to analyse in order to get feedback on the execution of their plans and activities. For each metric or performance indicator, multiple measurements need to be defined, implemented and measured.

Model a simple description of a system, used for explaining, calculating something.

Offering a service or group of services with a specific purpose and a specific audience.

Operational excellence ready to act with the quality of being extremely good or outstanding.

Outsourcing the activity of moving services (including the resources to provide these services) and/or competencies and/or assets from an internal service provider to an external service provider.

Out-tasking the activity of moving services (excluding the resources to provide these services) from an internal service provider to an external service provider.

Optimization to make information technology as good or as favorable as possible.

Partner the perception level at which IT service provisioning is considered to add value to the company at a level that is equal to the primary processes of the company.

Performance indicator see Metric.

Performance management the activity of planning and controlling the provisioning of information technology to a particular business.

Price an amount of money for which something may be bought or sold.

Portfolio (IT portfolio) the integral result of the continuous matching of IT demand and IT supply, and as such the major object for IT performance management.

Process (IT process) a series of actions or tasks performed in order to provide one or more IT services or IT service components.

Project an organized set of activities to achieve a predefined objective at a planned moment in time.

Professional development the activity of growing or causing somebody to grow gradually in his or her profession.

Quality of service the standard of service delivery when compared to similar services. Quality of IT service is expressed in service levels.

Service the perception level at which IT service provisioning is considered to be a supporting unit within a company that provides IT services.

Service (IT service) an identifiable, measurable, orderable and chargeable unit of service from the customer view, which provides a required capability. This can be, e.g., 'standard desktop service', 'application QQY support service', 'SAP consultancy service', etc.

Service component an identifiable and measurable unit of service from the provider's view, which can take part in one or more services. This can be, e.g., 'knowledge component', 'HW usage', 'SW licence fee', 'operational support', etc.

Service element a discrete part of a service with a defined number of units of the related service component. This can be, e.g., the average amount of 'HW usage' expressed in the unit of measure as defined in the service component 'HW usage' or the normative number of hours of support for 'operational support', etc.

Service group category of services which identifies specific groupings of offerings by the service provisioning organization. This can be, e.g., 'value added services', 'infrastructure services', 'professional services', etc.

Service level a defined level of service for a particular service or service element expressed in the unit of measure of the service level element. This can be, e.g., 'the agreed level of availability of SAP maintenance and support', 'the agreed service desk window for the desktop services', etc.

Service level agreement (SLA) or service agreement an agreement between a service requestor and a service provider that describes which services are delivered, when, at what quality/service level and at what price. An SLA can be a formal contract between two parties or it can be a specification within a 'frame agreement/frame contract'.

Service level element an identifiable, measurable, orderable and chargeable unit of the level of service from the customer's view. This can be, e.g., 'availability', 'service desk window', 'back-up frequency', 'information access authority levels', etc.

Service provider an organization that provides IT services to the company.

Sourcing the activity of obtaining services, competencies or assets from an external service provider.

Speed of new service introduction the ability to provide new IT services or service components at a speed that exceeds customer expectation.

Standardization to make information technology conform to a fixed standard, shape, quality, type, etc.

Strategy a set of comprehensive decisions on business and IT goals that provides for a target to the company.

Supply (IT supply) the activity of giving the end user IT functionality that is needed or useful.

Supported product a complex of technologies and competencies that are related to these technologies that deliver a predefined result.

Transparency the state or quality of being easily understood; accessible; simple or clear.

Value the worth attached by someone to something at a particular moment.

Appendix B:
Bibliography and reading list

Ansoff H.I. (1968) *Corporate Strategy: An Analytical Approach to Business Policy for Growth and Expansion*, Penguin Books, Harmondsworth, Reprint

Boynton A.C., Victor B. and Pine II B.J. (1993a) 'New competitive strategies: challenges to organizations and information technology', *IBM Systems Journal*, vol. 32 no. 1

Boynton A.C., Victor B. and Pine II B.J. (1993b) 'Making mass customization work', *Harvard Business Review*, September–October

CMM (1995) *The Capability Maturity Model, Guidelines for Improving the Software Process*, Carnegie Mellon University/Software Engineering Institute, Addison-Wesley

Cokins G. (1996) *Activity-Based Cost Management Making it Work: A Manager's Guide to Implementing and Sustaining an Effective ABC System*. Irwin Professional Publishing, Chicago

EIU (1999) *Assessing the Strategic Value of Information Technology*, The Economist Intelligence Unit and IBM Global Services, (www.eiu.com)

Hedley B., (1977) 'Strategy and the "business portfolio" ', *Longe Range Planning*, February, p. 12; as referenced in Kotler (1980)

Helfert Erich A. (1960) *Techniques of Financial Analysis*, 10th edition, 2000 McGraw-Hill

Henderson, Venkatraman (1993) 'Strategic alignment: leveraging IT for transforming organizations', *IBM Systems Journal*, vol. 33, no. 1, 4–16

ITPM (2000) 'Managing information technology in a new age', www.ibm.com/services/white_papers

ITIL (2002) *IT Infrastructure Library: Planning to Implement Service Management* and various other titles to be obtained from the Office of Government Commerce (www.ogc.co.uk)

Kaplan Robert S. and Cooper Robin (1998) *Cost and Effect, Using Integrated Cost Systems to Drive Profitability and Performance*, Harvard Business School Press, Boston

Kaplan Robert S. and Norton David P. (1992) 'the balanced scorecard: measures that drive performance', *Harvard Business Review*, January–February, 71–79

Kaplan Robert S. and Norton David P. (1996) *The balanced scorecard*, Harvard Business School Press.

Kotler Philip M. (1980) *Marketing Management*, 4th edition 1980, Prentice-Hall

Oxford (1995) *Oxford Advanced Learner's Dictionary*, fifth edition, Oxford University Press

Parker M.M., Benson R.J. and Trainor H.E. (1988) *Information Economics, Linking Business Performance to Information Technology*, Prentice-Hall

Porter M. (1980) *Competitive Strategy*, The Free Press, New York

Prior T. and Sahm J. (1995) *Using Activity Based Management for Continuous Improvement*, ISMS Inc., Arlington, Texas

Rappaport (1986) *Creating Shareholder Value*, The Free Press

Redman B., Kirwin B. and Berg T. (1998) *TCO, a Critical Tool for Managing IT*, Strategic Analysis Report, Gartner Group

Renkema Th. (2000) *The IT Value Quest*, Wiley & Sons, New York

Remeneyi, Money, Sherwood-Smith (2000) *The Effective Measurement and Management of IT Cost and Benefits*, Butterworth-Heinemann, Oxford

Rieger Chuck (1995) *IT Value and Contribution Model*, IBM Consulting Group, internal presentation

Stewart (1991) The Quest for Value, Harper Collins

Torgensen Paul E. and Weinstock Irwin T. (1972) *Management, an Integrated Approach*, Prentice-Hall

Treacy M. and Wiersema F. (1995) *The Discipline of Market Leaders*, Perseus Books, Cambridge, MA, USA

Urff Eric (2000) *Value Based Management*, Kluwer

WCCIO (2000) Executing Global IT Standardization, Working Council for CIOs, Global IT Series, Vol II. Corporate Executive Board, Cat. Nr. 072–244–634 (www.executiveboard.com)

Weill Peter and Broadbent Marianne (1998) Leveraging the New Infrastructure, *Harvard Business School Press*

Index

For Product Safety Concerns and Information please contact our EU
representative GPSR@taylorandfrancis.com Taylor & Francis Verlag GmbH,
Kaufingerstraße 24, 80331 München, Germany

Printed and bound by CPI Group (UK) Ltd, Croydon, CR0 4YY
08/05/2025
01864466-0001